Increasing Adult Learner *Persistence and Completion Rates*

A GUIDE FOR STUDENT AFFAIRS
LEADERS AND PRACTITIONERS

Marguerite McGann Culp *and*
Gwendolyn Jordan Dungy, *Editors*

NASPA™
Student Affairs Administrators
in Higher Education

Increasing Adult Learner Persistence and Completion Rates: A Guide for Student Affairs Leaders and Practitioners

Copyright © 2014 by the National Association of Student Personnel Administrators (NASPA), Inc. All rights reserved.

Published by
NASPA–Student Affairs Administrators in Higher Education
111 K Street, NE
10ᵗʰ Floor
Washington, DC 20002
www.naspa.org

Funded by a grant from the Lumina Foundation. Developed by NASPA–Student Affairs Administrators in Higher Education. Supported by the West Virginia Higher Education Policy Commission and the West Virginia Community and Technical College System.

Additional copies may be purchased by contacting the NASPA publications department at 202-265-7500 or visiting http://bookstore.naspa.org.

Library of Congress Cataloging-in-Publication Data

Increasing adult learner persistence and completion rates : a guide for student affairs leaders and practitioners / Marguerite McGann Culp and Gwendolyn Jordan Dungy, editors.
  pages cm
 ISBN 978-0-931654-97-8 -- ISBN 978-0-931654-98-5 -- ISBN 978-0-931654-96-1 1. Adult college students--Counseling of--United States. 2. Adult learning--United States. 3. Student affairs services--United States. I. Culp, Marguerite McGann, editor of compilation. II. Dungy, Gwendolyn Jordan, editor of compilation.
 LC5225.C68I53 2014
 378.1'982--dc23
              2014017737

Printed and bound in the United States of America

Print ISBN: 978-0-931654-97-8

Ebook (Mobi) ISBN: 978-0-931654-98-5

Ebook (ePub) ISBN: 978-0-931654-96-1

FIRST EDITION

Increasing
Adult Learner
Persistence and Completion Rates

NASPA.
Student Affairs Administrators
in Higher Education

CONTENTS

THE AUTHORS

Elizabeth Baldizan received her EdD in higher educational administration from the University of Nevada, Las Vegas (UNLV), her MA in education from the University of New Mexico, and her BA in communications and environmental studies from the University of Northern Colorado, magna cum laude. Baldizan has worked in student affairs at the University of New Mexico, the Seattle Community Colleges, and UNLV. She has taught at Seattle University and at UNLV in the Department of Educational Leadership. She is a past president of the Association for Student Conduct Administration and a former member of the board of directors of NASPA–Student Affairs Administrators in Higher Education. She is currently the executive director for Community2Campus in the UNLV Division of Educational Outreach.

Sarah Beasley is the director of statewide academic initiatives for the West Virginia Higher Education Policy Commission (HEPC). She holds a BA in psychology from Harvard University, an EdM from the Harvard Graduate School of Education, and a PhD in higher education from Boston College. Her interests include college access and success for low-income, first-generation, rural, and adult students. Before coming to the HEPC, Beasley worked for 6 years as a senior admissions officer at Harvard and served for 2 years as codirector of the Harvard Financial Aid Initiative, a program designed to expand recruitment, financial aid, and student services for low- and middle-income students. She is currently overseeing *DegreeNow*, the statewide adult learner initiative that seeks to re-enroll adults with some college credits but no degree.

Katie Busby is assistant provost for assessment and institutional research at Tulane University. She leads the Office of Assessment and Institutional Research and is responsible for planning and directing campuswide assessment and accreditation activities. Prior to joining Tulane, she was director of student affairs assessment and planning at The University of Alabama, and held a similar position at Indiana University–Purdue University Indianapolis. She spent 5 years as a member of the mathematics faculty at Baylor University and 4 years as a student affairs practitioner at James Madison University. She holds a BS and MS in mathematics from The University of Mississippi and earned her PhD in assessment and measurement at James Madison University. Busby currently serves as editor-elect of *Research & Practice in Assessment*.

Marguerite McGann Culp is currently partnering with NASPA and the state of West Virginia to implement *DegreeNow*, an innovative Lumina Foundation-funded initiative to strengthen persistence and completion rates for undergraduate adult learners. A former chief student affairs officer and faculty member in Florida and Texas, Culp has received numerous state and national awards recognizing her ability to design, lead, and assess innovative student affairs programs that transcend division boundaries. She coedited *Building a Culture of Evidence in Student Affairs: A Guide for Leaders and Practitioners* (NASPA, 2012), *Community College Student Affairs: What Really Matters* (Jossey-Bass, 2005), *Life at the Edge of the Wave: Lessons from the Community College* (NASPA, 1998), and *Promoting Student Success in the Two-Year College* (Jossey-Bass, 1995). Culp has presented more than 150 programs at state and national conventions and written dozens of book chapters and journal articles on a variety of topics including building teams and partnerships, creating cultures of evidence, and reinventing student affairs.

Kindra D. Degenhardt is the project specialist for the Fort Hays State University (FHSU) Alumni Association, where she plans and coordinates major events and promotes the active participation of future alumni. Previously, she worked as an administrative specialist in the Office of the Provost where she was responsible for the development and implementation of new technology-based communication tools and print-based publications for students, faculty, and staff. Degenhardt holds two bachelor's degrees from FHSU, one in communication studies/public relations and the other in English. She is scheduled to complete an online master's degree in human resource management in December 2014.

Gwendolyn Jordan Dungy served as executive director of NASPA from 1995 to her retirement in 2012. Currently, she serves as the primary consultant for the international collaboration between NASPA and the higher education graduate program at Colorado State University for the NASPA International Student Services Institute. She is a senior fellow at the Association of American Colleges and Universities in the Office of Diversity, Equity, and Student Success. In addition, she serves on the *Liberal Education* advisory board, the National Endowment for the Humanities Bridging Cultures advisory board, the advisory board for the Community College Roadmap Project, and as a faculty member for the High Impact Practices Institute. In addition to speaking and consulting, she recently coedited *Building a Culture of Evidence in Student Affairs: A Guide for Leaders and Practitioners* (NASPA, 2012).

Susan Gardner has more than 16 years of higher education experience in academic and student affairs. She has taught at the graduate and undergraduate levels in the areas of communications, social science, and leadership. Her experiences include serving as a community college vice president where she oversaw student affairs and enrollment. Prior to her community college work, Gardner served as assistant dean of students at the University of Charleston (UC). Recently she returned to UC and its School of Pharmacy where she is as an assistant professor and assistant dean for professional and student affairs. Gardner has published more than 100 articles related to enrollment, student success, and residence life. She earned her BA from Oakland University, MA from Central Michigan University, and PhD from Capella University.

Lawrence V. Gould is the former provost for Fort Hays State University (FHSU). Gould played a key role in the development of the FHSU distance learning environment, its undergraduate research initiative, internationalization of the campus, and the university's participation in the Higher Learning Commission's Academic Quality Improvement Program. In 1999, his initiative led the way in creating the university's academic programming in China and other countries. Gould is the recipient of the National Academic Advising Association's 2000 Pacesetter Award, the 2008 William M. Plater Award for Leadership in Civic Engagement, and the 2013 Brent Rubin Award, a special service recognition presented by the Network for Change and Continuous Innovation.

Adam S. Green currently serves as senior director of the West Virginia Higher Education Policy Commission's Division of Student Success and P–20 Initiatives, which focuses on increasing college access and higher education attainment rates among all West Virginia citizens. Additionally, he has contributed significant research focused on exploring high-quality student affairs assessment practices, including an article in the 2008 volume of the *NASPA Journal*. He earned both his bachelor's degree in journalism and his master's degree in educational leadership studies at West Virginia University. He also holds a postgraduate certificate in education awarded by the Manchester Metropolitan University in Manchester, England. He completed his doctoral degree in educational leadership studies at West Virginia University.

Tammy Johnson is executive director of admissions and international student services at Marshall University in Huntington, West Virginia. Her research interests include issues related to admissions, enrollment, international education, and access and retention initiatives for first-generation college students and adult learners. She is also an advocate for lesbian, gay, bisexual, transgender, and other underrepresented or minority populations in higher education. A native of West Virginia, Johnson earned her BS from the University of Charleston, MEd from Texas Woman's University, and EdD from Marshall University.

Leslie A. Laing is assistant director for adult learner programs and services in student affairs at The Pennsylvania State University (Penn State), a standing member on the Commission for Adult Learners, and the immediate past president of the Forum on Black Affairs. She was the 2013 recipient of the Shirley Hendrick Award for her work on the development and delivery of outreach programs for adult learners, encouraging a culture of innovation and collaboration, and providing visionary leadership. In addition, Laing founded the Adult Learner Opportunity Fund at Penn State and continues to solicit and award funds to deserving adult learners. An adult learner, she completed both her bachelor's degree (magna cum laude) and a master of arts in higher education administration at Montclair State University in New Jersey.

Tisa A. Mason is vice president for student affairs at Fort Hays State University, where she works with an integrated task group to assess and enhance support services for distance students. She recently coauthored a chapter on "Using Outcomes and Rubrics in Student Affairs" in *Building a Culture of Evidence in Student Affairs: A Guide for Leaders and Practitioners* (NASPA, 2012). Mason earned a doctorate from The College of William and Mary, where she received the Galfo Research Award, given annually to the graduate student who has demonstrated outstanding promise in educational research and helpfulness to fellow students. She holds a master's degree from Eastern Illinois University and a bachelor's degree from Transylvania University.

James Morales is vice president for student services at Utah State University. He earned a BA in speech communication from the University of Utah and an EdD in higher education policy and administration from the University of Minnesota. He served for more than 17 years in various admissions, enrollment management, and student services capacities in the University of Minnesota system and at the University of Connecticut. He also worked in human resources and as a private sector workplace issues consultant.

Pamela J. Schreiber received her EdD in adult education from The University of Georgia, her MA in student personnel administration from Bowling Green State University, and her BA in social welfare from the University of Wisconsin–Whitewater. She has worked in student affairs at Bowling Green, the University of Florida, The University of Georgia, Hodges University, and Florida Gulf Coast University. She currently serves as director of housing and food services at the University of Washington. Schreiber is cofounder of the National Housing Training Institute, now in its 23rd year. She has served on the board of the Association of College and University Housing Officers and has presented conference sessions and webinars on a variety of topics, including how to create effective learning experiences for adult learners.

Denise Swett has served as vice president of student services at Foothill College in Los Altos Hills, California, since July 2007. She has worked as a higher education administrator since 1998 and in positions in student services at the University of San Francisco, Chabot College, and Cañada College. Swett was Administrator of the Year at Foothill College in 2008–2009. In 2010–2011, she received the Educator of the Year award from the Association of Mexican American Educators of Silicon Valley as well as the National Community College Administrator of the Year award from NASPA. Swett earned her BA and MPA at San Jose State University and her EdD from the University of San Francisco.

David Vacchi, a retired U.S. Army officer with more than 20 years of service including combat deployments for Operations Enduring and Iraqi Freedom, is a doctoral candidate in the Educational Policy and Leadership program at the University of Massachusetts Amherst. He earned his BS from Purdue University and, while on active duty, an MS from Central Michigan University. Vacchi's scholarly work has focused solely on student veterans. He is the primary author of a chapter on student veterans in the *Higher Education Handbook of Theory and Research* (Vol. 29) (Springer, 2014) that provides a comprehensive history and literature review of scholarly activity on student veterans and features a more comprehensive explanation of the framework for student veteran success outlined in Module 6 of this tutorial.

Heidi Watson is a learning designer and research and evaluation scientist at the Clearinghouse for Military Family Readiness at Penn State. She earned a DEd in administration and leadership–higher education from Indiana University of Pennsylvania and an MEd in adult education from Penn State. Watson's research interests include benchmarking the needs of adult students working toward a bachelor's degree, student civic engagement, and understanding the use and effect of prior learning assessment. In addition to her 14 years in program design, development, and delivery at Penn State, Watson has worked with children and adults in a variety of settings including public schools, literacy centers, continuing education, and undergraduate higher education.

Judith Wertheim is senior fellow at the Council for Adult and Experiential Learning (CAEL). From 2006 to 2013, she was vice president for higher education services at CAEL, overseeing work with colleges, universities, consortia, and state systems to help adults return to school. She has presented workshops on prior learning assessment and the adult learning-focused institution and has consulted about policies, practices, and strategies to help adults continue their education. From 1980 to 2006, Wertheim was at Indiana University's School of Continuing Studies. Most recently, she was interim dean for the universitywide school and held the rank of professor. Her responsibilities included the general studies degree programs, the adult education master's program, Indiana University high school, distance courses at high school through graduate levels, and professional development programs.

MODULE 1

Adult Learners

Who They Are,
Why They Matter, and
What They Need to Succeed

Marguerite McGann Culp

ABSTRACT

Learners 25 to 64 years old are getting a lot of attention these days. Educators search for a comprehensive term to describe this population: Are they adult learners, lifelong learners, or post-traditional learners? Foundations compete to fund projects whose goal is to increase the number of adults with postsecondary credentials. States race to establish initiatives that encourage adults who left college before completing a degree to return and earn that credential. Colleges and universities struggle to better understand 25- to 64-year-old undergraduates and to create adult-friendly policies, procedures, and campuses. Researchers and theorists question whether instructional approaches, institutional processes, and nonclassroom support services that work for recent high school graduates also work for adults. This module assists readers in understanding why adult learners matter and assessing their own knowledge and skill sets in a variety of areas related to adult learners. The module also discusses the role that student affairs must play in supporting 25- to 64-year-old undergraduates and offers an introduction to the other modules in the tutorial.

HIGHER EDUCATION'S CHANGING LANDSCAPE

Data indicate that "powerful economic, demographic, and market trends are reshaping the landscape of higher education, particularly for adults" (Kazis et al., 2007). By 2018, more than 60% of jobs in the United States will require some type of postsecondary education (Carnevale, Smith, & Strole, 2010). Increasing the percentage of high school graduates who enroll in college or in postsecondary training programs is a step in the right direction, but is not enough to close the education gap (Brown, 2012). As demonstrated in *The 2012 Statistical Abstract of the United States* (U.S. Census Bureau, 2012), nearly 60% of Americans between the ages of 25 and 64 have no postsecondary degree. Assisting adults in continuing their education presents the United States with a classic win-win-win situation:

IN THE SPOTLIGHT

Haydee Nunuz, director of adult, commuter, and veteran student affairs at DePaul University, and James Stewart, assistant director at De Paul, share their perspective on working with adult learners.

- ⚙ Designing support services to meet the needs of adult learners is not only the right thing to do, it is the smart thing to do. In 10 years, there will be little difference between the support service needs and attendance patterns of traditional students and adult learners.

- ⚙ Do not assume there is only one type of adult learner or that all adult learners are uncomfortable with technology.

- ⚙ Do not try to retrofit existing services to meet the needs of adult learners. Talk with adult learners, gather data, and design support systems that meet their unique needs.

- ⚙ Provide extensive online support not only for administrative functions but also for support services.

- ⚙ Make sure that the institution offers essential services that require a campus visit (e.g., obtaining IDs) at times and places that are convenient for adult learners.

- ⚙ Provide faculty members with information and experiences to increase their ability to understand, appreciate, and teach adult learners.

- ⚙ Build internal and external partnerships: They are the keys to improving access and success for adult learners.

- ⚙ Do the research necessary to assess the effectiveness of programs and services created for adult learners. Use research results to strengthen programs and services. (personal communication, August 22, 2013)

Employers thrive when applicant pools are filled with well-educated and appropriately credentialed candidates, adults benefit because they can remain in or re-enter the job market with up-to-date knowledge and skills, and colleges and universities gain by demonstrating the benefits to society and the economy of investing in higher education.

The good news is that the number of undergraduate students classified as adult learners is growing. Signature Report 3 from the National Student Clearinghouse (2012) concluded that 38% of all college students are 25 or older, while Aslanian & Clinefelter (2012) reported that 80% of students enrolled in online programs are 25 or older. The average age of community college students, a group that represents 45% of all U.S. undergraduates, is 28; 57% of community college students are 22 or older, and 14% are 40 or over (American Association of Community Colleges, 2014). The bad news is that colleges and universities are struggling to meet the needs of, and improve persistence and completion rates for, this student population (Brown, 2012).

The Story Behind the Tutorial

In 2010, the West Virginia Higher Education Policy Commission (WV HEPC) and the West Virginia Community Technical College System (WV CTC) received a grant from the Lumina Foundation to launch *DegreeNow,* an ambitious 4-year initiative to improve higher education access and completion rates for adult learners. West Virginia partnered with NASPA–Student Affairs Administrators in Higher Education to design and implement the support services portion of the grant. As explained in further detail in Module 10, NASPA used a Train-the-Trainer approach to assist student affairs professionals, faculty, and staff to strengthen support services for adult learners in all of the state's public colleges and universities. In 2012, NASPA published *Building a Culture of Evidence in Student Affairs: A Guide for Leaders and Practitioners,* edited by Marguerite McGann Culp and Gwendolyn Jordan Dungy, which was designed to support *DegreeNow* and later released nationally. *Increasing Adult Learner Persistence and Completion Rates: A Guide for Student Affairs Leaders and Practitioners* is the companion tutorial to *Building a Culture of Evidence.* It addresses the heart of the *DegreeNow* grant: designing and implementing support services for 25- to 64-year-old undergraduates. It also shares some of the lessons learned while implementing the grant, lessons that may help student affairs professionals across the nation adjust the way they conceptualize and support adult learners.

Lesson 1: Definitions Matter, Divisions Don't

As written and funded, the *DegreeNow* grant focused on adults in West Virginia between the ages of 25 and 64 who had not earned a postsecondary credential. Participants in the first Train-the-Trainer workshops, however, pointed out that many students between the ages of 18 and 24 struggling to earn a degree would also benefit from the processes, programs, and services generated by *DegreeNow* (Sarah Beasley, personal communication, November 7, 2011). Train-the-Trainer participants also spent a significant amount of time discussing how West Virginia should refer to *DegreeNow*'s target population: Were they *adult learners* (Schlossberg, Lynch, & Chickering, 1989), *nontraditional learners* (Choy, 2002), or *lifelong learners* (Cross, 1991)? Since the grant application defined the target population as adult learners between the ages of 25 and 64, the decision was made to use the term *adult learner* and to focus primarily on 25- to 64-year-old undergradu-

QUICK TIP

"Presume that every one of your traditionally aged learners could be lifelong learners and, thus, *adult* (I hate that term) learners at some point. Think families, not individuals; think part-time, odd hours, and asynchronous learning; think financially challenged and debt averse; think veterans and reservists; think older, younger, and in between; think technologically advanced and limited; think motivated and fearful; think." —Larry Moneta, vice president for student services, Duke University (personal communication, June 17, 2013)

ates, even though many of the activities associated with the grant also would help 18- to 24-year-olds who did not enroll in college directly after high school. As *DegreeNow* evolved, so did the national conversation about adults in college. In 2013, Soares introduced the term *posttraditional learner,* and many Train-the-Trainer graduates gravitated toward the term because it seemed to more effectively describe students who did not enter college directly from high school, encouraged educators to view adult students as the "new normal" rather than as deviations from the traditional 18- to 22-year-old undergraduate norm, and challenged institutions to think twice before asking adults to fit into existing administrative, instructional, and support service models. Train-the-Trainer graduates also believed that the term *posttraditional* focused attention on new student attendance patterns that seem to be evolving into "a form of college-going that is . . . cross-generational and aligned with the innovation economy's emphasis on lifelong learning" (Soares, 2013, p. 5).

Through decades of educating adult learners, community college leaders discovered that dividing their institutions into departments and divisions (academic affairs, student affairs, continuing education, etc.) may be a convenient way for them to understand and govern the institution, but these distinctions are not that important to students. Adult learners want to make a significant connection with another person at the college; to experience integrated intake programs such as orientation, assessment, advising, and course placement; to follow a well-defined pathway from day one, even if they are not sure of their major or program of study; and to be a part of an institution that anticipates when students will need assistance and provides that assistance in an effective and timely manner (O'Banion, 2013). Adult learners do not care if the people with whom they connect are administrators, faculty members, support staff, or other students:

IN THE SPOTLIGHT

"Evidence indicates that traditional models of delivering student services by referral, or at the student's discretion, are not getting us to the level of success to which both students and colleges aspire. The emerging imperative is to take the services where the students are, which often means incorporating advising, tutoring, other academic supports, and even cocurricular supports into coursework. This redesign of students' educational experiences involves a whole new level of collaboration between student services and academic leaders." —Kay McClenney, director, Center for Community College Student Engagement, The University of Texas at Austin (personal communication, July 9, 2013)

They simply want to feel that they matter to someone. Adult learners do not care where support programs and services are housed, what they are called, or to whom they report: They just want them to work. Adult learners basically want to know that courses and support services are designed and delivered by professionals who are well trained in adult development theory and research, experienced in applying that theory and research to real-life situations, and dedicated to helping students identify and follow their individual paths to success. Adult learners also want to attend institutions that are learning-centered, capable of seeing life from an adult learner's perspective, and organized to promote their success.

Lesson 2: Building Capacity Is Essential

"Adult learners have typically been treated as an afterthought in higher education" (Pusser et al., 2007, p. 3); therefore, many higher education professionals possess limited (or outdated) knowledge of what this population needs to succeed in college. Exercise 1.1 provides an overview of theories and research focused on adult learners and invites readers to determine if their institutions offer programs and services to support adult learners that are consistent with these research results and theories. Exercise 1.1 also encourages readers to identify the programs and services their institutions must implement in order to respond effectively to the needs of 25- to 64-year-old undergraduates.

One of the most important messages that student affairs leaders can send to their team is that there is nothing more dangerous to students—and to the institution—than offering services that exceed staff capabilities or implementing processes that impede student access or success. To reinforce this message, student affairs leaders should use Exercise 1.1 to:

- Assist team members to realistically assess their knowledge of adult learner research and theories, create professional development plans to fill in critical gaps, and then hold staff members accountable for following their plan.
- Support the reallocation of resources to fund professional development activities and much-needed programs and services to support adult learners.
- Design data-driven programs and services to support adult learners that are consistent with the evolving knowledge and skill sets of the student affairs team.
- Develop a model to assess the effectiveness of processes, programs, and services designed to increase adult learner access and success. Use assessment results to add, eliminate, or redesign these processes, programs, and services.

 QUICK TIP

"Professional development is the Achilles' heel of the College Completion Agenda, a national effort to increase the number of students who complete 1-year certificates or associate's degrees, or who transfer and earn a credential at another college or university. Colleges must begin to take professional development seriously if they are going to have any chance of meeting the goals of the College Completion Agenda, which will fail or succeed based on the skills of the educators on the front lines who are responsible for making it work." —Terry O'Banion, president emeritus, League for Innovation; chair of the graduate faculty, National American University; and identified by *Change* in 1998 as 1 of 11 "Idea Champions" who set the agenda for all of higher education (personal communication, June 24, 2013)

QUICK TIP

"Students are different from one another, and these differences take a variety of forms. . . . For adult learners, giving credit for prior learning based on work and life experiences is important. Adult learners also need assistance putting together an individualized educational plan based on their goals and backgrounds. . . . The constraints for adult learners are more substantial than those for traditional students: They have work, family, and community responsibilities. In addition, their learning styles and motivational levels vary; many face the same existential challenges that traditional students face, but the form these challenges take will be very different. . . . Treating adult learners as individuals is the bottom line for improving graduation and completion rates." —Arthur W. Chickering, former professor of educational development and human leadership, George Mason University; coauthor, *Education and Identity* (Jossey-Bass, 1993) (personal communication, June 5, 2013)

- Launch strategic conversations within the college community about the needs of adult learners and how to meet these needs while remaining true to the institution's mission, vision, and values.

Student affairs leaders also need to encourage their college or university to build capacity across the institution by launching an on-campus professional development series that focuses on 25- to 64-year-old undergraduates; funding trips to state and national conferences for faculty and staff members; and appointing a cross-functional team to study adult learner theory and research, and then designing a program to integrate these students, whether they are enrolled in campus or Web-based courses, into the college community. Other options include developing blogs and supporting podcasts that allow faculty and support staff to share information on and experiences with adult learners and leveraging social media to both educate faculty and build e-communities dedicated to improving access and success for adult learners. Student affairs leaders also can partner with their faculty colleagues to introduce recently hired faculty and support staff to the topic. They can design small group or Web-based orientation experiences that send clear and consistent messages about the importance of learning, teaching, students, and partnerships; the unique needs of adult learners; and the institution's commitment to making data-driven decisions that increase the success of all learners.

Lesson 3: One Size Does Not Fit All

There is no typical adult learner (Pusser et al., 2007). Some adult learners need a great deal of support, others simply require occasional assistance, and a few do quite well on their own. However, because many colleges and universities were designed in another era to meet the needs of traditional students who enter college directly after graduating from high school, adult learners face a series of barriers. Exercise 1.2 offers a snapshot of some of these barriers, lists the strategies that institutions use to eliminate or reduce their impact, and invites readers to identify strategies that might prove effective at their institutions.

Just as there are no typical adult learners, there are no typical higher education institutions. Even within a state system, colleges and universities have different missions, cultures, infrastructures, and institutional memories. As a result, pedagogical approaches, administrative processes, and support services that work at one institution may not work at another. Fortunately, some universal approaches work across all institutional types to meet the needs of adult learners. Institutions use these approaches to:

- Send clear messages to faculty, staff, administrators, and students about the institution's commitment to adult learners by referencing adult learners in the institution's mission or vision statements, including adult learner initiatives in the institution's strategic plan and performance benchmarks, and tracking the effectiveness of these initiatives in the institution's annual report.

- Pay attention to existing and emerging adult learner research, translate the research into systems and services that work for adult learners at their institution, and rigorously assess the results of their efforts.

- Ask adult learners about their goals, aspirations, and needs—avoid viewing them as students whose only requirement is short-term job training.

- Offer more flexible approaches to learning (e.g., blended, online, and self-paced instruction; accelerated course formats; and customized courses, certificates, and degrees).

- Provide adult learners with clear pathways to success that are grounded in both research (national, state, and local) and reality (e.g., the institution's culture, priorities, and resources).

- Reward collaboration within the college and across the community that improves access and success for adult learners.

- Influence local, state, and national public policy debates that deal with issues that affect adult learners (e.g., prior learning assessment, credit transfer among institutions, developmental education requirements, and federal financial aid policies).

QUICK TIP

The flood of data available today means more noise but not necessarily more signal. Data and predictions can only be as good as we are. Humans have a "limiting ability": they can be fallible, biased, and slipshod. They expect too much of computers and not enough of themselves. "People blame the data when they should be asking better questions." —Nate Silver (in an interview with Jon Gertner in the June 2013 issue of *Fast Company*)

Lesson 4: Asking—and Answering—the Right Questions Is Important

The essential questions in higher education have not changed much in the past century: (1) What is the purpose of a college education, and how can we most effectively organize and present the curriculum to achieve this purpose? (2) What is our institution's specific mission? (3) Who are our students and what support services do they need to succeed in college? (4) How can we demonstrate to ourselves and to the communities we serve that our institution is efficient, offers quality instruction and support services, and can effectively support access, success, and learning for all student populations? (5) How do we use technology to help us meet the needs of our students in a manner consistent with the purposes of higher education and our institution's mission, philosophy, goals, and resources?

In addition to assisting institutions in responding to those questions, student affairs educators must address four additional questions: (1) Are the processes, programs, and services we offer designed to

IN THE SPOTLIGHT

William Carter, vice chancellor of information technology for the Houston Community College System, shares that in implementing software to support the new student services model, the institution made a conscious decision to leverage technology and to involve students in designing and testing the software.

- ✿ The goal was to provide seamless experiences to all users.

- ✿ No single department owned the model; everyone "drove" the model.

- ✿ The model was designed to provide users with immediate feedback and allow managers to make timely, data-driven decisions.

- ✿ The network and technology were agnostic, allowing students to bring their own devices.

- ✿ Every application was device-ubiquitous and personalized based on student feedback.

- ✿ Student surveys identified what students liked and disliked about the college's website and interfaces as the online experience evolved.

- ✿ Current and prospective students tested the website and provided invaluable feedback that was used to modify the site. (personal communication, August 22, 2013)

respond to student needs, or do they reflect the outdated preferences of student affairs professionals? (2) Do student affairs staff members have the skills and the knowledge to provide the support services required by students—and the faculty who work with them? (3) How do student affairs professionals demonstrate that they make data-driven decisions; remain up to-date on theories, research, and technology; and look objectively at what they do and how they do it? (4) Do student affairs leaders demonstrate their commitment to student learning and success by reallocating resources to support new programs and services; collaborating with faculty to design programs and services that benefit all students, wherever they are and however they choose to learn; and partnering with information technology (IT) to intelligently leverage technology?

Lesson 5: e-Learning and Technology Are Game Changers for Student Affairs

The winds of change have been blowing for a while. More than a decade ago, Arthur Levine (2000) cautioned the higher education community that it had only a small window of opportunity to determine its role in relation to distance learning, and that decision might well determine the future of higher education. Ten years later, the American College Personnel Association and NASPA (2010) issued a joint report on the future of student affairs that bluntly stated, "At no other time in history has the incentive for real change been more powerful or the consequences for not changing more significant" (p. 7). In 2011, Christiansen and Eyring announced that online learning was higher education's disruptive innovation, warned that current higher education models were unsustainable, and urged colleges and universities to create a new DNA that was student-centric and committed to quality, efficiency, and usefulness.

The number of students taking one or more courses online grows each year, as does the number of students enrolling in blended courses. As colleges and universities move entire degree programs online, student affairs is scrambling to define its role in supporting students—and the faculty who teach them—in an ever-changing, technology-driven world. Technology offers powerful tools to help the profession respond to the needs of e-learners as well as the needs of students taking on-campus classes. Technology supports more efficient, effective, and targeted processes, programs, and services. It allows student affairs to disseminate information quickly and to communicate with on- and off-campus populations in a variety of ways. It permits an endless array of innovative strategies to increase student development, engagement, and learning. It supports data gathering and analysis at levels never before seen. What technology does not do is compensate for weak or outdated organizational structures, prop up ineffective programs and services, or answer the million-dollar question: How should student affairs leverage technology to improve access and success for all students in a manner that is consistent with the mission and goals of the institution and the guiding principles of the profession? To answer that question, student affairs professionals will need to do the following.

Know themselves. The constantly evolving technology scene presents a significant challenge to student affairs. The processes, programs, and services that student affairs offers are often the first that students experience—and send a powerful message about the institution's ability to offer seamless, personalized experiences that use technology effectively. Exercise 1.3 offers student affairs leaders and practitioners the opportunity to evaluate their readiness to partner with IT and to use technology effectively. Exercise 1.4 invites readers to assess their current technology skills. Both exercises help student affairs leaders and practitioners to build capacity within student affairs and to identify and respond to internal challenges that limit their ability to use technology effectively.

Understand technology's capabilities. Websites like http://www.howstuffworks.com offer easy-to-grasp insights into the complex world of computer hardware and software, peripherals, security, and the Internet (click on "Computers") and tips to manage the technology in your life (click on "Electronics"). The site http://www.zdnet.com features reviews of hardware and software, technology news, and position papers on a variety of technology-related topics. The *Journal of Technology in Student Affairs*, http://www.studentaffairs.com/ejournal, provides up-to-date information on higher education research and technology related to student affairs as well as descriptions of innovative applications; the journal's website includes an archive of issues from 2000 to the present. *The Chronicle of Higher Education* publishes current news on technology and higher education at http://chronicle.com/blogs/wiredcampus. NASPA's Technology Knowledge Community, http://www.naspa.org/constituent-groups/kcs/technology, offers resources for professionals interested in exploring the impact of technology on higher education. When combined with coaching from IT staff, these resources, among others, allow student affairs leaders and practitioners to use technology more effectively.

QUICK TIP

"Technology is seductive. . . . The pressure to succumb to the latest and greatest technology can be overwhelming—and expensive! It is ever more critical that student affairs staffs focus on the outcomes intended by our various services and let the technology follow—not lead—a thoughtful consideration of the roles and relationships associated with our profession." (Moneta, 2005, p. 13)

Know their students. Technology allows student affairs to offer customized services, but these services are effective only if they are grounded in theory and research and demonstrate a clear understanding of the target population's needs and the levels of proficiency with technology. Levine and Dean (2012) described traditional 18- to 22-year-old students as "digital natives," a "24/7 generation" that operates around the clock, whose members favor "concrete (practical) and active (hands on)" approaches to learning (pp. 20–22). If traditional students are digital natives, adult learners are digital immigrants. Some enjoy using online services exclusively. Others prefer blended support services (basic information via podcasts coupled with opportunities to ask questions in a mediated chat room or small group session). Many, however, prefer face-to-face interactions, especially at the start of their college careers. There are five keys to effectively using technology with adult learners: (1) Do not assume that all adult learners fear technology; many are avid online shoppers, e-mailers, and texters; (2) help adult learners assess and then build on their knowledge of and proficiency with technology; (3) do not force adult learners to move out of their technology comfort zones too quickly; (4) provide adequate and timely support; and (5) include the equivalent of a panic button in technology applications (e.g., a box to click to talk with someone or obtain help).

Engage in strategic conversations. Magolda and Magolda (2011) described the evolving roles that student affairs played in colleges and universities over the past 50 years. In the beginning, student affairs provided high-quality services in nonacademic functional areas. In the second phase, student affairs professionals became "noncognitive human development specialists"; in the third phase, student affairs focused on learning as "the epicenter of the cocurriculum with development and service as its foundation" (p. xviii). All of these phases were played out against the backdrop of a fairly stable higher education system. As Christiansen and Eyring (2011) and Levine and Dean (2012) so capably demonstrated, higher education is no longer stable and will change more in the next two decades than it has in the past two centuries. Student affairs' role in the colleges and universities of the future is uncertain. A few things, however, are clear: Student affairs professionals must engage in strategic conversations that produce a consistent, coherent strategy for supporting adult learners; design personalized support services for both online and campus-based learners; and partner with their faculty colleagues to design, deliver, and assess student-centered learning experiences and support services.

USING THE TUTORIAL

Increasing Adult Learner Persistence and Completion Rates: A Guide for Student Affairs Leaders and Practitioners is designed to increase the ability of student affairs professionals to develop, implement, and assess the effectiveness of processes, programs, and services for undergraduates between the ages of 25 and 64. Although the nine modules that follow focus on different topics, they send five consistent messages: (1) Colleges and universities need to build on the knowledge and experiences that adult learners bring to their institutions; (2) no one can do it alone: collaboration, both internal and external, matters; (3) student affairs must partner with adult learners to determine what they know, what their goals are, and what they need to succeed; (4) support services must be intentionally designed, intelligently delivered, and thoughtfully assessed; and (5) the future of student affairs may well depend on its ability to understand and effectively leverage technology. Embedded in each module is another powerful message: The time for incremental change is over.

QUICK TIP

"The instructor as lone cowboy cannot move the herd roughly west without the help of others. In fact, piecemeal reform, boutique programs, and the applications of a practice by an individual faculty member or college will not bring about significant change in an institution." (O'Banion, 2013, p. 16)

Throughout the tutorial, readers will find sections dedicated to advice from experienced professionals (Quick Tips), concrete examples of how institutions have applied the concepts or used the tools described in the module (In the Spotlight), and exercises to help them assess their knowledge and skill sets in a variety of areas related to adult learners (Apply the Concepts). The tutorial also introduces readers to a variety of resources, both electronic and print, and research related to adult learners.

In Module 2, Judith Wertheim explores the roles that both academic and student affairs play in increasing adult learner completion rates; offers insight into using Council for Adult and Experiential Learning principles to build capacity within student affairs and partnerships with faculty; and provides a snapshot of the types of processes, programs, and services that institutions must create to increase adult learner completion rates. The module also describes how individual institutions are addressing some of the major challenges associated with improving adult learner completion rates.

Community colleges have decades of experience working with adult learners. Denise Swett and Marguerite Culp describe these experiences in Module 3, review strategies to remove the institutional barriers that undergraduate adult learners face, and suggest a mental model for working with adult learners. Module 3 also examines relevant community college research and offers examples of innovative approaches community colleges use to increase adult learner persistence and completion rates. Finally, the module provides readers with an opportunity to assess their knowledge of adult learner theory and research as well as their institution's ability to serve adult learners.

Module 4 tackles the challenging subject of translating adult learner theory and research into programs and services in colleges and universities. Leslie Laing and Heidi Watson explore the way colleges and universities build on theory and research to create programs and services for adult learners. Module 4 also describes innovative state and local initiatives, offers a fresh perspective on the role that student affairs must play in increasing access and success for adult learners, and introduces the REAL approach to designing and implementing support services for adult learners.

In Module 5, Lawrence V. Gould, Tisa Mason, and Kindra D. Degenhardt explain why adult student support services enabled by technology are transforming the student learning experience. The module explores the importance of developing a comprehensive adult learner strategy to provide online support services, moving from a "prevent failure" approach to a proactive "success agenda" approach in student affairs, and accepting the premise that "the user is king." Module 5 also identifies benchmark institutions that have successfully developed support systems for online learners and offers an introduction to the practice of "service blueprinting."

Module 6 turns the spotlight on one of the fastest-growing adult learner subpopulations: veterans. David Vacchi outlines the unique needs of veterans entering or returning to college, assesses the strengths and weaknesses of existing student success models in relation to veterans, and proposes a data-driven support service model for veterans and their families. In addition, Module 6 explores the role that student affairs professionals play in increasing access and success for student veterans and urges institutions to move away from an inflexible, institution-centric support services model for veterans.

Effective learning-centered institutions are built on shared goals, outcomes, and definitions. Module 7 describes the relationships that student affairs professionals must build with colleagues across the institution, especially faculty colleagues, in order to develop processes, programs, and services that are relevant to the institution's academic mission and its adult learner population. Written by Marguerite Culp and James Morales, Module 7 offers guidelines for developing partnerships, provides tools to assess partnership climates as well as the readiness of student affairs professionals to build these partnerships, and describes innovative higher education partnerships that benefit adult learners.

Where Module 7 focuses on internal partnerships, Module 8 explores the benefits of external ones. Elizabeth Baldizan and Pam Schreiber examine the wide variety of off-campus partnerships that are essential to recruiting, retaining, and graduating adult learners. Module 8 also suggests strategies to deal with the barriers to effective off-campus partnerships, explores the important role of boundaries in effective partnerships, and provides concrete examples of external partnerships that benefit adult learners.

In Module 9, Katie Busby and Adam Green apply the concepts presented in *Building a Culture of Evidence in Student Affairs* (Culp & Dungy, 2012) to programs and services for adult learners. Emphasizing the importance of carefully articulated research questions, Module 9 describes what adult learner data are available at the institutional, state, and federal levels; explores how technology can assess student learning and evaluate the effectiveness of programs designed to increase adult learner completion rates; and provides concrete examples of how some institutions demonstrate the effectiveness of processes, programs, and services for adult learners—and how they determine if programs and services designed for all students meet the needs of adult learners.

Finally, Module 10 analyzes the progress West Virginia has made since 2010 in improving access and completion rates for adult learners; designing innovative processes, programs, and services to increase adult learner completion rates; and building capacity among student affairs leaders and practitioners. Sarah Beasley joins Susan Gardner and Tammy Johnson in sharing the West Virginia story.

APPLY THE CONCEPTS

Exercise 1.1—*Translating Theories and Research into Programs and Services for Adult Learners*

Directions: Many theories and research results have programming implications for student affairs professionals working with adult learners. Column A describes some of these theories or research results and provides the name of the author or researcher associated with them. Read the brief description. Use your smartphone, tablet, desktop, laptop, or college library to locate additional information, as needed. In Column B, list any initiatives already in place at your institution that demonstrate how your college or university translated a specific theory or research finding into a process, program, or service to benefit adult learners. In Column C, identify three theories or research results that you consider most important for your institution. For each one, recommend programs or services for adult learners that your college or university could design to operationalize it. *See item 6, Column C for a sample response.*

A	B	C
Theory or research result	**A process, program, or support service at your institution based on this theory or research finding**	**Processes, programs, or services your institution should consider implementing based on this theory or research finding**
1 $B = f(P \times E)$ Behavior *(B)* is a function *(f)* of the interaction of a person *(P)* with his or her environment *(E)*. In many situations, change involves two opposing forces: driving forces that push individuals toward change, and restraining forces that encourage individuals to maintain the status quo. (Lewin, 1936)		
2. Three conditions increase the chances that students will grow and develop in college: readiness, challenge, and support. Young students benefit from maturation; adult students benefit from supportive environmental conditions. (Sanford, 1966)		
3. External environments play a role in the developmental issues adults face during their lives. There are eight stages of development. Generativity versus stagnation is where most adult learners find themselves. However, adult learners may revisit earlier stages to resolve conflicts (e.g., identity versus role confusion could surface when adult learners lose their jobs or are engaged in the job-search process). (Erikson, 1980)		

A	B	C
Theory or research result	A process, program, or support service at your institution based on this theory or research finding	Processes, programs, or services your institution should consider implementing based on this theory or research finding
4. Adults do not learn the same way that children learn and prefer a problem-centered approach to learning. Andragogy is the art and science of helping adults learn. (Knowles, 1978)		
5. "When they can control the pace, most adults in their 40s and 50s have about the same ability to learn as they had in their 20s and 30s." (Knox, 1977, p. 422)		
6. Adult learners deal with three types of barriers: (a) personal or situational (e.g., lack of time or money), (b) attitudinal (e.g., fear of failure), and (c) structural or institutional (e.g., 16-week semesters or daytime-only sections of some classes). (Cross, 1992)		Appoint a cross-functional team to identify and prioritize barriers for adult learners, identify strategies to remove or reduce these barriers, and develop a plan to increase adult learner completion rates.
7. To change the environment for adult learners, educators must take four basic steps: (a) identify obstacles to change; (b) gather data to assess the impact of existing processes, programs, and support services on adult learners; (c) design and implement a change process consistent with current research and theories on change; and (d) design and implement adult-learner-focused professional development activities for the entire college community. (Schlossberg, Lynch, & Chickering, 1989)		
8. Educators need to validate the student as knower, situate learning in the student's experiences, and define learning as jointly constructed meaning. (Baxter Magolda, 1992)		
9. There are seven vectors of development, seven aspects of a college environment that influence the development of adult learning, and three important principles for working with adult learners. The three principles are: recognition and respect for individual differences, helping students integrate work and learning, and acknowledging the cyclical nature of work and development. (Chickering & Reisser, 1993)		
10. *Transitions matter*—any event or nonevent that results in changed relationships, routines, assumptions, or roles affects adult learners. *Sense of belonging matters*—adult learners must believe that they matter and are valued. (Schlossberg et al., 1989)		

Theory or research result	A process, program, or support service at your institution based on this theory or research finding	Processes, programs, or services your institution should consider implementing based on this theory or research finding
A	B	C
11. Attrition for undergraduate nontraditional students is a byproduct of four factors: (1) background variables, (2) academic variables, (3) environmental variables, and (4) psychological outcomes. Being engaged academically is more important to an adult learner than social involvement. Adult students are more likely to remain enrolled and achieve their educational goals if they have the support of their family. (Bean & Metzner, 1985)		
12. Adult learners who receive prior learning assessment (PLA) credits have significantly better completion rates than students who do not receive PLA credits. (Klein-Collins, 2010)		
13. Piloting "best practices" and then trying to bring them to scale does not significantly increase community college completion rates. Community colleges should follow a "best process" approach that invites the entire college community to review, realign, and redesign processes, programs, and support services to accelerate student access and completion rates. (Jenkins, 2011)		
14. Research in behavioral economics and other fields indicate that students perform better when offered a limited set of clearly defined program options that have well-structured or prescribed paths to completion. (Scott-Clayton, 2011)		
15. Community college students are more likely to benefit from student support services that are integrated into their educational experiences and help them to create social relationships; clarify aspirations and increase their commitment to education; develop college know-how; and address the conflicting demands of work, family, and college. (Karp, 2011)		

APPLY THE CONCEPTS

Exercise 1.2—*Significant Barriers for Undergraduate Adult Learners*

Directions: Review the strategies institutions have used to eliminate or reduce barriers. Identify strategies with the potential to work at your institution.

Barriers	Strategies to eliminate or reduce barriers	Strategies that might work at my institution
Processes, programs, and services based on research and theories associated with traditional students who enter college directly after graduating from high school.	• Use a service blueprinting approach to assess the effectiveness of current policies, processes, and support services for adult learners, both online and on campus. • Conduct collegewide process improvement activities to review, redesign, and realign processes, programs, and services. • Expand data-gathering techniques to build a more complete picture of adult learner needs and concerns. • Research processes, programs, and support services at institutions with high adult learner completion rates. • Implement workshops, seminars, and reading programs to update educators' skills and increase their knowledge of adult learners.	
Pedagogical approaches that reflect the needs and learning preferences of students who enter college directly after graduating from high school.	• Assess the faculty's knowledge of adult learner theory and research. • Design opportunities for faculty members to increase their knowledge of adult learner theory and research, and to apply that knowledge to both the curriculum and the classroom (virtual as well as brick-and-mortar). • Host informal activities designed to encourage cross-department discussions about the most effective way to meet the needs of adult learners. • Disaggregate existing data to better understand the needs and perceptions of adult learners. • Create clear pathways to completion for all degrees, certificates, and programs of study. • Focus on learner-centered instruction.	
Family and work responsibilities	• Identify and provide targeted services to meet the needs of student parents. • Design and implement intrusive advising, counseling, and educational planning models, both on campus and online. • Build internal and external partnerships that help adult learners balance their many responsibilities. • Send clear messages to adult learners that they are valued—and that they belong in college. • Create a family-friendly campus.	

Barriers	Strategies to eliminate or reduce barriers	Strategies that might work at my institution
Financial and time challenges	• Structure admissions, financial aid, recruitment, and registration procedures (online and on campus) to meet the needs of adult learners. • Offer flexible scheduling, self-paced courses, and online programs and services. • Publish clearly defined and streamlined pathways to every degree and certificate. • Build community partnerships that increase financial support for adult learners. • Improve credit-transfer policies among institutions. • Establish an emergency loan fund. • Support Pell Grant changes at the national level as well as flexible scheduling and accelerated programs at the state level.	
Confined to a specific geographic location	• Develop transfer agreements with local public and private institutions. • Increase online, blended, self-paced, and off-campus learning opportunities. • Increase the support services available to students taking advantage of online, blended, self-paced, and off-campus learning opportunities.	
Poor grades and/or low scores on college placement tests	• Examine placement policies for adult learners, especially in relation to developmental courses. • Provide a variety of academic support services (e.g., "brush-up" sessions, learning labs, tutoring) at times and in locations convenient to adult learners. • Prepare adult learners to take college placement tests. • Embed developmental courses in programs of study. • Partner with area K–12 systems to strengthen English, math, and reading preparation for all students.	
Difficulty obtaining credit for prior learning experiences	• Streamline the awarding of credit for prior learning experiences. • Establish clear and consistent guidelines for assessing and awarding credit for prior learning experiences.	
Not understanding how to navigate the higher education system	• Design and implement an integrated, personalized set of campus-based and online support services that help adults understand the institution (orientation and peer support groups), make sound educational choices (advising, career counseling, and educational planning), and deal with challenges that may interfere with their ability to learn (personal and crisis counseling). • Conduct process improvement studies of major campus-based and online systems that affect students. Identify ways to streamline and improve these systems.	
Uncomfortable with technology	• Provide opportunities for adult learners to assess and update their technology skills before starting classes and throughout their college career.	
Doubt they belong in college	• Create an institution where 25- to 64-year-old students feel comfortable and valued.	

APPLY THE CONCEPTS

Exercise 1.3—Readiness Checklist

Directions: Selecting appropriate technology requires a partnership between student affairs and information technology (IT) areas. The partnership works best when student affairs professionals prepare for technology discussions with IT staff. Use this checklist to determine student affairs readiness to partner with IT at your institution.

	Done	In progress	Not done
The student affairs team has:			
Analyzed and updated work processes and practices in all areas			
Assessed the effectiveness of major programs and services and taken the appropriate action (to maintain, strengthen, or eliminate)			
Identified and prioritized technology needs for each area			
Defined major outcomes and outcomes measures for each area			
Determined how students use technology and what students like or dislike about current technology applications (e.g., portals, Web pages, etc.)			
A critical mass of staff members knowledgeable about and proficient with technology			
Key staff members who have participated in IT information sessions that describe what is happening in technology at the institution and across the country			
Leaders who understand technology and change theory and know how to manage change			
Demonstrated that all members understand and adhere to the institution's data security and authentication rules			

APPLY THE CONCEPTS

Exercise 1.4—Assess Your Technology Knowledge and Skills

Directions: Rate your ability to use the following technology tools to interact with or create support services for adult learners. The skill levels are defined as:

- **Developing:** Limited knowledge or skills but willing to learn.
- **Proficient:** Able to use knowledge and skills to interact with or create support services for adult learners.
- **Exemplary:** Capable of helping others acquire skills and knowledge in this area.

	Developing	Proficient	Exemplary
Accessibility tools (e.g., speech-to-text)			
Blogging platforms (e.g., Blogger, Tumblr, Wordpress)			
Communication software (e.g., e-mail, texting, Skype, podcasts, online discussion boards)			
Content management systems (e.g., Squarespace, SharePoint, Azure, Joomla, Drupal Gardens)			
Design or image editing software (e.g., Adobe Photoshop, Image Now)			
Enterprise resource planning systems (e.g., Banner, Datatel, PeopleSoft)			
Predictive analytics (e.g., IBM data mining, predictive analytics, statistical toolkits)			
Presentation software (e.g., Keynote, Prezi, Microsoft PowerPoint)			
Productivity software (e.g., Microsoft Office)			
Project management software (e.g., Team Dynamics Higher Education, Microsoft Project, eBuilder)			
Reporting tools (e.g., Microsoft Excel, Microsoft SharePoint)			
Social media (e.g., Facebook, YouTube, LinkedIn, Twitter)			
Smartphones (e.g., Apple iPhone, Samsung Galaxy) and tablets (e.g., Apple iPad, Google Nexus, Microsoft Surface Pro)			
Software unique to specific areas of responsibility within student affairs (e.g., admissions, career center, financial aid, housing and residence life, orientation, records, registration)			
Other (please identify)			

REFERENCES

American Association of Community Colleges. (2014). *2014 fact sheet.* Retrieved from http://www.aacc.nche.edu/AboutCC/Documents/FactSheet_2014_bw_r2.pdf

American College Personnel Association, & National Association of Student Personnel Administrators. (2010). *Envisioning the future of student affairs.* Retrieved from http://naspa.org/consolidation/tf-final-narr.pdf

Aslanian, C. B., & Clinefelter, D. L. (2012). *Online college students 2012: Comprehensive data on demands and preferences.* Louisville, KY: The Learning House.

Baxter Magolda, M. (1992). *Knowing and reasoning in college: Gender-related patterns in students' intellectual development.* San Francisco, CA: Jossey-Bass.

Bean, J. P., & Metzner, B. S. (1985). A conceptual model of nontraditional undergraduate student attrition. *Review of Educational Research, 55*(4), 485–540.

Brown, P. A. (2012). *Degree attainment for adult learners.* Retrieved from http://www.acenet.edu/news-room/Documents/Degree-Attainment-for-Adult-Learners—Brown.pdf

Carnevale, A. P., Smith, N., & Strohl, J. (2010). *Help wanted: Projections of jobs and educational requirements through 2018.* Washington, DC: Georgetown University Center on Education and the Workforce.

Chickering, A. W., & Reisser, L. (1993). *Education and identity* (2nd ed.). San Francisco, CA: Jossey-Bass.

Choy, S. (2002). *Nontraditional undergraduates.* Washington, DC: U.S. Department of Education, Institute of Education Sciences, National Center for Education Statistics.

Christiansen, C. M., & Eyring, H. J. (2011). The *innovative university: Changing the DNA of higher education from the inside out.* San Francisco, CA: Jossey-Bass.

Cross, K. P. (1992). *Adults as learners: Increasing participation and facilitating learning.* San Francisco, CA: Jossey-Bass.

Culp, M. M., & Dungy, G. J. (Eds.). (2012). *Building a culture of evidence in student affairs: A guide for leaders and practitioners.* Washington, DC: National Association of Student Personnel Administrators.

Erikson, E. H. (1980). *Identity and the life cycle.* New York, NY: W.W. Norton and Company.

Gertner, J. (2013, June). The data demystifier. *Fast Company, 176,* 70–73.

Jenkins, D. (2011). *Get with the program: Accelerating community college students' entry into and completion of programs of study* (CCRC Working Paper No. 32). New York, NY: Community College Research Center, Teachers College, Columbia University.

Karp, M. M. (2011). *How non-academic supports work: Four mechanisms for improving student Outcomes* (CCRC Brief No. 54). New York, NY: Community College Research Center, Teachers College, Columbia University.

Kazis, R., Callahan, A., Davidson, C., McLeod, A., Bosworth, B., Choitz, V., & Hoops, J. (2007). *Adult learners in higher education: Barriers to success and strategies to improve results.* Retrieved from http://files.eric.ed.gov/fulltext/ED497801.pdf

Klein-Collins, R. (2010). *Fueling the race to postsecondary success: A 48-institution study of prior learning assessment and adult student outcomes.* Chicago, IL: Council for Adult and Experiential Learning.

Knowles, M. S. (1978). *The adult learner: A neglected species.* Houston, TX: Gulf Publishing.

Knox, A. B. (1977). *Adult development and learning: A handbook on individual growth and competence in the adult years for education and the helping professions.* San Francisco, CA: Jossey-Bass.

Levine, A. (2000). Higher education in the digital age. *Student Affairs On-Line, 1*(1). Retrieved from http://www.studentaffairs.com/ejournal/Spring_2000/article1.html

Levine, A., & Dean, D. R. (2012). *Generation on a tightrope: A portrait of today's college student.* San Francisco, CA: Jossey-Bass.

Lewin, K. (1936). *Principles of topological psychology.* New York, NY: McGraw-Hill.

Magolda, P. M., & Baxter Magolda, M. (2011). *Contested issues in student affairs: Diverse perspectives and respectful dialogue.* Sterling, VA: Stylus.

Moneta, L. (2005). Technology and student affairs redux. In K. Kruger (Ed.), *Technology in student affairs: Supporting student learning and services* (New directions for student services, No. 112, pp. 3–14). San Francisco, CA: Jossey-Bass.

National Student Clearinghouse Research Center. (2012). Signature report 3. Retrieved from http://nscresearchcenter.org/wp-content/uploads/NSC_Signature_Report_3.pdf

O'Banion, T. (2013). *Access, success, and completion: A primer for community college faculty, administrators, staff, and trustees.* Chandler, AZ: League for Innovation in the Community College.

Pusser, B., Breneman, D. W., Gansneder, B. M., Kohl, K. J., Levin, J. S., Milan, J. H., & Turner, S. E. (2007). *Returning to learning: Adults' success in college is key to America's future.* Indianapolis, IN: Lumina Foundation for Education.

Sanford, N. (1966). *Self and society: Social change and individual development.* Hawthorne, NY: Aldine.

Schlossberg, N. K., Lynch, A. Q., & Chickering, A. W. (1989). *Improving higher education environments for adults.* San Francisco, CA: Jossey-Bass.

Scott-Clayton, J. (2011). *The shapeless river: Does a lack of structure inhibit students' progress at community colleges?* (CCRC Working Paper No. 25). New York, NY: Community College Research Center, Columbia University, Teachers College.

Soares, L. (2013). *Post-traditional learners and the transformation of postsecondary education: A manifesto for college leaders.* Retrieved from http://www.acenet.edu/news-room/documents/soares-post-traditional-v5-011813.pdf

U.S. Census Bureau. (2012). *The 2012 statistical abstract of the United States.* Retrieved from http://www.census.gov/compendia/statab/2012edition.html

MODULE 2

Principles for Effectively Serving Adult Learners

Judith Wertheim

ABSTRACT

For 40 years, the Council for Adult and Experiential Learning (CAEL) has been helping colleges and universities identify and remove barriers to adult learning. Because many of these barriers are institutional, CAEL has developed a taxonomy of nine principles for effectively serving the adult learner. This module identifies and discusses the principles, presents examples of how they can be implemented, and describes how student affairs leaders and practitioners can help ensure that their institutions more effectively recruit, retain, and graduate adult students.

ADULT LEARNERS ARE DIFFERENT

As Module 1 makes clear, the programs and services that adult learners need are different from those in place for traditional students who enter college directly after graduating from high school. The Council for Adult and Experiential Learning (CAEL) has long recognized that adult learners come to their postsecondary studies with learning experiences, life circumstances, goals, and needs that may be very different from those of traditionally aged students. Beginning in 1974 as a project funded by the Carnegie Corporation and housed at Educational Testing Service, CAEL (at that point in its history named the Cooperative Assessment of Experiential Learning) initially sought to identify and make more widely known the best practices in assessment of experiential learning (CAEL, 1999).

"Experiential learning" is learning that is acquired through on-the-job experiences, corporate training, military service, volunteer activities, or independent study. The original CAEL project demonstrated that such learning can validly and reliably be assessed as equivalent to college-level learning and, consequently, awarded college credit. Given its emphasis on experiential learning, CAEL quite naturally focused on adult learners, individuals returning to school after having had many learning experiences outside the classroom. Today, as noted on its website (http://www.cael.org/home), CAEL's vision has evolved to "linking learning and work"—providing meaningful learning, credentials, and work for every adult.

The major impetus for the initial CAEL project was to remove barriers for adults seeking to continue their education. CAEL and its early supporters believed that helping adults earn college credit for their prior learning experiences would accelerate their progress toward a degree and increase their chances of success. The project's nationwide study of prior learning assessment (PLA) and learning outcomes confirms this assumption: Adults who earn credits for prior learning graduate in significantly higher percentages than those who do not earn PLA credit.

Figure 2.1

Comparison of Graduation Rates

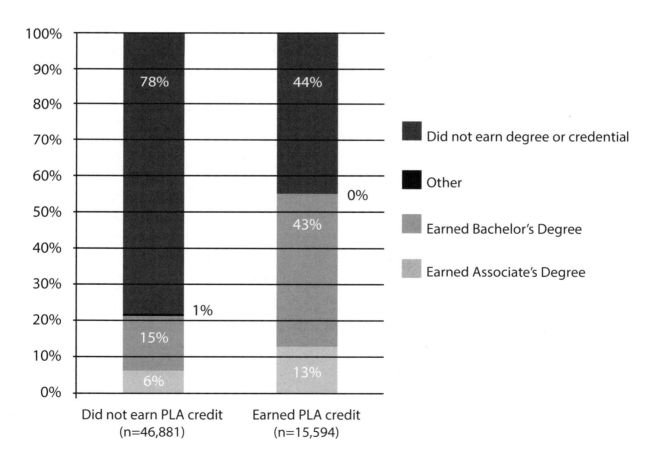

Source: Klein-Collins, 2010, p. 34. Reprinted with permission.

PRINCIPLES OF EFFECTIVELY SERVING ADULT LEARNERS

However, offering students the opportunity to earn PLA credit is clearly not the only way for institutions to effectively meet the needs of their adult learners. As those who work with adult learners know so well, recruiting, retaining, and graduating these students is a complex process, involving a wide range of services tailored to their particular needs. This acknowledgment, however, is not sufficient; it is also essential to ask what those needs are.

To answer this question, CAEL launched the Adult Learner Focused Institution (ALFI) initiative in 1999. Recognizing that some institutions are more successful than others in identifying and meeting the needs of their adult learners, CAEL partnered with the American Productivity and Quality Center (APQC) to conduct a benchmarking study with the following six institutions:

- Athabasca University
- The College of New Rochelle/School of New Resources
- DePaul University/School for New Learning
- Marylhurst University
- Sinclair Community College
- State University of New York Empire State College (Flint, 1999)

Building on this six-institution study, CAEL clarified the findings and identified eight specific principles addressed by institutions that effectively serve adult learners. These principles are:

1. Outreach
2. Life and Career Planning
3. Financing
4. Assessment of Learning Outcomes
5. Teaching-Learning Process
6. Student Support Systems
7. Technology
8. Strategic Partnerships (Flint, 2005)

Soon afterward, while working on a Lumina Foundation-funded project that focused on implementation of the principles among 25 community colleges, CAEL identified yet another principle:

9. Transitions

With further investigation, CAEL determined that implementation of the transitions principle is applicable to both institutions offering an associate's degree and those offering a baccalaureate degree (Frey, 2007). Thus, there are nine CAEL principles that are essential for effectively serving adult learners.

Defining the CAEL Principles

The importance of these nine principles is not intuitive. If it were, more institutions would be successful in retaining and graduating their adult learners. Similarly, the operational definitions of the principles are not intuitive. Here, then, are the working definitions of the CAEL principles for effectively serving adult learners:

- **Outreach:** The institution conducts its outreach to adult learners by overcoming barriers in time, place, and tradition in order to create lifelong access to educational opportunities.

- **Life and Career Planning:** The institution addresses adult learners' life and career goals before or at the onset of enrollment in order to assess and align its capacities to help learners reach their goals.

- **Financing:** The institution promotes choice by using an array of payment options for adult learners in order to expand equity and financial flexibility.

- **Assessment of Learning Outcomes:** The institution defines and assesses the knowledge, skills, and competencies acquired by adult learners—both from the curriculum and from life and work experience—in order to assign credit and confer degrees with rigor.

- **Teaching-Learning Process:** The institution's faculty uses multiple methods of instruction (including experiential and problem-based methods, as well as online and hybrid models) for adult learners in order to connect curricular concepts to useful knowledge and skills.

- **Student Support Systems:** The institution assists adult learners by using comprehensive academic and student support systems in order to enhance students' capacities to become self-directed, lifelong learners.

- **Technology:** The institution uses technology to provide relevant and timely information and to enhance the learning experience.

- **Strategic Partnerships:** The institution engages in strategic relationships, partnerships, and collaborations with employers and other organizations in order to develop and improve educational opportunities for adult learners.

- **Transitions:** The institution supports guided pathways that lead to and from its programs and services in order to ensure that students' learning will apply usefully to achieving their educational and career goals. (Frey, 2007, pp. 4–5)

Practitioners may ask whether the order of the above list is significant. As mentioned earlier, Transitions was the last principle identified, but there are no other priorities implied in the sequence of the list. The nine principles are equally important. Indeed, those who work with adult learners will recognize that many—if not all—of the principles overlap in practice. A basic CAEL tenet for understanding and implementing the principles is that they are interrelated and work as a whole. Thus, institutional strengths and challenges frequently reflect performance on more than one principle. Even at the beginning of the project, when the National Center for Higher Education Management Services (NCHEMS) worked with CAEL to assign scores to institutional performance on the ALFI principles, statisticians noted that individual items on the self-assessment could, on occasion, relate to more than one benchmark (Frey, 2003).

Table 2.1 indicates how some of these interactions might work. The first column lists an activity that is part of the ALFI Toolkit, which is described in more detail later in this module. The second column identifies the CAEL principles that each activity addresses. The third column offers insights and observations on how student affairs professionals can contribute to specific institutional activities. Table 2.1 clearly demonstrates how the CAEL principles work together and are, in many respects, inseparable.

Table 2.1

Synergies among the CAEL Principles

Institutional activity	Principles addressed	Insights, comments, and observations
A *commitment to serving adult learners* is emphasized in the institutional mission statement, catalogs, brochures and view books, websites and online materials, public statements by top administrators, and orientation materials and handbooks for faculty, staff, and students.	• Assessment of Learning Outcomes • Financing • Life and Career Planning • Outreach • Teaching-Learning Process • Student Support Systems	**Institutions:** Too frequently, institutions neglect some of the outreach materials listed in the first column and demonstrate only a superficial commitment to serving adult learners. For example, institutions may not picture older students in their literature, or key Web search words may omit terms like *adult, returning,* or *older.* In a similar vein, catalogs may refer to adult learners as an afterthought or provide incomplete or misleading information about the possibility of earning credit for prior learning experiences. **Student affairs:** Student affairs leaders can make a difference by collaborating with colleagues in information technology and institutional research to gather, analyze, and share data about the number, needs, and importance of adult learners. Leaders also can draw attention to how the institution unconsciously neglects adult learners and can arrange formal and informal opportunities for institutional leaders to interact with and listen to current and former adult learners.
Typical features of the curriculum include *accelerated approaches, a flexible academic calendar with continuous offerings,* or *cohort-based approaches.*	• Outreach • Teaching-Learning Process • Student Support Systems	**Institutions:** Creative, flexible approaches to the teaching-learning process are important to adult learners. Given their multiple responsibilities in addition to school, adult learners seek ways to maximize their time and accommodate other responsibilities, which may change during the course of a semester or quarter. Institutions can recruit and retain adult learners by developing flexible modes of instruction, with regard not only to timing but also ease of entry and exit. For example, identical sections of one course, offered at different times and on different days of the week, can accommodate a shift worker whose schedule changes. Institutions also need to realize that even though cohort groups may provide less flexibility than independent study, they can provide crucial support that may make the difference between adult learners' completing a course or giving up in the face of competing demands. **Student affairs:** While faculty members are responsible for developing flexible modes of instruction, student affairs leaders are responsible for designing services that support adult learners enrolled in campus-based, distance learning, e-learning, or blended courses. Student affairs professionals need to recognize that peers, as well as trained professionals, can provide significant support to adult learners and should be an integral part of any support service strategy for undergraduate adults. Finally, when designing creative learning experiences, academic and student affairs professionals can partner to: • Capitalize on the value of cohort groups in helping to retain adult learners. • Design and implement targeted orientation and college success experiences for adult learners. • Identify nonclassroom-based support services that adult learners need, and then create incentives for them to use these services. • Gather and analyze data to determine how effectively the institution is meeting the needs of adult learners.

Institutional activity	Principles addressed	Insights, comments, and observations
The institution offers part-time faculty workshops on *mentoring adult learners.*	• Life and Career Planning • Teaching-Learning Process • Student Support Systems	**Institutions:** Often, institutions provide only cursory training for part-time faculty, and this training does not specifically address the needs of adult learners. Yet, appropriate faculty development for part-time and adjunct instructors can yield important benefits, not only in supporting students but also in strengthening the bonds among the part-time or adjunct faculty, their students, and the institution. This can contribute to increased retention for students as well as for part-time faculty. **Student affairs:** Faculty members are subject-matter experts. Student affairs professionals have a great deal of expertise in learning theory and adult development. Each group can contribute to strengthening the persistence and completion rates of adult learners. Working together, both groups can design and implement innovative workshops that help adjunct faculty members increase their understanding of and ability to work with adult learners. By leveraging technology (e.g., online streaming video), the workshops need not be bound by time or place.

Meeting the Adult Student's Needs

After identifying the first eight principles, CAEL joined with NCHEMS and Noel-Levitz Higher Education Consulting to develop the ALFI Toolkit. This kit, updated after transitions was added as a principle, focuses exclusively on the principles and helps institutions assess how they are performing as Adult Learner Focused Institutions. The toolkit consists of two surveys: one completed by adult learners, the other by a small team of representatives of the various offices that may deal with adults at the institution. Each survey consists of approximately 50 questions, and the results identify perceptions of institutional performance vis-à-vis adult learners. Results are compared between groups and against other institutions. The real power of the ALFI Toolkit data comes from the internal group comparisons, which institutional administrators can use to identify areas of agreement—for both strengths and challenges—as well as disagreement. Institutions can subsequently emphasize and market their strengths, prioritize and work to improve challenges, and clarify the reasons for disagreements.

Because CAEL's nine Principles for Effectively Serving Adult Learners are so inextricably linked to the ALFI Toolkit, the principles have come to be referred to as "the ALFI principles." They can help student affairs leaders and practitioners become aware of areas to which they can direct their expertise to help adult learners at their institutions. Moreover, the principles can help them identify how they can work at the institution to help support adults in less obvious, albeit just as effective, ways.

Incidentally, it is important to note that in nearly all ALFI administrations, CAEL has identified another value of the institutional self-assessment: conversations among institutional members. Because their primary responsibilities are often not student affairs, many members of these institutional teams report that their discussion about the ALFI survey is the first time they have truly focused on the adult learner. Certainly it is the first time that they as a group have focused on the adult learner. Their

IN THE SPOTLIGHT

Changing the culture at Northwestern State University (NSU) in Louisiana has been an ongoing process. Yet the institution has made significant strides toward recognizing the changing nature of its student population and creating awareness of the needs of adult learners. Darlene Williams, vice president for technology, research, and economic development, is encouraged by the progress at her institution. The developments affect many policies and practices—some of which have been in existence for many years.

Recognizing that other institutions are dealing with similar challenges, Williams recommends several strategies for changing campus perceptions, using the ALFI principles as a framework.

- ☼ Begin the change process with caution and with a plan.

- ☼ Develop a leadership team that includes a range of stakeholders. This will ensure that the team is representative of all relevant units of the institution and that they are all on the same page. Assign to the team administrators and faculty as well as those who deal directly with students.

- ☼ Review best practices at institutions across the country.

- ☼ Brainstorm with the team. Encourage them to look at new opportunities for adults.

- ☼ Proceed with caution. Be patient and do not expect major change to happen quickly.

- ☼ Inform adults of the opportunities available to them. Convey the message that university faculty and staff want them to succeed and are there to help.

Williams notes that as awareness of the needs of adult learners has grown at NSU, her colleagues have realized that many of the changes will also benefit traditional students. Thus, the institutional goal is to sustain the changes and, in the long run, serve all students more effectively. (D. Williams, personal communication, March 25, 2014)

interactive ALFI discussions have, thus, been crucial to raising awareness among campus personnel of adult student needs and the synergies that can help meet those needs.

ADDRESSING THE ALFI PRINCIPLES IN PRACTICE

The goal of reviewing the ALFI principles is—in a word—action. Results of the ALFI surveys, coupled with understanding of the principles, give institutions data to use toward identifying and marketing institutional strengths, prioritizing challenges, and developing strategies to improve specific services to adult learners. These strategies can range from the relatively low-cost to those that are far more resource-intensive. Yet even for costly plans, budget requests accompanied by data can make a convincing case for additional funding.

Low-Cost ALFI Initiatives

Because budgetary concerns are nearly universal, here are some low-cost strategies to address the ALFI principles and improve services to adult learners.

Redesign orientation. Even when they are carefully designed, orientation sessions for new adult learners may not actually address students' major concerns and needs. For example, Continuing Education at The Pennsylvania State University learned that its orientation sessions assumed students knew more about financial aid resources than they actually did. Consequently, Penn State redesigned its orientation sessions to enlighten students about financing (e.g., financial aid opportunities, deadlines, and regulations). The redesign had no additional cost, but it improved the odds of retaining adult students and helping them leverage available financial aid resources (Rebecca Beatty, associate director, Office of Continuing Education at University Park, Penn State University, personal communication, April 2007).

Another way institutions have redesigned student orientation sessions is by making them mandatory, either face-to-face or online, and to offer information that is essential to the target population. In the case of adult learners, most students want to:

- Learn how to navigate and effectively use the institution's website.
- Identify the assistance available to them in the areas of advising, counseling, financial aid, technology, and tutoring.
- Learn how to access these services outside the typical 9 a.m. to 5 p.m. time frame.
- Understand the requirements for their degree, when specific courses will be offered, and which courses have unique patterns (e.g., offered only once a year or only at a specific time or on a specific campus).
- Learn about prerequisites and recommended course loads.
- Understand general college or course expectations and requirements, such as attendance, participation, and deadlines.
- Learn how to contact and interact with faculty.

It is prudent to assume that students come to an institution with little knowledge about the institution itself, about its culture, and about success strategies. It is also prudent to assume that busy adults will not have the time or the confidence to access all the important information available to them—or even to realize that the information is important. Consequently, moving away from flexibility and instead requiring completion of an orientation session have helped several institutions ensure that returning adult learners begin their studies with information they will need to succeed and knowledge about how to access additional information when they need it.

Create a student mentor program. Although adult programs frequently provide informal opportunities for students to meet and exchange experiences and strategies for success, a formal student mentor program can go a long way toward engaging both new students and those who are more established. A "buddy" program can effectively help new students learn about the institution from peers whose experiences are similar to their own. Such support may be invaluable to new students who do not have the discretionary time to take advantage of a student lounge or student get-togethers, and can be aided by the convenience of social media. The connection to a mentor will help adults learn the ropes and will provide a support system that they might not otherwise have. Moreover, the training of the mentors that is integral to such a program will provide the mentors themselves with a cohort group and will also help strengthen their connections to the institution.

Establish an adult learner committee. Participants in the ALFI surveys, who have included faculty, administrators, advisors, financial aid personnel, bursars, veterans' affairs officers, admissions staff, and marketing professionals, typically report that the discussions among ALFI committee members are extremely productive, for both raising awareness about the needs of adult learners and developing initiatives to meet those needs. Consequently, many institutions have named those participants as charter members of an Adult Learner Committee, charged with focusing on returning students. These committees meet regularly, thus helping the institution maintain its commitment to—and focus on—adult learners.

QUICK TIP

"Preparing for and administering the ALFI surveys at Eastern Kentucky University encouraged campuswide conversations about the unique needs of adult learners. Building on this dialogue, the university established the Student Outreach and Transition Office, a one-stop shop for adults and transfer students that offers individualized guidance and support." —Lisa Cox, director, Student Outreach and Transition Office, Eastern Kentucky University (personal communication, March 27, 2014)

Convene student focus groups. CAEL recommends that after institutions complete the ALFI surveys and receive their results, they convene focus groups of students, staff, and administrators to discuss their divergent perceptions of institutional strengths and challenges. In addition, within the framework of the ALFI principles, CAEL also advises institutions that have not completed the surveys to convene such groups. The discussions that ensue will help the institution identify strengths and challenges, perceptions and misperceptions held by students, and priority areas for student support and advising. Moreover, convening the same focus groups semiannually can help institutions measure progress in meeting objectives and addressing concerns related to adult learners. For students to participate fully and frankly, they need to see evidence of progress and feel that their voices are being heard.

ALFI Initiatives Requiring Additional Resources

Some approaches to implementing the ALFI principles are cost-free or low-cost, but others require additional human and financial resources. At a time of concerted efforts throughout the country to recruit and retain adults, many institutions have determined that the return on investment is worth the cost. For example, several institutions have funded one or more of the following initiatives designed to increase the persistence and completion rates of undergraduate adult learners.

Create new and expand existing course delivery options. Recognizing the relevance of the principles of outreach, teaching-learning process, technology, and strategic partnerships for their adult learners, many institutions have initiated programs such as Saturday and Sunday course offerings,

"Friday night" degree programs, accelerated degree programs, hybrid courses, modular courses, credit for massive open online courses, and courses offered at employment sites immediately before or after the workday. Indeed, many of these delivery options are no longer considered innovative and are available even at traditional institutions for traditional students.

CAEL applauds these efforts to offer flexible academic programming to adults with busy schedules and multiple responsibilities. Yet CAEL also cautions institutions to ascertain the demand for such alternatives before implementing them. It is not necessarily true that "if you build it, they will come." In fact, several institutions report that demand for some of their innovative programs is lower than anticipated and that the programs are, consequently, unnecessarily costly. Demographic research and additional focus groups can help determine the demand for specific delivery options. Moreover, institutions would do well to consider a gradual introduction of alternate delivery options, accompanied by formative evaluations, before fully committing to the changes.

In addition, advisors should be particularly alert to the need for support services for students who enroll in classes that are delivered via alternate methods. For example, is there online advising for those who take online courses? How do employees taking college courses at the workplace access advising and other support services? Are advising, tutoring services, and food services available on Friday evenings or weekends for those who choose to attend classes at those times? In short, adding creative course options is not a simple answer to the complex matter of meeting the needs of adults.

QUICK TIP

Diane Dingfelder, executive director of outreach and continuing education at Winona State University, addresses the need for advising services dedicated to adults and their specific concerns by hiring student affairs professionals with specialized skills and approaches. Winona State University also introduced proactive advising to help its adult students attend to their concerns before they become problems (Diane Dingfelder, personal communication, September 29, 2013).

Hire a retention coordinator or an advising professional who can focus on adult learners. Although one theme throughout this tutorial is that adult learners are different from traditional postsecondary students, institutional hiring policies do not always reflect this insight. Many hiring practices imply that an advisor = an advisor = an advisor, even though this is not always the case. Institutions that are serious about focusing on improving services for adult learners will hire specialists. For example, William L. (Lance) Ikard, director of the prior learning assessment program at Middle Tennessee State University, indicated that the university determined that advising nontraditional/adult/online students is different from advising traditional students and added dedicated advisor positions to accommodate adult students (personal communication, September 27, 2013).

Expanding its hiring practices in creative ways while addressing the ALFI principles, Continuing Education at Penn State hired a financial literacy coordinator to build a foundation of resources, webinars, and workshops around personal finance and budgeting, credit card use/debt, and student loan debt. Martha Jordan, director of adult learner advocacy at Penn State, reported that this initiative has been warmly welcomed by adults throughout the university community, even those not enrolled in the continuing education unit (personal communication, September 27, 2013).

IN THE SPOTLIGHT

Dalton State College in Georgia has begun an innovative program to support the Life and Career Planning needs of its *prospective* students. Andrew Meyer, assistant vice president for academic affairs at Dalton State, reports that the impetus for this program was the recognition that adult learners are frequently unclear about their career goals and do not know how to select an appropriate institution. Consequently, Dalton State is joining with regional technical colleges to work with adults before they enroll in postsecondary education. In this program, begun in the spring of 2014 and funded by a U.S. Department of Education College Access Challenge Grant, career counselors help prospective Dalton State students assess their aptitudes and interests and identify possible careers. The counselors then refer the students to the appropriate academic program, either at Dalton State or at one of the cooperating institutions. Institutional representatives who planned this program included vice presidents of the institutions, representatives of the enrollment services units, counselors, and program specialists from related academic departments. All collaborated to ensure that prospective students make reasonable life and career plans and then enroll in the institution that is right for them, thus also enhancing strategic partnerships and student support services (Andrew Meyer, personal communication, March 25, 2014).

Designate life and career planning resources for adults. Advisors can play a vital role in helping adults, even those with jobs, address the principles of life and career planning, learning outcomes, and transitions by focusing on helping the students articulate their career plans and integrate their coursework and their careers. Research conducted by Noel-Levitz and CAEL (2013) consistently showed that adult learners are most dissatisfied with the ways in which their need for life and career planning is being met by institutions, whether that institution is a two-year college, a four-year college, or a university. Given the skills of advising professionals in this area, CAEL recommends that institutions develop programs to help their adult students with career planning as soon as possible. Again this is a priority for all higher education institutions: community colleges, 4-year colleges, and universities. CAEL also recommends that institutions share resources to see if they can collaborate to offer these services. Because large numbers of students need help with life and career planning, exploring ways to scale up efficiently may well benefit not only the students, but also the institutions.

Moreover, help with life and career planning is integrally related to the principle of transitions. In a 2007 CAEL report, Frey noted that "adult students have little patience for courses that do not help them progress toward their degree" (Frey, 2007, p. 8). A question adults repeatedly ask is "How long will this take me?" They want to be sure that their previous learning will apply to their degree, that the path to their educational objective is clear, and that their coursework will prepare them for their next steps.

Develop an adult orientation class (either on site or online). Bainbridge College in Georgia developed a class for adult learners that focuses on helping returning students cope with test anxiety, negative thinking, lack of support from employers, costs, day care and transportation options, and career readiness. Although the program is still in its early stages, initial results indicate that it has a significant impact on student retention. For example, from fall 2011 to fall 2012, retention for adults who completed the class was 56%, compared with a retention rate of 15% for adults who did not complete the class (Trish Paterson, executive director, College Access Initiatives, University System of Georgia, personal communication, September 25, 2013).

ALFI Principles for the 21st Century

As noted earlier in this module, CAEL's research at the end of the 20th century led to the identification of the ALFI principles. But years have passed. Are the principles still relevant? Yes, they are. The answer is affirmative for two important reasons:

1. Institutions continue to find the principles helpful in designing services for their adult learners.
2. Even at this point, many institutions have not fully implemented ALFI-based activities that can effectively help them recruit, retain, and graduate adult learners.

Quick Tip

Martha Jordan, director of adult learner advocacy at Penn State, believes that institutions should focus on helping adult learners plan for life and for careers. Colleges and universities also need to assist adult learners to understand the transitions to the next stage of their lives. Continuing Education at Penn State, for example, recognized soon after administering the ALFI Toolkit that the institution lacked appropriate career-oriented services and immediately hired a career counselor for returning adults. Since that time, Penn State has added two adult-learner-focused career counselors (Martha Jordan, personal communication, September 27, 2013).

The principles remain relevant, even though specific activities within them may change over the years. For example, MOOCs (massive open online courses) meant nothing in the late 1990s, but today discussion of them is everywhere. The principles provide a framework for understanding how MOOCs—and other new developments—affect adults. MOOCs link to the ALFI principles of outreach, technology, assessment of learning outcomes, teaching-learning process, and life and career planning. One of the principles' strengths is that they can accommodate changes in the learning environment and continue to suggest a context for effective strategies.

Consideration of MOOCs raises the larger question of how the ALFI principles apply to e-learning in all its variations (e.g., synchronous courses, asynchronous courses, or hybrid courses). Although CAEL initially developed the ALFI tools with a focus on campus-based programs, the principles also apply to distance programs. Particularly now, when so many adults are finding it helpful to enroll in classes that they can complete any time at any place, it is important to reflect on how to apply the principles to distance learners. Perhaps most important is the principle of student support systems. Unfortunately, even in a campus-based program, adults may feel that they are peripheral and that student support services do not accommodate their needs or recognize their constraints. It is therefore important to enhance student support systems for adults who have limited face-to-face interaction with each other, as well as with faculty and staff. Sometimes, those enhancements can be relatively easy to achieve. For example, at the October 24, 2013, meeting of the Association of Jesuit Colleges and Universities, Robert Deahl, dean of the College of Professional Studies at Marquette University, noted that simply personalizing e-mail communications to current and prospective adult learners results in improved recruitment and retention.

Yet a focus on only student support systems would be misplaced, for distance learners and for all adult students. This module has emphasized how the ALFI principles are interrelated. Because of this, student affairs leaders must be involved in advancing all the principles in order to help adults succeed at their institutions. The principles work as a whole.

Just as the CAEL principles are interdependent, so, too, are the roles of those who work with adult learners to help them succeed. Although student affairs professionals are most often assigned responsibility for supporting adult learners, the list of principles implies that many institutional representatives—faculty, staff, and administrators—also play a vital role in helping adults. For example, representatives of a variety of areas within academic affairs, business services, information technology, institutional research, and student affairs can influence the students' perceptions of the institution and how the institution is responding to their specific advising and educational planning needs. Student affairs professionals can help educate their colleagues about the unique needs of adults. They can, for example:

- Make presentations at faculty and academic department meetings.
- Highlight student success stories on the institutional website and other publications.
- Post information about adult learners and adult learning on the faculty website.
- Encourage administrators to include information about adult learners and adult learning in orientation for new faculty and staff.
- Advocate for or independently convene an adult learner committee, including faculty, staff, and administrators from across the institution.
- Engage faculty, staff, and administrators in short-term planning projects to help adults.
- Accept appointment to institutional committees that focus on adult learners.
- Publicly recognize faculty, staff, and administrators who have provided support to adult learners.
- Advocate for recognition of adults at commencement and awards ceremonies.

Within the framework of the ALFI principles, student affairs professionals are singularly well situated to take the lead in helping the institution identify effective strategies to help adult learners. O*Net OnLine (2010), for example, listed the following among the skills required for academic advisors:

- Active listening
- Speaking
- Social perceptiveness
- Critical thinking
- Judgment and decision making
- Complex problem solving
- Service orientation

Coupled with professional training in advising and with an understanding of the culture of one's own institution, these skills can help the advising professional emphasize the importance of serving the adult learner, garner support for the adult learner, and succeed in enhancing the educational experience of the adult learner.

When they understand and implement the principles, student affairs leaders and their colleagues can succeed in recruiting, retaining, and graduating adults—goals that are identical to those of their institutions. Indeed, by linking ALFI strategies to broad institutional goals, student affairs professionals can leverage their positions to enhance their services to adult students and to the institution. Measuring success against the ALFI principles can also provide accountability data that are so often required. And by tailoring their activities around the nine principles, student affairs leaders and other student affairs professionals can help their institutions become exemplary ALFIs—Adult Learner Focused *Innovators*—at a time when there is a nationwide demand for helping adult learners earn their postsecondary credentials or degrees.

 IN THE SPOTLIGHT

Diane Dingfelder, executive director of outreach and continuing education at Winona State University (WSU) in Minnesota, refers to institutional efforts to engage in meaningful conversations about effectively serving adult learners as a "journey." Although not complete by any means, the journey is well underway as the university reviews ALFI data related to its performance on the nine principles.

High on the list of priorities at WSU is Assessment of Learning Outcomes. In the spring of 2014, faculty leadership appointed an advisory taskforce, charged with recommending how credit for prior learning can contribute to program requirements and degree completion. In addition, the university is partnering with three community and technical colleges to offer a regional workshop on earning credit for prior learning. Demonstrating the synergies of the ALFI principles, this workshop addresses transitions, outreach, and strategic partnerships, as well as assessment of learning outcomes.

Other activities initiated at WSU in response to the ALFI data are:

○ Additional outreach via evening registration—a first for adult learners on a traditional campus

○ An online orientation for adult learners, addressing both the outreach and technology principles

○ A revision of the Individualized Studies baccalaureate degree to engage more faculty in serving adult learners and address the teaching and learning process

(Diane Dingfelder, personal communication, March 26, 2014)

10 PITFALLS AND HOW TO AVOID THEM

Since identifying the nine principles, CAEL has worked with hundreds of institutions as they try to improve their services to adult learners and thereby improve their performance in recruitment, retention, and graduation. Over the years, CAEL has encountered many institutions that implement best practices, some of which are noted in this module. However, CAEL has also encountered practices that are less than ideal. The following 10 suggestions are offered as cautionary notes. Noting them will help institutions avoid some pitfalls while moving forward more quickly and successfully to embed the ALFI principles in their services to adult learners.

1. Remember to identify and market institutional strengths. Inform internal, as well as external, constituencies about the institution's or the unit's strengths. Do not focus solely on challenges.
2. Prioritize strategies and activities. Do not try to tackle all challenges at once. Although there are nine principles, institutions must prioritize their efforts and deal with two or three principles at a time.
3. Involve institutional stakeholders throughout the process. Consider creating a standing committee or an adult learner task force.
4. If the perceptions of students and those of faculty, staff, and administrators are not congruent, convene focus groups to discuss the discrepancies. Do not assume that one group or the other has "the answer."
5. Use student input to deliver the message that "We are listening to you." If the institution convenes focus groups, respond to those groups with specific, measurable objectives.
6. Look for no-cost or low-cost initiatives. In times of tight budgets, remember that there are adult-learner-focused initiatives that are not costly.
7. Work on related principles at the same time. An advantage of the interrelationship of the principles is that progress on one can often mean progress on another.
8. Use data about the principles and the institution's performance on them as a basis for budget requests.
9. Assess progress. Make changes in activities as needed. Publicize your progress.
10. Share successes with others at the institution and colleagues at other institutions.

APPLY THE CONCEPTS

Exercise 2.1—Apply ALFI Principles to Your Institution

Directions: Look carefully at your own institution, review the ALFI principles, and respond to the following questions:

1. Within the framework of the ALFI principles, what are the institution's strengths and challenges?

    a. How can you capitalize on the strengths?

    b. How would you prioritize the challenges?

    c. Can you address the challenges by grouping them according to the ALFI principles, thereby coordinating activities?

    d. Can you join with other institutions to address the challenges, rather than duplicating efforts?

2. Given that adult students are typically dissatisfied with the ways their institution helps them with life and career planning, how would you evaluate what your institution is doing?

    a. Which activities would you keep?

    b. What would you change? How?

3. How can you, as a student affairs leader, engage other stakeholders at your institution to address the needs of adult learners with more energy?

4. How will you measure progress?

    a. What are your specific goals?

    b. What is your timeline?

RESOURCES

Adult College Completion Network. (n.d.). Retrieved from http://adultcollegecompletion.org

Council for Adult and Experiential Learning website. (n.d.). Retrieved from http://www.cael.org

Council for Adult and Experiential Learning. (2007). *Summary of CAEL's adult learning focused institution (ALFI) initiative activities.* Retrieved from http://www.cael.org/pdfs/ AFLI-Lumina-Summary

Council for Adult and Experiential Learning. (2010). *Duty, honor, country . . . & credit: Serving the education and learning needs of active military and veterans.* Retrieved from http://www.cael.org/ pdfs/128_2010dutyhonorcountryandcreditforumandnews

Lumina Foundation. (n.d.). *Lumina Foundation publications.* Retrieved from http://www. luminafoundation.org/publications.html

Tate, P. J. (2013). *Keeping college within reach: Improving higher education through innovation.* Written Statement before the Education and Workforce Committee, U.S. House of Representatives. Retrieved from http://www.cael.org/pdfs/WrittenStatement

REFERENCES

Council for Adult and Experiential Learning. (1999). *25th anniversary timeline 1974–1999.* Chicago, IL: Author.

Flint, T. (Ed.). (1999). *Best practices in adult learning: A CAEL/APQC benchmarking study.* Chicago, IL: Council for Adult and Experiential Learning.

Flint, T. (2005). *Principles in practice: Assessing adult learning focused institutions, case studies.* Chicago, IL: Council for Adult and Experiential Learning.

Frey, R. (2003). *ALFI report, appendix A: Construction of ISAS benchmarks.* Chicago, IL: Council for Adult and Experiential Learning.

Frey, R. (2007). *Helping adult learners succeed: Tools for two-year colleges.* Chicago, IL: Council for Adult and Experiential Learning.

Klein-Collins, R. (2010). *Fueling the race to postsecondary success: A 48-institution study of prior learning assessment and adult student outcomes.* Chicago, IL: Council for Adult and Experiential Learning.

Noel-Levitz, & Council for Adult and Experiential Learning. (2013). *National adult learners satisfaction-priorities report.* Retrieved from http://www.noellevitz.com/Benchmark

O*Net OnLine. (2010). *Summary report for educational, guidance, school, and vocational counselors.* Retrieved from http://www.onetonline.org/link/summary/21-1012.00

MODULE 3

Increasing Access and Success for Adult Learners

Lessons From Community Colleges

Denise Swett and Marguerite McGann Culp

ABSTRACT

Community colleges have a long history of access, inclusion, and opportunity. They have built a path to higher education for a wide spectrum of students: those with disabilities, veterans, immigrants, and first-generation, low-income, minority, and adult learners. While many factors influence year-to-year priorities within individual community colleges, their essential mission remains unchanged: to provide postsecondary education opportunities to all who can benefit. This module introduces community college practices and programs that effectively support adult learners, provides opportunities for readers to assess their knowledge and skills in a variety of areas related to supporting adult learners, and shares research results that demonstrate what colleges and universities can learn from their community college colleagues.

ADULT LEARNER COMPLETION RATES

Research conducted by the National Student Clearinghouse Research Center discovered that the success of adult learners depends on the type of institution they attend. The gap between the completion rates of adult learners and the completion rates of traditional students at 4-year private colleges is 22%; the gap at 4-year public institutions is 18.5%. Only 2-year colleges post comparable completion rates for adult learners and traditional students (Shapiro & Dundar, 2012). These findings reinforce the need for strategic conversations between community colleges and other higher education institutions, highlight the effectiveness of the support systems that community colleges build with and for adult learners, and underscore the importance of collaboration across institutional types. These findings also demonstrate why *Forbes* magazine views community colleges as an overlooked national asset (Shapiro, 2012).

'TYPICAL' ADULT LEARNERS

The average age of students attending community college is 29 (American Association of Community Colleges, n.d.), and between 2009 and 2019, adult community college enrollment is projected to increase by almost 23% (Kelly & Strawn, 2011). Adult students over the age of 25 comprise 40% of the total enrollments in U.S. community colleges, and adults over 50 comprise 5% (Integrated Postsecondary Education Data System, 2009). Of these adult students, 59% attend part time, 23% are parents, 33% work full time, and 47% live on their own and are financially independent from their parents (Center for Law and Social Policy, 2011; National Center for Education Statistics, 2011). Adult learners also are more likely than traditional-age students to be female and students of color (National Center for Education Statistics, 2011).

Community colleges are often the first choice for adult learners because they focus on basic skills, award certificates as well as degrees, and generally make success more achievable in a short period of time. Cost, location, flexible class scheduling, and a focus on teaching also make community colleges a good choice for adult learners (Hagedorn, 2005; Laanan, 2006). Many adult learners hope to earn a bachelor's degree, but their family and work responsibilities frequently derail these plans. In fact, compared with community college students who enroll soon after high school, adults who start college at a later age (25 to 64) are more likely to earn a certificate and less likely to earn an associate's degree (Prince & Jenkins, 2005).

QUICK TIP

"Community colleges are the pathway for adult learners to retool their education and their careers. It is a collegewide responsibility to provide guidance and support to ensure their success, even with the ongoing funding challenges we face." —Judy Miner, president, Foothill College (personal communication, June 2, 2013)

The majority of adult students have significant family, work, and financial responsibilities, which means that adult learners bring a more complicated set of life circumstances to college (Kasworm, 1990). In their early days, many community colleges, believing that one size fits all, offered adult learners the same processes, programs, and services developed for traditional students. They soon learned that adult learners were different, both as a cohort and within that cohort, and required more customized approaches. The challenge then became transforming community colleges in order to provide adult learners with both the incentive to seek postsecondary education and the support they required to succeed. Although the challenge was daunting, community college faculty and staff believed that the outcome was worth the effort: helping millions of adult learners realize their educational potential and substantially benefit themselves, their families, their communities, and the national economy (Pusser et al., 2007).

 IN THE SPOTLIGHT

"We cannot continue to treat all students alike. . . . The American Association of Community College's *21st Century Report* talks about structured pathways for all students, and we must take into account the unique needs of adult learners. . . . Many states are looking at different diagnostic exams for returning students or adult learners. Others are taking a hard look at developmental education. The bottom line is that we need different pathways for adult learners—some require more support and some need less—but all benefit from appropriate counseling and intrusive advising." —Walter Bumphus, president and CEO, American Association of Community Colleges (personal communication, June 5, 2013)

UNIQUE CHALLENGES

Community colleges serve more adult students who have disabilities, who need basic skills remediation, or who attend part time than do 4-year colleges and universities. Community colleges also serve many adult learners who are seeking not a degree or certificate, but simply skills improvement in order to earn a promotion or start a new career. Adult learners attending community colleges frequently have significant child care and transportation challenges. In fact, the primary reason given by adult students for dropping out of community college is the stress of combining both work and school (Public Agenda, 2009). These findings are part of the reason a growing number of educators question whether Tinto's model of engagement applies to adult learners in the community college, because these students tend to attend part time and have significant outside responsibilities (Karp, 2011b).

Now more than ever, community colleges must develop new and innovative approaches that address the growth in adult student enrollment; implement strategies that increase adult learner persistence and completion rates; and reduce or eliminate institutional barriers to student access, persistence, and completion. The list of challenges and suggested reforms is long and costly, making a unified commitment to supporting adult student success imperative. The challenge, of course, is accomplishing all of this in the face of declining local, state, and federal resources.

IN THE SPOTLIGHT

"It takes great courage for adults to become beginners again. We strive to welcome and honor the rich experiences older students add to our campuses. We steer those needing a boost in their skills, confidence, or support systems to adult re-entry seminars or counseling classes. We've found that, if they tap into their inmost desires to improve their lives and design their own learning environments, adult students can grow into extraordinary learners, campus leaders, and role models for younger students." —Cindy L. Miles, chancellor, Grossmont-Cuyamaca Community College District (personal communication, September 3, 2013)

RESEARCH ON ADULT LEARNERS IN COMMUNITY COLLEGE

Research demonstrates that adult learners are more likely to persist in community college if they receive focused counseling and intrusive advising combined with individualized financial aid (Richburg-Hayes et al., 2009). Strong outreach initiatives led by knowledgeable, well-trained staff who are skilled at connecting with adult learners and assisting them to overcome systemic barriers are an essential first step. For adult learners to succeed, however, colleges must follow up on these outreach initiatives by providing adult learners with targeted advising, assessment, counseling (both career and personal), educational planning, orientation, and support services that meet their unique needs.

The Advisory Committee on Student Financial Assistance (2012) confirmed that keeping adult learners in college is a significant challenge, one created by a combination of factors: the adult student's individual situation, his or her reason for attending college, and the institution's inability to remove barriers or develop practices that improve support. For many years, the Community College Research Center (CCRC; http://ccrc.tc.columbia.edu) has provided invaluable feedback to community colleges on the effectiveness of their policies, processes, and support services in increasing student access and success. This feedback, when coupled with research at the local level, allows community colleges to answer three essential questions: (1) Do current college policies, practices, and support services increase adult learner persistence and completion rates? (2) Are there policies, practices, and support services that the college needs to modify or eliminate to better serve its adult learner population? (3) What new policies, practices, and support services have the potential to increase the persistence and completion rates of the college's adult learner population? Exercise 3.1 provides a snapshot of major CCRC findings

QUICK TIP

"We think we are helping students with online forms and computer-based registration when we are actually making it much more difficult for returning adult students who just do not have the skills to navigate these systems successfully." —Pam Walker, vice president of student services, American River College (personal communication, July 8, 2013)

and invites readers to identify the actions their institution has taken that are consistent with the findings. The exercise allows student affairs professionals to determine how effectively their institution supports students who are adult learners. Completing the exercise also helps readers to identify areas where their institution may need to add programs or services.

MENTAL MODEL FOR WORKING WITH ADULT LEARNERS

As described in detail in Module 2, the Council for Adult and Experiential Learning (CAEL) has developed nine principles for effectively serving adult learners (Klein-Collins, 2011). Over the years, student affairs professionals have drawn on their knowledge of these principles, national research findings, and their experiences with adult learners to develop a mental model of what matters most in helping adult learners make the decision to continue their education and to successfully earn a certificate or a degree. Figure 3.1 introduces the mental model. Exercise 3.2 invites readers to determine how effectively their institution addresses the essential elements of the model.

Figure 3.1

What Drives Adult Learner Success in the Community College: A Mental Model

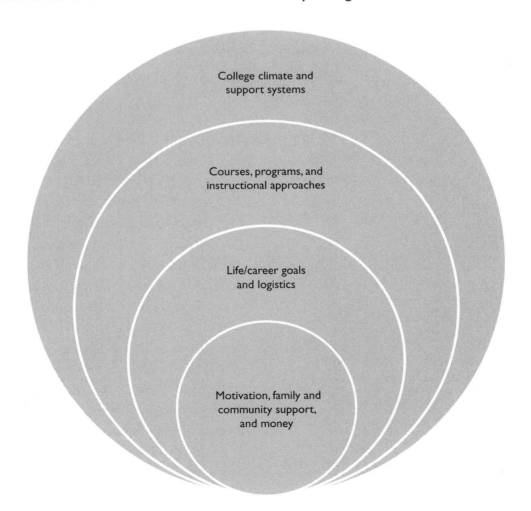

After completing Exercise 3.2, readers can continue the process of assessing their institution's effectiveness in supporting adult learners by reflecting on their responses; examining their institution's mission, culture, and adult learner population; and completing Exercises 3.3, 3.4, and 3.5. These exercises assist readers in identifying their institution's top priorities in relation to adult learners, the major barriers to supporting adult learners, and the first steps their institution must take to increase its capacity to attract, support, and graduate adult learners.

NATIONAL SUPPORT FOR COMMUNITY COLLEGE ADULT LEARNERS

The American Association of Community Colleges (AACC, http://www.aacc.nche.edu) and the Lumina Foundation (http://www.luminafoundation.org) have had—and continue to have—a major impact on community colleges' ability to support and graduate adult learners. Acting independently, in partnership with one another, or in partnership with other foundations or national groups, AACC and Lumina have made it possible for hundreds of community colleges to design, pilot-test, and assess the effectiveness of innovative approaches to connecting with and supporting adult learners. The vehicles developed to assist community colleges include, but are not limited to, the following programs: Achieving the Dream, the Adult College Completion Network, the Dreamkeepers and Angel Fund Emergency Financial Aid Program, and the Plus 50 initiatives.

Achieving the Dream *(http://www.mdrc.org/publication/turning-tide)*

The Lumina Foundation launched this ambitious data-driven initiative in 2004 in collaboration with AACC, the Community College Leadership Program (http://www.utexas.edu/academic/cclp), the Community College Research Center (http://ccrc.tc.columbia.edu), Jobs for the Future (http://www.jff.org), MDC, Inc. (http://www.mdcinc.org), and Public Agenda (http://www.publicagenda.org). The goal of the initiative was to improve the success of community college students, especially those students belonging to groups historically underserved by higher education.

Approximately 130 institutions in 24 states and the District of Columbia have participated in this initiative. One of Achieving the Dream's (ATD's) goals is to help institutions build cultures of evidence, and the research on ATD institutions provides evidence of what works in relation to increasing persistence and completion rates of community college students, many of whom are adult learners.

Impact: Drawing on the experiences of ATD institutions, Lumina identified strategies that significantly increase student success. Seven of these strategies speak directly to colleges and universities just beginning the process of building adult-friendly institutions and support

QUICK TIP

"Many adult students are challenged in translating skills from the workforce into the classroom. Help adult learners understand two things: (1) Hard work, perseverance, communication, and collaboration will always lead adult students in the right direction; and (2) transitioning to a successful college career is much like navigating the culture of a new job." —Brett Campbell, provost of the Southeast Campus, Tulsa Community College (personal communication, September 4, 2013)

systems. These strategies include the following: (1) Directly engage faculty, staff, and lower-level administrators in planning, implementation, and assessment processes; (2) focus more directly on improving instruction and student services; (3) involve adjunct faculty and staff; (4) provide in-depth and meaningful professional development to all college personnel; (5) pay more attention to institutional research capabilities; (6) develop more nuanced measures of student outcomes that relate directly to classroom practices and students' learning and progress; and (7) design more systematic approaches to evaluating interventions (Richburg-Hayes et al., 2009, pp. 146–154).

Adult College Completion Network *(http://www.adultcollegecompletion.org)*

Funded by the Lumina Foundation and facilitated by the Western Interstate Commission for Higher Education (http://wiche.edu), the Adult College Completion (ACC) Network provides a forum for organizations and agencies that are exploring strategies to increase college completion rates for adults with prior college credits but no degree. The ACC Network shares promising ideas and proven practices, assists members in expanding their knowledge of adult learners, and allows members to connect with one another and share ideas. The ACC Network also supports Project Warehouse, a repository of information on what colleges are doing to increase adult learner completion rates.

Impact: The network provides colleges and universities with up-to-date information on innovative approaches for increasing adult learner completion rates. It also identifies and provides contact information for administrators, faculty, and staff involved in designing, implementing, and assessing these initiatives.

Dreamkeepers and Angel Fund Emergency Financial Aid Programs
(http://www.knowledgecenter. completionbydesign.org/resources/498)

Dealing with unexpected financial crises is a challenge for community college students, many of whom are also parents. To help colleges meet this challenge, the Lumina Foundation created the Dreamkeepers and Angel Fund Emergency Financial Aid Programs. Dreamkeepers focuses on community colleges and is administered by Scholarship America; Angel Fund targets tribal colleges and is administered by the American Indian College Fund. Both require colleges to raise funds from internal (e.g., college foundation) or external (e.g., business or civic groups) sources in order to retain the grant in years 2 through 5. Both allow participating colleges to establish their own eligibility criteria and application procedures.

Impact: In their first 2 years, the programs awarded more than $845,000 in emergency financial aid to more than 2,400 students. Research indicates that students typically requested funds for housing and transportation expenses. Research also demonstrates that Dreamkeepers recipients were more likely to be older than traditional students, in their first year of college, parents of dependent children, and enrolled in a vocational field of study. As a result of the aid, recipients reenrolled in college at rates comparable to the overall average reenrollment rates of students at their institutions.

Plus 50 *(http://plus50.aacc.nche.edu)*

Launched in 2008 by AACC with funding from The Atlantic Philanthropies, Plus 50 initially involved 15 community colleges and focused on helping adults with prior college credit prepare for new careers. In 2009, AACC expanded the program to include anyone 50 or older who wanted to acquire new skills or strengthen existing skills in order to enter or re-enter the workforce. That year, 12 additional colleges joined Plus 50, and all the members began to focus on preparing adults for high-value careers. In 2010, with support from the Lumina Foundation, AACC was able to launch the Plus 50 Completion Strategy, add 32 institutions to the initiative, and establish a peer mentoring approach that paired one of the original Plus 50 institutions with a new Plus 50 institution. Recently, AACC announced another expansion of the initiative with the addition of 100 more colleges (Plus 50 Encore Completion Program).

Impact: The original 18 Plus 50 institutions reached their goals 2 years ahead of schedule. Over a 3-year period, these institutions served 54% more students than originally planned and awarded 50% more certificates or degrees than originally projected. Plus 50 also had a significant positive impact on the number of workforce training courses available to older adult learners.

INDIVIDUAL COMMUNITY COLLEGE INITIATIVES

Individual institutions use one of two approaches in designing policies, processes, and support services for adult learners. The first approach involves adopting or adapting tried and true methods that have stood the test of time; the second approach focuses on creating innovative strategies that fit the unique history, culture, and needs of an institution. Whether adopting, adapting, or innovating, community colleges adhere to two basic guidelines: (1) The approach must be consistent with the institution's mission and culture, and (2) the approach must be research-based, outcomes-oriented, and data-driven. Table 3.1 describes tried and true approaches used by a significant number of community colleges to support adult learners. Table 3.2 provides a snapshot of some of the innovative strategies individual community colleges have designed and implemented to increase adult learner persistence and completion rates.

Table 3.1

Tried and True Approaches for Increasing Adult Learner Persistence and Completion Rates

Increase Access	Increase Success	Increase Access and Success
Include adult learner outreach and recruitment in the institution's enrollment management plan.	Offer college success courses specifically for adult learners or include an adult learner component in existing courses.	Appoint cross-functional work groups to analyze adult learner needs and make recommendations to the college.
Train staff members in admissions and financial aid to understand, value, and work effectively with adults.	Provide student affairs professionals with workshops designed to strengthen their knowledge of adult learners.	Appoint process improvement teams to assess the impact of current policies, practices, and processes on adult learner access and success.
Offer campus-based services that the college requires adult learners to use at convenient times and locations.	Assign specific staff members in the financial aid office to work with—and become experts in—the financial needs of adult learners.	Offer courses in a variety of formats (e.g., evening, weekend, online, blended, off-campus).

Increase Access	Increase Success	Increase Access and Success
Provide 24/7 Web access to information and support.	Implement an early warning academic alert system.	Develop dedicated websites for adult learners.
Include pictures of adult learners in all recruitment materials. Communicate with adults in a manner that makes sense to them (not just the college).	Identify internal and external sources of funding for child care initiatives, student parent programs, and other approaches with the potential to increase adult learner completion rates.	Assist faculty, support staff, and administrators to understand, value, and work effectively with adults.

Table 3.2

Innovative Approaches to Increasing Adult Learner Persistence and Completion Rates

Area	Approach/Community College
Advising	Define clear pathways that assist students to achieve their goals. • Miami Dade College, Florida (O'Banion, 2013) Develop an online advising system (LifeMaps). • Valencia College, Florida (http://www.valenciacollege.edu/lifemap/pbs/damodel.htm) Prepare adult learners to succeed in college. • Project Independence at Portland Community College, Oregon (http://www.pcc.edu/resources/women/cascade/project-independence.html) • SMART Program at Lakeland Community College, Ohio (http://lakelandcc.edu/comeduc/women/smart.pdf) Train faculty advisors to work with adult learners. • Bellevue Community College, Washington (http://www.bellevuecollege.edu/adcurriculum/default.asp)
Basic skills preparation	Establish decision zones, a score range below the state cutoff scores on the college's assessment test. Allow advisors to use additional methods to determine course placement for students whose scores fall within the zone. • Numerous New Jersey community colleges (http://ccrc.tc.columbia.edu/publications/designing-meaningful-developmental-reform.html) Mainstream upper-level developmental students into college-level courses with mandatory support services. • Community College of Baltimore County, Maryland (http://ccrc.tc.columbia.edu/publications/designing-meaningful-developmental-reform.html) Partner with an external entity to establish a College Preparatory Academy that offers an off-campus developmental education option to selected students. • Austin Community College and Capital IDEA, a nonprofit organization in Texas (http://www.capitalidea.org/college-prep)
Career counseling	Develop an online career exploration system. • Valencia College, Florida (http://www.valenciacollege.edu/lifemap) Offer career counseling boot camps. • Lorain County Community College, Ohio (http://www.loraincc.edu/.../Looking+for+work/workshops/Career+Boot+Camp.htm)

Area	Approach/Community College
Child care	Create early childhood learning centers on campus.
	• LaGuardia Community College, New York (http://www.lagcc.cuny.edu/advisingcentral/aca-support.aspx?id=10737418975)
	• Rancho Santiago Community College District, California (http://www.rsccd.edu/For-students/Pages/Child-care.aspx)
	Collaborate with the college foundation to finance some of the expenses associated with operating a child development center.
	• Johnson County Community College, Kansas (http://www.ccc.edu/childcare and http://www.ccc.edu/foundation)
	Offer low-cost child care on selected campuses.
	• Lone Star College System, Texas (http://www.lonestar.edu/child-care.htm)
	Partner with local businesses to finance special projects related to child care centers.
	• Truckee Meadows Community College, Nevada (Boressoff, 2013)
	Pay student employees at the college day care center from the college's general fund.
	• Truckee Meadows Community College, Nevada (Boressoff, 2013)
	Use federal funds to provide child care.
	• Madison Area Technical College, Wisconsin (http://www2.ed.gov/programs/campisp/index.html and http://madisoncollege.edu.cfc)
	Provide on-campus child care resources and referral center.
	• Lane Community College, Oregon (http://www.lanecc.edu/lfc)
Connecting students to the college and to one another	Connect adult learners to one another and to events, seminars, and workshops to assist them with the challenges associated with starting college.
	• Montgomery College, Maryland (http://cms.montgomerycollege.edu/edu/department.aspx?id=13525)
	Use social network sites to connect students with the college and one another.
	• Getting Connected Project, currently being field-tested by eight community colleges (https://gettingconnected.arizona.edu)
	Establish an adult student lounge.
	• Montgomery College, Maryland (http://cms.montgomerycollege.edu/edu/department.aspx?id=13525)
Degrees and scheduling	Offer customized degrees or certificates.
	• Inver Hills Community College, Minnesota (http://www.inverhills.edu/ProgramsAndMajors/ASAP)
	• Portland Community College, Oregon (http://www.catalog.pcc.edu/programsanddisciplines/employmentskillstraining)
	Offer multiple start and stop times throughout the year.
	• Rio Salado College, Arizona (http://www.riosalado.edu)
	Offer accelerated programs and nontraditional scheduling
	• Inver Hills Community College, Minnesota (http://www.inverhills.edu/ProgramsAndMajors/ASAP)
	Offer online degrees and certificates, not just courses.
	• Foothill College, California (http://www.Foothill.edu/fgu/degrees.php)

Area	Approach/Community College

Early warning systems 2.0	Develop a next-generation early alert system that identifies, tracks, and intervenes early.
	• Frederick Community College, Maryland
	  (http://www.frederick.edu/student-services/counseling-policies-early-alert.aspx)
	• LaGuardia Community College, New York
	  (http://www.laguardia.edu/student-Services/Academic-Early-Alert)
	• Sinclair Community College, Ohio
	  (http://www.sinclair.edu/support/success/ea with a demonstration
	  at http://studentsuccessplan.org)

Financial assistance and planning	Offer an online resource called Cash Course to assist adult learners with financial planning and budgeting. • Norwalk Community College, Connecticut (http://www.cashcourse.org/ncc) Partner with local foundations to generate funding for student parent assistance. • Norwalk Community College, Connecticut (http://www.ncc.commnet.edu/fesp)
Orientation	Provide targeted orientation experiences for adult learners. • Anne Arundel Community College, Maryland (http://www.aacc.edu/orientation) Offer a stand-alone orientation for student parents. • Anne Arundel Community College, Maryland (http://www.aacc.edu/orientation)
Personal counseling	Link the services of a counselor experienced in recognizing and responding to the unique needs of adults to learning communities established for adult learners. • Accelerated Learning Program (ALP) at the Florissant Valley Campus of St. Louis Community College, Missouri (Worth & Stephens, 2011)

Student parents	Offer targeted programs and support services for student parents.
	• Central New Mexico Community College, New Mexico
	  (http://www.cnm.edu/student-resources/get-help/our-story)
	• Front Range Community College, Colorado
	  (http://www.frontrange.edu/Current-Students/...Programs/Single-Parent-Program)
	• McLennan Community College, Texas
	  (http://www.mclennan.edu/student-development/support)
	• Norwalk Community College, Connecticut (http://www.ncc.commnet.edu/fesp)

Student veterans	Design and open a services center for veterans. • Gulf Coast College, Florida (http://www.gulfcoast.edu/veterans) • Mississippi Gulf Coast Community College, Mississippi (https://www.mgccc.edu/veterans-services) • Lone Star College System, Texas (http://www.lonestar.edu/veterans-services.htm) • Mesa Community College, Arizona (http://www.mesacc.edu/veteran-services) Develop a systemwide approach to expediting certificates and degrees for veterans. • Texas Community Colleges (https://collegecreditforheroes.org) Pilot-test expedited certificates and degrees for veterans. • Lone Star College System, Texas (http://www.lonestar.edu/veterans-services.htm)

CHANGING TO MEET THE NEEDS OF ADULT LEARNERS: A CASE STUDY

How do individual institutions evolve to meet the needs of adult learners without neglecting traditional students? What is the most effective way for colleges to adopt strategies that are consistent with their mission and culture? How important—and challenging—is building capacity and commitment across the college? Foothill College in Los Altos Hills, California, a large publicly supported community college established in 1957, recently faced these questions. Foothill has a reputation for innovation: It was the first California community college to offer online courses (http://www.edutrek.com/california/school/summary/foothill-college). Foothill also is one of the top 10 institutions in terms of sending transfer students to University of California campuses (http://datamart.cccco.edu/DataMart.aspx). In addition, 100% of the students who successfully complete programs in dental hygiene, diagnostic medical sonography, pharmacy technician, respiratory therapy, radiologic technology, or veterinary technology successfully pass their licensing board exams—far exceeding the national average (Nanette Solvason, division dean, Biological and Health Sciences, Foothill Community College, personal communication, October 29, 2013).

After a data review clearly demonstrated that Foothill's adult student population represented nearly 50% of its total enrollment, the college launched a major Adult Learner Initiative (ALI). In late fall 2012, the college formed a cross-functional work group to analyze adult learner needs and to identify the most effective and innovative approaches Foothill could use in meeting these needs. Using principles developed by the Council for Adult and Experiential Learning (CAEL) to evaluate programs and services, the ALI work team determined that Foothill College needed to strengthen targeted support services in order to help adult learners reach their career and educational goals. Table 3.3 outlines the 10 recommendations developed by the ALI work team and presented to the college's Planning and Resource Council.

Table 3.3

Recommendations of the Adult Learner Initiative Work Team

The following recommendations are based on an extensive review of the literature and an analysis of national, state, and institutional data:
1. Add a statement about adult learners to the college's mission statement.
2. Review, evaluate, and revise current student support services and resources to meet adult learner needs.
3. Create a specialized orientation for adult students.
4. Review college costs up front and identify payment options.
5. Focus on prospects for career advancement and provide reliable links to workplace-related course work and degrees and current pathway opportunities.
6. Create partnerships between student services and instruction to develop learning communities and program cohorts.
7. Offer a variety of learning options including evening, weekend, short-term, late start, and accelerated classes as well as online, face-to-face, and hybrid courses.

8.	Review and modify student leave possibilities to add flexibility and provide adult learners with alternatives.
9.	Provide professional development workshops and training for faculty and staff that focus on adult learner needs and success strategies.
10.	Undertake continuous assessment and recalibrate programs and services in response to the data.

Initial Changes

Student services managers at Foothill College took the lead role in examining and evaluating existing support services. Using an adult learner lens, they gathered and reviewed additional data, contacted peer institutions to learn about their adult learner initiatives, and conducted interviews with adult learners. The managers then presented the ALI work team with recommended approaches to strengthening support services for adult learners. At their spring 2013 meeting, the ALI work team developed an action plan and adopted an implementation timeline for executing the recommended approaches. To date, Foothill College has taken the following steps to strengthening support services for undergraduate adult learners:

1. In fall 2013, the ALI work team agreed to work collaboratively through student services, instruction, and marketing to create an Adult Learner Program Web page listing all the current programs and services for adult students.
2. Student services designated a contact person in each department for adult learners.
3. An interdisciplinary group developed an orientation program to meet the needs of adult learners that the college implemented in spring 2014.
4. Career counselors partnered with the Career Technical Education faculty to develop interactive career pathway modules directed at adult students.
5. The financial aid staff agreed to review current funding options for adult students and develop recommendations for alternative payment and financing opportunities.
6. Foothill opened a new student success center that provides workshops, training, and peer-to-peer support for adult students.
7. Instructional deans were asked to work with faculty to develop additional evening, weekend, and late start classes.
8. Foothill added online professional development workshops focusing on adult and nontraditional students to the college's program (e.g., Understanding the "New" Nontraditional Student: Supporting Their Success In and Out of the Classroom).
9. In collaboration with Foothill's institutional researcher, student services managers developed a new program review template for Student Learning/Service Area Outcomes that included an assessment component specifically focused on adult learners.

Cultural Shift

Foothill College remains committed to institutionalizing a comprehensive approach to serving adult learners while retaining its commitment to maintaining its well-established and coveted identity as a top transfer institution for traditional 18- to 24-year-old students. The efforts of the ALI work group have met occasional resistance: Some members of the college community believe that the college cannot effectively serve both traditional and posttraditional students, while others are reluctant to change processes, practices, and support services that have been in place for decades. Supported by the college's leadership, however, the ALI team continues to work within the college community to increase understanding of and acceptance for the changes that need to happen. The ultimate goal is to build on what is already in place, develop additional support services to fill in the gaps, and increase capacity across the college by providing ongoing professional development activities that focus on adult learners. In addition, the ALI work team is committed to helping Foothill College assess adult learner programs and services and use data to drive change.

LEARNING FROM SUCCESSES—AND FAILURES

This module demonstrates that a commitment to adult learners is part of a community college's DNA and that there are many approaches to working with these students. These approaches are built on adult learner theories and strengthened over time as institutions use local, state, and national research to identify programs and services that work and to eliminate ineffective programs and services. Over the years, community colleges have launched many successful initiatives and survived many failed attempts to assist adult learners. In preparing to write this module, the authors asked scores of community college leaders to reflect on their experiences with adult undergraduate learners and to share with college and university colleagues the most important lessons they learned from these experiences. The following 10 lessons were the ones most frequently mentioned.

Lesson 1: Seize the challenge presented by the growing adult learner population in higher education to examine how student affairs is organized, delivers programs and services, and partners with faculty. Move away from a single-source support service model designed to prevent failure, to an integrated model that focuses on student success and is designed and delivered in collaboration with adult learners, faculty colleagues, and community partners.

Lesson 2: Maps matter to adult learners, to the faculty who teach them, and to the student affairs professionals who support them. Everyone needs to know where they are going, how to get there, and why a particular route works best for them. Provide each student with an educational plan that clearly identifies the individual path the student must follow to earn a degree or certificate. Link the educational plan with a support service plan designed to meet each adult learner's individual needs.

Lesson 3: Adult learners have too many demands on their time to do "optional." Make using or participating in important activities or support services (e.g., advising, career counseling, orientation, targeted support groups, tutoring) mandatory.

Lesson 4: Advising, career counseling, educational planning, and financial planning assistance, whether delivered in person or online, are the "secret sauce" that community colleges use to increase adult learner success.

Lesson 5: If advising, educational planning, and career counseling are the "secret sauce," then data are often the missing ingredient. It is imperative that colleges assess the impact of policies, processes, and support services on the success of adult learners and use the results to strengthen existing—or create new—services and systems.

Lesson 6: Early warning systems coupled with policies and procedures that require adult learners to use the support services that they need are essential.

Lesson 7: Partnerships matter, whether internal (e.g., academic and student affairs) or external (e.g., the career center and the local workforce development board). No one can (or should want to) do it alone!

Lesson 8: Creative child care solutions and support for student parents are a must as more and more adult learners start college as parents or become parents during their undergraduate years.

Lesson 9: Pay attention to the money. Not only must institutions help adult learners evaluate options for financing college and dealing with unexpected financial challenges, they also must teach many students how to manage their money.

Lesson 10: Lifelong learning is the ultimate goal. Higher education's role is not limited to helping adult learners acquire a set of skills related to a specific job that could disappear in a few years. Colleges must help adult learners understand the need for—and build a foundation that supports—a commitment to lifelong learning.

 IN THE SPOTLIGHT

"Regardless of the model a college adopts, its components need to be designed and treated as an integrated, cohesive, systemic, connected series of experiences the students and the college will use to map out the route students need to navigate to reach desired student and college goals and milestones. Connecting students to services across the college must be intentional and purposeful. The pathway needs to have on- and off-ramps to make it easier for students to exit and re-enter when the realities of their lives demand it. Students do not move from one component to another in a synchronized sequence. Their progress is more like entering a roundabout where they swirl in and out, making wrong exits and entrances, and running into dead ends. It is the college's responsibility to facilitate the ebb and flow of traffic to ensure that each student reaches the desired destination as smoothly as possible." (O'Banion, 2013, pp. 15–16)

APPLY THE CONCEPTS

Exercise 3.1—Translating Research into Policies, Processes, Programs, and Services

Directions: The findings of the Community College Research Center at Teachers College, Columbia University have many implications for institutions with large adult learner populations. Review the findings in Column A. In Column B, list any actions your institution has taken to translate these findings into policies, processes, programs, or services that benefit adult learners. *See item 5, Column B for a sample response.*

A	B
Community College Research Center (CCRC) findings	**Actions taken at your institution that are consistent with CCRC findings and benefit adult learners**
1. Community colleges need to strengthen connections with local K–12 systems, their chief suppliers (Jenkins, 2011, p. 15).	
2. "Building capacity is an essential prerequisite to changing any organization" (Jenkins, 2011, p. 10).	
3. Piecemeal changes are not enough to improve student learning. Community colleges must implement innovations "in a coordinated manner so they support students' progression and success at each stage of their experience with the college" (Jenkins, 2011, p. 36).	
4. Tinto's theory does not provide "practical guidance to community colleges" because it is based on the experiences of traditional students and does not address the unique needs of part-time, commuter, and under-represented minority students (Karp, 2011b, p. 3).	
5. Four mechanisms appear to increase student success. These are most effective when integrated into the student's educational experience, and they help the student to: • Create relationships with other students and with faculty and staff. • Develop clear goals and a commitment to higher education. • Develop college know-how. • Overcome challenges they face outside the classroom. (Karp, 2011b, p. 6)	• Implemented a college success course specifically designed for adult learners

A	B
Community College Research Center (CCRC) findings	**Actions taken at your institution that are consistent with CCRC findings and benefit adult learners**
6. To improve student outcomes, community colleges need to: • Streamline and personalize advising and counseling. • Force students to use nonacademic support services. • Create more structure and fewer decision points for students. (Karp, 2011a, p. 3)	
7. Community colleges "need to implement a 'best process' approach in which faculty, staff, and administrators across the college work together to review programs, processes, and services . . . and rethink and better align their practices to accelerate entry into and completion of programs of study that lead to credentials of value" (Jenkins & Cho, 2012, p.4).	
8. "Students who entered a program of study in their first year were much more likely to complete a credential or transfer to a four-year institution within five years than were students who did not enter a program until their second year or later" (Jenkins & Cho, 2012, p. 19).	
9. "Piloting 'best practices' and then trying to bring them to scale will not 'move the needle' on overall rates of student completion" (Jenkins & Cho, 2012, p. 19).	
10. Community colleges must provide students with clear expectations, give examples of these expectations, and offer students the opportunity to acquire the skills needed to meet these expectations (Karp & Bork, 2012, p. 36).	

APPLY THE CONCEPTS

Exercise 3.2—Meeting the Needs of Adult Learners

Directions: Use a think–pair–share approach to this exercise.

    Step 1: Ask each person in the group to complete the exercise independently.

    Step 2: Ask participants to share their individual responses with the group.

    Step 3: Reflect on everyone's responses, and develop a list that represents the consensus of the group.

	Current strategies (What your institution does now to attract adult learners and help them succeed)	**Future strategies** (What your institution could do to improve adult learner access and success)
Motivation, family and community support, money		
The institution reaches out to adult learners.		
The institution demonstrates to adult learners that they are valued and respected.		
The institution assists adult learners to estimate the costs associated with college.		
The institution develops a variety of scholarships, awards, and payment options for adult learners.		
The institution provides adult learners with opportunities to learn how to manage their financial resources.		
The institution collaborates with business and community groups to generate support for adult learners.		
The institution helps adult learners build or maintain existing family and community support systems.		
Other (please identify).		

	Current strategies (What your institution does now to attract adult learners and help them succeed)	**Future strategies** (What your institution could do to improve adult learner access and success)
Life/career goals and logistics		
The institution helps adult learners effectively manage child care issues.		
The institution helps adult learners deal with transportation issues.		
The institution helps adult learners balance family, work, and college.		
The institution provides adult learners with career counseling and educational planning services.		
The institution provides adult learners with academic advising services.		
The institution provides adult learners with the opportunity to realistically assess their current knowledge and skill sets.		
Other (please identify).		
Courses, programs, and instructional approaches		
The institution offers credit for prior learning experiences.		
The institution offers classroom, online, and distance learning opportunities and blended courses.		
The institution outlines clear pathways to each degree or certificate for both full- and part-time students.		
Faculty members use multiple instructional methods that reflect the way adults prefer to learn.		
Faculty members connect adult learners with the support services they need by incorporating these services into their course syllabi.		

	Current strategies (What your institution does now to attract adult learners and help them succeed)	**Future strategies** (What your institution could do to improve adult learner access and success)
Faculty members are skilled at establishing mentoring relationships with adult learners.		
Other (please identify).		
Institutional Climate and Support Systems		
The institution disaggregates data to develop an accurate picture of its adult learner population and the institution's effectiveness in serving this population.		
The institution has procedures in place to identify and remove institutional barriers to adult learner access and success.		
The institution offers opportunities for adult learners to strengthen their reading, writing, and math skills before starting classes.		
The institution offers opportunities for adult learners to acquire the computer skills they need to succeed in college.		
The institution intentionally connects adult learners with one another, with the faculty, and with support services.		
The institution has an early warning system in place that includes prompts related to the success of adult learners at their institution.		
Student affairs professionals create and continually assess the effectiveness of support services and systems designed for adult learners.		
Student affairs professionals create opportunities for adult learners to provide feedback to institutional leaders about their needs and their experiences at the institution.		
Partnerships between academic and student affairs to increase adult learner success are expected and rewarded.		
Other (please identify).		

APPLY THE CONCEPTS

Exercise 3.3—Establishing Priorities

Directions: The president of your college has asked you to develop a "top 10" list for strengthening programs and services for adult learners. She has requested that you identify barriers and implementation strategies. Take a few minutes to reflect on your responses to Exercise 3.1 and to think about your institution's mission, culture, and adult learner population. Review the strengths and weaknesses identified in Exercise 3.2. Use your analysis of Exercises 3.1 and 3.2 to identify the 10 most important steps your institution can take to improve access and success for adult learners.

1.
2.
3.
4.
5.
6.
7.
8.
9.
10.

APPLY THE CONCEPTS

Exercise 3.4—Identifying and Eliminating Barriers

Directions: Review your responses to Exercises 3.1, 3.2, and 3.3. List the five most significant barriers to increasing access and success for adult learners at your institution. Identify strategies to remove or reduce the impact of each barrier.

Barrier	Strategies to remove or reduce the barrier's impact
1.	
2.	
3.	
4.	
5.	

APPLY THE CONCEPTS

Exercise 3.5—Building Capacity Across the Institution

Directions: Review your responses to Exercises 3.1, 3.2, 3.3, and 3.4. Identify the five steps your institution needs to take to increase the ability of faculty, staff, and administrators to work with adult learners.

1.
2.
3.
4.
5.

RESOURCES

Adult Student.com
http://www.adultstudent.com

Adult Student Connect: Online Forum
http://connect.adultstudent.com

Association for Nontraditional Students in Higher Education
http://www.antshe.org

Coalition of Adult Learning Focused Institutions
http://www.cael.org/Whom-We-Serve/Colleges-and-Universities/Adult-Student-Services/ALFI-Assessment-Tools/ALFI-Coalition

College Scholarships.org
http://www.collegescholarships.org/grants/adult.htm

Cape Cod Community College
http://www.capecod.edu/web/adult-learner

LearningCounts.org
http://www.learningcounts.org

Nontraditional Students Website
http://www.nontradstudents.com

REFERENCES

Advisory Committee on Student Financial Assistance. (2012, February). *Pathways to success: Integrating learning with life and work to increase national college completion.* Retrieved from http://www2.ed.gov/about/bdscomm/list/acsfa/ptsreport2.pdf

American Association of Community Colleges. (n.d.). *Students at community colleges.* Retrieved from http://www.aacc.nche.edu/AboutCC/Trends/Pages/studentsatcommunitycolleges.aspx

American Association of Community Colleges. (2009). *Educating plus 50 learners: Opportunities for community colleges.* Retrieved from http://plus50.aacc.nche.edu/aboutplus50/Pages/default.aspx

Boressoff, T. (2013, June). *Financing child care for college student success.* Retrieved from http://www.iwpr.org/publications

Center for Law and Social Policy. (2011). *Policy solutions that work for low income people.* Retrieved from http://www.clasp.org/about

Hagedorn, L. S. (2005). How to define retention: A new look at an old problem. In A. Seidman (Ed.), *College student retention: Formula for student success* (pp. 89–106). Westport, CT: ACE/Praeger.

Integrated Postsecondary Education Data System. (2009). Retrieved from http://nces.ed.gov/ipeds

Jenkins, D. (2011). *Redesigning community colleges for completion: Lessons from research on high-performance organizations* (CCRC Working Paper No. 24). New York, NY: Community College Research Center, Columbia University, Teachers College.

Jenkins, D., & Cho, S. (2012). *Get with the program: Accelerating community college students' entry into and completion of programs of study* (CCRC Working Paper No. 32). New York, NY: Community College Research Center, Columbia University, Teachers College.

Karp, M. M. (2011a). *How non-academic supports work: Four mechanisms for improving student outcomes (2011)* (CCRC Brief No. 54). New York, NY: Community College Research Center, Columbia University, Teachers College.

Karp, M. M. (2011b). *Toward a new understanding of non-academic student support: Four mechanisms encouraging positive student outcomes in the community college* (CCRC Working Paper No. 28). New York, NY: Community College Research Center, Columbia University, Teachers College.

Karp, M. M., & Bork, R. H. (2012). *They never told me what to expect, so I didn't know what to do: Defining and clarifying the role of the community college student* (CCRC Working Paper No. 47). New York, NY: Community College Research Center, Columbia University, Teachers College.

Kasworm, C. (1990). Adult undergraduates in higher education: A review of past research perspectives. *Review of Educational Research, 60*(3), 345–372. Retrieved from http://www.jstor.org/discover/10.2307/1170758?uid=2129&uid=2&uid=70&uid=4&sid=21102595746941

Kelly, P., & Strawn, J. (2011). *Not just kid stuff anymore: The economic imperative for more adults to complete college.* Retrieved from http://www.clasp.org/admin/site/publications/files/NotKidStuffAnymoreAdultStudentProfile-1.pdf

Klein-Collins, R. (2011). Strategies for becoming adult-learning focused institutions. *Peer Review, 13*(1), 4–7.

Laanan, F. S. (Ed.). (2006). *Understanding students in transition: Trends and issues* (New directions for student services, No. 114). San Francisco, CA: Jossey-Bass.

National Center for Education Statistics. (2011). *Digest of education statistics, 2010* (NCES 2011-015). Retrieved from http://nces.ed.gov/programs/digest/d10

O'Banion, T. (2013). *Access, success, and completion: A primer for community college faculty, administrators, staff, and trustees.* Chandler, AZ: League for Innovation in the Community College.

Prince, D., & Jenkins, D. (2005, April). *Building pathways to success for low-skill adult students: Lessons for community college policy and practice from a longitudinal student tracking study.* Retrieved from http://www.sbctc.ctc.edu/docs/education/ford_bridges/bldg_pathways_to_success_for_low-skilled_adult_stdts.pdf

Public Agenda. (2009, December). *With their whole lives ahead of them*. Retrieved from http://www.publicagenda.org/pages/with-their-whole-lives-ahead-of-them

Pusser, B., Breneman, D. W., Gansneder, B. M., Kohl, K. J., Levin, J. S., Milam, J. H., & Turner, S. E. (2007, March). Returning to learning: Adults' success in college is key to America's future. *Lumina Foundation for Education New Agenda Series*. Retrieved from http://www.luminafoundation.org/publications/ReturntolearningApril2007.pdf

Richburg-Hayes, L., Brock, T., LeBlanc, A., Paxson, C., Rouse, C. E., & Barrow, L. (2009, January). *Rewarding persistence effects of a performance-based scholarship program for low-income parents*. Retrieved from http://www.mdrc.org/publication/turning-tide

Shapiro, D., & Dundar, A. (2012). *Completing college: A national view of student attainment rates*. Retrieved from http://nscresearchcenter.org/signaturereport4/#AboutThisReport

Shapiro, G. (2012, February 29). Innovation and community colleges—The overlooked national asset. *Forbes*. Retrieved from http://www.forbes.com/sites/garyshapiro/2012/02/29/innovation-and-community-colleges-the-overlooked-national-asset

Worth, J., & Stephens, C. J. (2011). Adult students: Meeting the challenge of a growing student population. *Peer Review, 13*(1), 23–25.

MODULE 4

The Campus Climate for Adult Students

Cloudy with a Chance of Success

Leslie A. Laing and Heidi Watson

ABSTRACT

In the context of the major demographic shifts, technological advances, and funding shortfalls currently reshaping higher education, it is imperative that colleges and universities understand the importance of designing support systems for adult learners that are data-driven, outcomes-oriented, and well-grounded in theory and research. This module offers an overview of theory and research related to undergraduate adult learners and identifies strategies for developing policies, processes, and support services consistent with established and emerging knowledge about this population. The module also describes innovative approaches that colleges and universities across the country are using to increase access and success for undergraduate adult learners and invites readers to assess their institution's ability to effectively serve this growing population.

ADULT LEARNERS MATTER TO THE ACADEMY

The National Center for Education Statistics (2011) projected that between 2009 and 2020, enrollment will increase 9% for traditional 18- to 24-year-old students, 21% for 25- to 34-year-old students, and 16% for students 35 and older. These figures underscore the importance of adult learners and the need for colleges and universities to pay more attention to this growing segment of the postsecondary population. After obtaining self-reported data from 355 colleges and universities, Watson (2012) concluded that the majority (58.5%) allocated less than 25% of their marketing budget to the adult student segment of their target market. In that 2012 study, Watson also discovered that while 92% of the 320 self-reporting 4-year institutions supported online applications, 84.1% did not offer flexibility regarding the admissions process for adult learners and only 20.9% tracked adult student admissions. It seems that a decade after Sissel, Hansman, and Kasworm (2001) theorized that colleges and universities pursued a policy of neglect in relation to adult students, many institutions continue to undervalue this population.

As Module 1 demonstrates, the similarities between traditional undergraduate populations and adult learner populations increase each year, primarily because students of all ages are juggling multiple roles and working more hours while seeking a degree. Adult learners, however, do have additional challenges: behaviors, mindsets, and responsibilities that may impede their persistence, restrict their involvement in campus life, or limit their vision of success. It is imperative that colleges and universities understand emerging adult learner theory and research, assess the impact of the institution's current climate on 25- to 64-year-old students, and identify and remove barriers that stand between adult learners and a 4-year degree.

 ## In the Spotlight

"Colleges and universities should not stop supporting 18- to 22-year-old traditional students, but they must start supporting posttraditional students as well. Posttraditional students cannot navigate the systems we have created: We must change these systems from within. Advising and early intervention initiatives are essential. Helping posttraditional students become more financially literate is a must. Eliminate barriers. Make sure there is a good fit between the student and the college. Posttraditional students do not have a lot of time to spend on campus; build cohorts and teach faculty to create a community within each class. Early intervention is critical." —Lynn Gangone, dean, The Women's College of the University of Denver (personal communication, June 27, 2013)

SNAPSHOT OF ADULT LEARNER RESEARCH AND THEORY

In her seminal work *Adults as Learners: Increasing Participation and Facilitating Learning,* Cross (1981) reinforced the importance of a learning society and challenged educators to "develop lifelong learners who possess the basic skills for learning plus the motivation to pursue a variety of learning interests throughout their lives" (p. 249). Cross pointed out that it was essential to build programs and services for adult learners that are based on theory and research, since "theory without practice is empty, and

IN THE SPOTLIGHT

"Within the higher education arena, it is imperative to provide access to anyone who desires to learn—whether it is training for a new job, the beginnings of a career, or just for the joy of being a better educated person. Age should not be a restrictive factor in opportunities to learn. As administrators, we continually strive to remove barriers for adults who enter the gates of a traditional college setting, providing appropriate support services to ensure their success. Many times we find that the services we provide to adult learners benefit all learners and create efficiencies for an overall better college experience." —Martha Jordan, director of adult learner advocacy and outreach, The Pennsylvania State University (personal communication, November 13, 2013)

practice without theory is blind" (p. 110). Cross also theorized that adult learners face three types of barriers to continuing their education: situational, institutional, and dispositional. Situational barriers emerge from the context of a person's life at a specific point in time: child care, transportation, money, and time, for example. Institutional barriers are built by colleges and universities: admissions offices that open from 9 to 5 and close on the weekends, financial assistance available primarily to full-time students, and the absence of readily available support services designed specifically for adult learners. Dispositional barriers are "related to attitudes and self-perceptions about oneself as a learner" (p. 98); they include fear of failure, lack of confidence in the ability to deal with college, and a belief that adults may be too old to learn.

Knowles (1978) proposed a framework for understanding adult learners that has become one of the most used and frequently cited frameworks (Merriam, 2001). According to Knowles, adult learners as a group tend to prefer active, self-directed learning that takes their life experiences into account and is problem-centered rather than subject-centered. Recent research (Ross-Gordon, 2003) confirms the importance of Knowles's framework, while pointing out that adult learners also desire structure and cannot be viewed through a single lens: There is no such thing as the typical adult learner.

Bean and Metzner (1985) developed a conceptual model to explain attrition among undergraduate nontraditional (i.e., older, part-time, and commuter) students. The model theorizes that students are affected by their external environments and that both academic and nonacademic variables contribute to attrition. Academic variables include limited interaction with peers, faculty, or support staff; infrequent use of campus services; and little connection between class-related activities and the student's life. Nonacademic variables include enrollment status, the distance from campus to the student's residence, unclear educational and career goals, and previous academic performance. Both academic and nonacademic variables are compounded by gender, ethnicity, and the educational experiences of the student's parents.

In exploring the support service needs of adult learners, Schlossberg, Lynch, and Chickering (1989) stressed the importance of transitions as motivating factors in an adult learner's life and challenged higher education institutions to provide the support services adult learners require as they are "moving in, moving through, or moving on" (p. 32). Among the many suggestions offered to help higher education institutions understand and support adult learners, five must be essential components of any mental model developed by today's student affairs professionals: (1) Talk to adult learners about their experiences entering and navigating the institution, and listen carefully to their responses; (2) assess prior learning experiences in a way that sends a message that the institution values and respects adult learners; (3) view each adult learner as an individual, and resist the temptation to choose administrative convenience over personalized experiences; (4) design and implement support services that adult learners need to successfully complete each phase of their educational journey; and (5) provide adult learners with "recognition and a sense that they occupy a viable place in the institution" (p. 144).

Although based primarily on studies of traditional college students, Tinto's (1993) model contributes two significant ideas to the adult learner debate: (1) Helping students have high-quality interactions with faculty, staff, and peers is important; and (2) any student's decision to leave is a long-term process that is influenced by the quality of day-to-day interactions, the student's personal situation, and the presence (or absence) of supportive policies, procedures, programs, and services. Graham and Gisi's (2000) study of nearly 2,000 college students to determine the effect that student involvement in out-of-the-classroom programs and services has on academic success demonstrated that adult learners most involved in college life did as well or slightly better than traditional students on four measures of academic development.

In the past decade, researchers and theorists have begun to pay more attention to the needs of specific adult learner subpopulations. Hamrick & Rumann's (2013) *Called to Serve* explored the support service needs of student veterans on college and university campuses. Ross-Gordon (2005) examined the college climate for adult learners of color. Rocco (2001) assessed the importance of helping faculty members respond appropriately to disability disclosures related to adult learners. The California Postsecondary Education Commission (2009) offered recommendations for meeting the needs of college and university students with disabilities, while Betts et al. (2013) explored strategies for responding to online learners with disabilities. However, much work remains to be done in examining the needs of specific adult learner subpopulations, especially adult learners of color and adult learners with disabilities.

STUDENT AFFAIRS' ROLE IN SUPPORTING ADULT LEARNERS

At first glance, much of what colleges and universities need to do to improve the institutional climate for adult learners seems to be outside the purview of student affairs. Adult learners want accelerated degree programs; alternatives to the standard 16-week semester; night, weekend, and online course offerings; and credit for prior learning. They also seek flexible scheduling, funding streams for tuition, internships, child care subsidies and facilities, and targeted support services (Watson, 2012). Thoughtful reflection, however, soon produces two valuable insights: (1) Access and success for adult learners depends on all areas of the institution working together; and (2) student affairs professionals are experienced in dealing with nontraditional students, a population that includes adult learners. Modules 7 and 8 focus on the importance of partnerships to adult learner success and student affairs' role in those partnerships, while this module explores the overall role that student affairs plays in the institution's ability to serve adult learners and the effect this role may have on the profession.

Student affairs professionals are in a unique position to collaborate with their colleagues in institutional research and information technology to gather, sort, and present data to the college or university on the characteristics and needs of adult learners. To adult learners, student affairs professionals represent the institution through the many systems they design (e.g., admissions, advising, registration, orientation), the websites and portals they create, and the programs and support services they implement with and for adult learners. For colleges and universities, student affairs professionals are in a position to design and implement many of the high-quality support services that are becoming increasingly important to prospective students (Hanover Research, 2012).

Whether student affairs professionals are able to leverage the opportunities presented by the growth of the adult learner population depends on their ability to accomplish three tasks. The first task simply requires student affairs professionals to take an honest look in the mirror to determine if they "have become defensive of what they enjoy doing at the expense of acquiring skills to accomplish what needs to be done" (Bresciani, 2012, p. 40). The second task challenges student affairs professionals to focus on the future, embrace change, and strengthen their skill sets (Moneta & Jackson, 2011). The third involves leveraging the increase in the undergraduate adult learner population and the explosion in online and distance learning to:

- Rethink what procedures, processes, and support services are essential.
- Identify when, where, and how to deliver essential services.
- Leverage technology to both support and deliver innovative support services.
- Develop strategies that allow adult learners to personalize processes and services.

Building on the work of Knowles (1978) and other adult learning pioneers mentioned in this module, Figure 4.1 presents a REAL approach for student affairs professionals to follow in designing processes, programs, and support services for adult learners. The REAL approach challenges student affairs professionals who wish to work effectively with adult learners to:

- Adopt policies and procedures and design support services that are **relevant** to the experiences and needs of adults.
- Develop programs and support services that **engage** adult learners and assist them in actively applying what they are learning.
- Build **assessment** into procedures, programs, and support services. Analyze assessment results and use them to improve adult learner access and success.
- Design processes, programs, and services that are **learning-centered** and support the mission of the institution.

Figure 4.1

Keep It REAL: Designing Cocurricular-based Processes, Programs, and Services for Undergraduate Adult Learners

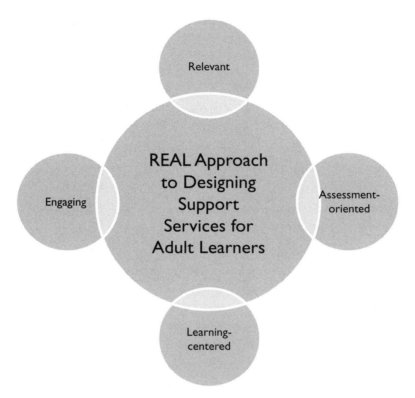

As with any student affairs activity, the REAL approach starts with evaluating existing policies, procedures, and support services in relation to the needs of the institution's adult learners. The second step involves helping team members to realistically assess their knowledge and skill sets in relation to adult learners and to increase both their knowledge of adult learners and their ability to design and deliver services to this student population. Once the required knowledge and skill sets are in place, staff members can initiate step three: redesigning policies, processes, and support services to meet the needs of the institution's adult learner population. The final, and frequently the most difficult, step involves reallocating resources to strengthen existing initiatives or to create new programs and services. Two sources of assistance for student affairs professionals committed to using a REAL approach for this are the Council for Adult and Experiential Learning (CAEL) and the Council for the Advancement of Standards in Higher Education (CAS).

- As Module 2 explains, CAEL developed the Principles of Effectiveness for Serving Adult Learners, nine principles for colleges and universities to better understand and meet the needs of adult learners (Flint, 2000). CAEL also partnered with the National Center for Higher Education Management Systems and Noel-Levitz to create the Adult Learner Focused Institutions (ALFI) Toolkit to help colleges and universities assess their effectiveness in serving adult learners (http://www.cael.org/ALFI/tools.html).

- The eighth edition of the *CAS Professional Standards for Higher Education,* published in 2012, offers guidelines for 43 functional areas within student affairs, including four related to adult learners: (1) adult learner programs and services, (2) parent and family programs, (3) veterans and military programs and services, and (4) transfer student programs (http://www.cas.edu/index.php/about/applying-CAS). CAS also provides *Self-Assessment Guides* for colleges and universities. Published in 2013, version 5.2 of the guides includes a CD with an e-learning tutorial on how to conduct a self-assessment activity as well as a PowerPoint presentation on CAS and the assessment process (https://store.cas.edu/catalog/index.cfm).

THE FIRST STEPS

Many colleges and universities, recognizing the value of improving access and success for adult learners, already have taken steps to strengthen their ability to understand and intelligently support this growing student population. Table 4.1 analyzes three of the strategies institutions frequently employ to launch new or strengthen existing adult learner initiatives.

Table 4.1

Improving Access and Success for Undergraduate Adult Learners: The First Step

Approach	Strengths	Weaknesses
Invite an outside consultant to evaluate current efforts and recommend strategies to increase adult learner access and success.	• Brings objectivity, a fresh perspective, and new expertise • Limits the influence of history, tradition, and internal politics • Validates what the institution does well, while motivating it to move to the next level	• Learning curve in relation to institutional history and data • Important internal constituencies may ignore the recommendations from outside • Tendency to offer prepackaged options
Send teams to other institutions to study their policies, processes, programs, and support services.	• Exposes college and university leaders to innovative ideas and applications • Develops links between the university and other institutions • Expands team members' knowledge of and perspective on adult learners • Identifies possible benchmark institutions	• Best practices do not always transfer well between institutions • Results depend on the composition of the team and the institutions selected • Other members of the university community may not accept the team's recommendations
Appoint a cross-functional team to study adult learner theory and research, assess the institution's current response to adult learners, and offer recommendations to help the university strengthen this response.	• Builds capacity among team members in three areas: adult learner theory and research, institutional data on adult students, and the current state of adult learner programs and services • Creates adult learner champions across the university • Develops recommendations that are based on data and experience	• Negative outcomes are possible if the university does not appoint objective, principled team members who represent a cross-section of the institution and are respected by their peers • Members of the college or university community may not value the recommendations of their peers

Readers of this tutorial have another option: Complete Exercises 4.1 and 4.2 at the end of this module to assess the institution's efforts to translate theory and research into policies, procedures, and support services for adult learners. Exercise 4.1 focuses on access initiatives; Exercise 4.2 explores success initiatives for retention. Both exercises are suitable for small or large groups and invite participants to celebrate current efforts and identify areas where action is required.

THE MOST PROMISING APPROACH

There are many ways to translate theory and research into policies, procedures, and support services for adult learners. Just as no two adult learners are exactly alike, no two colleges or universities share the same history, mission, or student populations. Consequently, there is no "right" way to organize support for adult learners. The key is to develop programs and services that are relevant to and reflect the mission, culture, and history of the institution; respond to the institution's changing student demographics; and factor in the effect of public policy initiatives, funding challenges, and emerging technology. Table 4.2 outlines strategies dozens of colleges and universities have used that are consistent with theory and research and have proven effective in increasing adult learner access and completion rates. Table 4.3 provides a snapshot of innovative approaches adopted at individual colleges or universities.

Table 4.2

Effective Strategies for Increasing Adult Learner Access and Success

Recommendation based on theory and research	Strategy
Assist adult learners with challenges, both expected and unexpected, that have the potential to interfere with their educational goals.	• Mandate participation in specific programs or services that are tied to the success of adult learners (e.g., advising, college success courses, orientation). • Sponsor support service fairs to connect adult learners to important community resources (e.g., child care, medical care, social services). • Provide ongoing counselor-led support groups for adult learners. Allow students to drop in and out of the group as needed. Offer child care to support group participants. • Develop a website or an adult learner portal that becomes a one-stop resource for important information and dates. • Provide detailed information about on- and off-campus child care options. • Negotiate reduced rates with reputable child care centers in the area. • Establish a revolving emergency loan fund for adult learners. • Identify (or create) options for students who are no longer eligible for Pell Grants or supplemental state grants.

Recommendation based on theory and research	Strategy
Assist adult learners in defining and working toward specific career and educational goals.	• Provide adult learners with up-to-date information on degree requirements, when courses are offered, and course prerequisites. • Develop degree plans for every major. Include options for part-time students as well as full-time students. • Require every adult learner to develop and continually update a realistic educational and support service plan. • Design career exploration courses, seminars, and resources specifically for adult learners.
Build incentives for working with adult learners into the institution's culture.	• Mention adult learners in the institution's mission statement. • Include adult learner initiatives in the strategic and operational plans. • Set aside money from the operating budget to fund initiatives designed to increase access and success for adult learners. • Recognize and reward partnerships between academic and student affairs that increase adult learner completion rates. • Send clear and consistent messages to the college or university community that adult learners matter.
Connect adult learners to the institution.	• Create work-study positions, part-time jobs, or campus-based internships for adult learners. • Design service learning opportunities that fit adult learners' needs and time constraints. • Provide adult learners with opportunities to serve in leadership positions within university clubs and organizations. • Establish an adult learner advisory group to assist the university with designing and implementing programs that matter to adult learners. • Use technology to develop personalized methods of communicating with adult learners and connecting them to the institution.
Connect adult learners to faculty members.	• Help faculty members create learning communities within their classes. • Build cohorts of adult learners majoring in the same subject and connect the cohorts to designated faculty members. • Fund periodic, informal lunches for adult learners to meet with faculty members to discuss college survival skills. • If faculty members serve as advisors, train them to practice intrusive advising when working with adult learners.

Recommendation based on theory and research	Strategy
Connect adult learners to other adults with similar interests, life experiences, and challenges.	• Create a space (or several spaces) for adult learners on campus. Make sure these spaces are child-friendly. • Establish clubs and organizations for adult learners, student parents, transfer students, and veterans. • Host quarterly brown-bag lunches for specific adult learner groups (e.g., student parents, veterans). Provide speakers willing to organize a presentation on a topic of interest to everyone, but allow time for individual pairing and sharing. Offer child care services when possible, and allow participants to bring their children. • Schedule reduced-rate community activities for adult learners and their families (e.g., movies in the park, a visit to the zoo, a trip to the aquarium). • Use social media platforms like Facebook, Twitter, or Tumblr to help students with similar interests connect with one another.
Educate campus leaders, faculty, support staff, and the community.	• Disaggregate institutional data to reflect access and success rates for adult learners. Share this information with influential groups in the college and the community. • Invite faculty members who demonstrate a high level of effectiveness in teaching adult learners to share their knowledge with peers via seminars, blogs, webinars, YouTube videos, or mentoring. • Convene annual adult learner focus groups. Train selected campus leaders to facilitate these groups and to create one report that summarizes focus group findings. Share the report with senior staff, faculty leaders, and others throughout the university community. • Schedule an annual dialogue between a representative group of adult learners and senior staff. • Schedule professional development activities for all areas of the university that focus on adult learner theory and research.
Increase the visibility of adult learners.	• Provide opportunities for groups representing adult learners to meet with senior staff and the president's cabinet. • Feature adult learner success stories on the institution's website and in alumni magazines. • Update the student handbook to include information for and pictures of student parents, student veterans, and other adult learners. • Establish Nontraditional Student Recognition Week. • Acknowledge adult learners, student parents, and veterans at convocations, orientation sessions, graduation ceremonies, and other campus events.
Provide adult learners with opportunities to acquire "university know-how."	• Develop an orientation session specifically for adult learners. • Set aside a section of a college success course exclusively for adult students or identify existing sections with large adult learner enrollments and include targeted information for adults in these sections. • Develop a website to help adult learners navigate and understand the institution. • Establish a mentoring program that pairs experienced adult learners with adult learners new to the institution. • Use social media platforms to connect adult learners with one another, share information, and track student needs.

Recommendation based on theory and research	Strategy
Recognize adult learner achievements.	• Establish a local chapter of Alpha Sigma Lambda, the national honor society for adult learners. • Establish awards specifically for adult learners, student parents, and student veterans. • Schedule recognition ceremonies that include the extended families of adult learners. • Help adult learners identify and celebrate milestones. • Encourage adult learners to create e-portfolios that: o Record their accomplishments; o Improve technical skills; and o Build a professional presence by creating an archive of successful projects, internships, research, or leadership achievements.
Shift adult learners' perspectives.	• Offer workshops and seminars to help adult learners increase their confidence and expand their horizons. • Invite adult learners who succeeded at your institution to share their stories. Feature these stories in print and e-material. • Develop a "success story" website that links current and former adult learners. • Coach adult learners through the process of applying to graduate school, taking the GRE, or sitting for the LSAT.
Use data to drive change.	• Disaggregate institutional data to reflect access and success rates for adult learners. • Schedule periodic presentations to the president's cabinet that describe shifting student demographics and how peer institutions are responding to these changes. • Subject National Survey of Student Engagement data to subgroup analysis. Identify how adult learners differ from traditional learners and the support services they need to succeed. Share this information with strategic partners and campus leaders.

Table 4.3

Innovative Adult Learner Practices or Support Services at Peer Institutions

Institution	Practice or support service
Arizona State University	• Offers a Family Resource Program that connects students to on- and off-campus child care resources (Schumacher, 2013).

The Pennsylvania State University	• Established a Commission for Adult Learners in 1998. Comprised of faculty, staff, and administrators from 23 campuses, the commission provides a visible body whose primary purpose is to contribute to a supportive climate for adult learners by:
	
	   o Monitoring adult learner recruitment, retention, customer satisfaction, and status.
	
	   o Recommending changes in policy, practice, and procedures.
	
	   o Advocating for adult learners.
	
	   o Serving as a repository and coordinating body for all adult learner-focused initiatives at Penn State (http://wpsudev1.vmhost.psu.edu/dev/pdf/Complete_History_of_CAL_07052012.pdf).
	
	   o Sponsors Non-Traditional Student Recognition Week each November, planned and hosted by Adult Learner Programs and Services. Each day focuses on a different group: student parents, student veterans, international students, etc. The week includes workshops, social events, and an adult learner listening luncheon with high-level administrators (http://studentaffairs.psu.edu/adults).

St. Catherine University (Minnesota)	• Has a child-friendly space adjacent to the Access and Success Center that contains computers and other resources for parents on one side and toys, beanbag chairs, dress-up clothes, and a TV/DVD player for children on the other. A glass wall separates the two sides. Parents are responsible for supervising their children (Carissa Morris, personal communication, September 17, 2013).
Texas A&M University System	• Launched a Military Friendly e-mail list in 2010 to allow support service staff working with student veterans to share information across the Texas A&M System. The e-mail list grew to include 325 participants from colleges and universities as well as local, state, and federal agencies. In July 2013, Texas A&M joined with Operation College Promise (OCP) to establish the Veterans Education Support Network, a national e-mail list open to anyone in higher education who has completed the OCP's Certificate for Veterans' Services Providers training (http://www.kbtx.com/home/headlines/the-Texas-AM-system-and-operation).
University of Akron (Ohio)	• Created *Express for Success*, a course that allows adult learners to review their knowledge of specific subjects before taking for-credit exams and to assess their chances of passing the exams (http://uakron.edu/express).
University of Alabama	• The Undergraduate and Graduate Parent Support programs sponsor Sitters for Service, a program that provides student parents with 30 hours of free babysitting each semester (Schumacher, 2013).
University of Illinois	• Sponsors a Facebook page for adult learners and nontraditional students that invites students to connect with one another, share experiences, identify challenges, find support, and keep up with college activities and events (Schumacher, 2013).
University of Michigan	• Provides child care subsidies through the financial aid office for full- and half-time students (Schumacher, 2013).
University of Toledo (Ohio)	• Established the College of Adult and Lifelong Learning (CALL) to provide access, career and life coaching, and academic support to new, continuing, and returning adult learners. CALL offers interdisciplinary and individualized degrees as well as scholarships and workforce credit programs for adult learners (http://www.utoledo.edu/call).

Institution	Practice or support service
University of Wisconsin	• Appointed a statewide committee to analyze, evaluate, and make recommendations concerning prior learning assessment (PLA) for adult learners. The goal is to expand PLA opportunities for adult learners and to design consistent policies and procedures across the system for evaluating and transferring PLA credit (Schumacher, 2013).
Widener University (Pennsylvania)	• Provides a variety of learning options for adults, including Saturday Studies (7-week courses that combine in-class instruction and independent study), WebStudy (online), and Accelerated Studies (blend of on-campus and online learning) (http://www.widener.edu/admissions/adult_undergraduate).

CASE STUDIES

Colorado State University and the University of California, Berkeley, followed different paths in developing support services for adult learners. Both institutions produced effective programs.

Colorado State University

Twelve percent of students at Colorado State University (CSU) are adult learners, 9% are student parents, and 4% are veterans. To support this fast-growing population, CSU developed the office of Adult Learner and Veteran Services (ALVS). Housed in the student affairs division, ALVS supports the transition, education, leadership, and involvement of adult learners and is committed to strengthening adult learner persistence and completion rates (http://alvs.colostate.edu/home.aspx). Table 4.4 offers a snapshot of some of the services that ALVS provides.

Table 4.4

Services Provided to Adult Learners at Colorado State University

Area	Adult Learner and Veteran Services (ALVS)
Assistive technology	• Provides assistive technology through the ALVS Office.
Child care	• Provides supervised educational activities on a drop-in basis for children ages 1 to 11 while parents study in the library (Ram Kidz Village). • Offers access to two child care centers on campus and one off campus.
Connect with other adults	• Sponsors an organization for older adult students and another organization for student veterans.
Expand horizons	• Provides study abroad opportunities and support.

Financial assistance	• Offers bookstore awards of $400 each semester to eight adult students.
	 • Provides scholarships to the following adult learner subpopulations:
	    o Former military (Veterans Scholarship Fund, eight per year)
	    o $2,500 to adult students with a more than 5-year gap in enrollment (Osher Fund)
	    o 100% tuition return to student veterans deploying
	 • Sponsors workshops to help adult learners manage their finances. The workshops include information related to budgeting, retirement, completing the Free Application for Federal Student Aid, managing debt, and buying a home (first-time home buyers).

Area	Adult Learner and Veteran Services (ALVS)
Information and input	• Publishes a newsletter with information about deadlines, programs, services, activities, jobs, and issues of importance to adult learners and veterans. • Appoints an ALVS Advisory Board composed of students and staff to ensure that CSU is meeting the needs of adult learners and veterans.
Mentoring	• Offers a peer-mentoring group for women transitioning to CSU. • Provides personalized coaches, liaisons, or case managers to assess students' needs, identify barriers, and refer to on- and off-campus support services.
Navigating the university	• Sponsors adult student welcome and orientation sessions. • Designs and presents custom on- and off-campus workshops and seminars for adult learners.
Recognition	• Sponsors recognition ceremonies, Pinnacle (the honor society for adult learners over 25 with a 3.0 GPA), and SALUTE (the honor society for veterans with an undergraduate GPA of 3.0 or a graduate GPA of 3.5). • Provides adult learners with the opportunity to be recognized as academically excellent nontraditional students at graduation.
Support services	• Designs and offers custom on- and off-campus workshops for adult learners. • Provides a Student Parent Success Program that reaches out to student parents, connects them with university and community resources, and offers a variety of services. • Provides a Veteran Success Program that reaches out to student veterans and assists them in accessing resources.
Transition after graduation	• Partners with the CSU Career Center and the Colorado Department of Labor and Employment to offer Education to Employment (E2E), an opportunity for adult learners to explore their future, participate in job-search workshops, attend networking events, and benefit from a Dress for Success program.
Tutoring	• Organizes study groups for adult learners. • Loans handheld survey response devices and calculators to adult learners, as needed. • Provides tutoring in mathematics and writing.

University of California, Berkeley

Trailblazer Alice Jordan, founder and director of the Transfer, Re-entry, and Student Parent Center at the University of California (UC), Berkeley (http://trsp.berkeley.edu), used her personal experience and advocacy to champion access, achievement, and success for undergraduate student parents in 1988, which makes the UC Berkeley's Student Parent program one of the oldest and most respected in the country. Jordan began by identifying differential treatment and a lack of access for student parents and helped students organize themselves. She sought allies within the College of Education and established a re-entry network and informal committees while building a culture of evidence to demonstrate the importance of providing support services for student parents. Jordan documented financial need for low-income, first-generation, student parents that ultimately resulted in UC Berkeley providing a university-funded $8,000 annual scholarship to student parents who file a FAFSA and qualify for financial aid. UC Berkeley also developed family housing, drop-in crisis intervention, counseling, and three credit-bearing courses to assist student parents. The courses are:

- **Once Upon a University**—A survival skills course that introduces student parents to the university and the resources available to them.

- **It Takes a Village**—A course designed to build community and teach students how to successfully combine school, work, and family.
- **Beyond the Village**—A course that addresses career and graduate school preparation and planning, offered in partnership with career services.

UC Berkeley also offers several unique services to student parents:

- Baby Bears @ Cal Project offers information, assistance, and peer support to student parents.
- Bear Necessities provides donated food and clothing to student parents.
- Service-learning internships specifically designed for student parents.
- SPARR: The Student Parent Association for Recruitment and Retention is a registered student group with funding from the UC Berkeley Student Government Association that provides a place for student parents to connect with one another and identify and advocate for their needs. (UC Berkeley, n.d.)

Jordan's legacy lives on: The student parent program has grown into the Transfer, Re-entry, and Student Parent Program and is now housed in the Cesar Chavez Student Center. As Table 4.5 demonstrates, it has become a comprehensive program that provides a variety of services for adult learners in addition to the services for student parents.

QUICK TIP

Alice Jordan, founder and former director of the Transfer Re-Entry Student Parent Center at the University of California, Berkeley, stresses that from admissions to graduation, it takes a village to foster institutional inclusion. Student affairs professionals must keep moving forward and continue to elevate the issues and mobilize students in order to change the culture and remove barriers for student parents (Alice Jordan, personal communication, October 11, 2013).

Table 4.5

Snapshot of Support Services That UC Berkeley Provides to Adult Learners

Adult Learner Subpopulation	Support Services Provided
Re-entry students	• Academic skills workshops • *Culminating the Cal Experience*: a 1-unit capstone experience for re-entry students • *EDUC 198: Adult Learners in Higher Education* (a first semester course) • Links with key campus resources (Berkeley International Office, Career Center, Student Learning Center, Multicultural Student Development, Student Life Advising/Educational Opportunity Program (EOP) Services, Disabled Student Program, and the Gender Equity Resource Center) • Mentoring • New student reception and recognition events (e.g., Transfer, Re-Entry, and Student Parent Achievement Celebration; the Judith L. Stronach Prize for Poetry and Prose) • Opportunities to serve as peer mentors or co-facilitators of classes or groups • Outstanding Faculty Series • Re-entry Transfer Student Association • Scholarships for re-entry learners (Beverly Mullins Memorial Scholarships, Osher Re-entry Scholarship Program) • Workshops to help adult learners to transition to college, identify sources of financial assistance, and connect with other students
Student veterans	• Access to scholarships and awards established for adult learners and re-entry students • Cal Veterans Student Services • Cal Veterans Group (Mission = successful transition and advocacy) • *Culminating the Cal Experience*: a 1-unit capstone experience for student veterans • *EDUC 198: Veterans in Higher Education* (takes a boot-camp approach to the student veteran's first semester) • Links with key campus resources (Berkeley International Office, Career Center, Student Learning Center, Multicultural Student Development, Student Life Advising/EOP Services, Disabled Student Program, and Gender Equity Resource Center) • Mentoring • Opportunities to serve as peer facilitators in the Veterans in Higher Education classes or as peer mentors to other student veterans • Recognition events • Timely processing of paperwork so that student veterans may access their benefits in a timely manner

Adult Learner Subpopulation	Support Services Provided
Transfer students	• Academic and Enrichment Workshop series (focus on travel abroad, opportunities for internships and undergraduate research studies, and graduate school) • Community-building events (advertised on the Transfer, Re-Entry, and Student Parent [TRSP] Facebook page) • Commuter student website • *Culminating the Cal Experience*: a 1-unit capstone experience for transfer students • *Education 198: Transitioning to Cal: An Introduction to the Research University for Transfer Students* • Internship opportunities within the Transfer, Re-entry and Student Parent Center • Links with key campus resources (Berkeley International Office, Career Center, Student Learning Center, Multicultural Student Development, Student Life Advising/EOP Services, Disabled Student Program, and Gender Equity Resource Center) • Major Insights Mentoring Program (pairs transfer students with students from their major) • Peer leadership and peer mentoring opportunities • Starting Points Mentoring Program (pairs current and new transfer students) • Summer orientation program • Transfer Student Association • Transfer Student Guide • Transitioning to Berkeley workshops • Welcome week workshops for transfer students

STATE INITIATIVES

Recognizing the importance of educated citizens to their economic future, several states have launched comprehensive initiatives to increase the number of adults with college degrees. This module highlights initiatives in Florida, Kentucky, and South Carolina; Module 10 will describe the unique approach pioneered in West Virginia.

Finish Up, Florida!

Finish Up, Florida! (FUF) involves 28 state (formerly community) colleges and is designed to entice students who either stopped out or dropped out of college before earning a degree to return to college. The initiative focuses on 87,000 students who left college within the past 2 years after completing 36 semester hours or more. Leaders at the 28 participating institutions received data relevant to their institutions, information about forming local FUF teams, and an invitation to share successful strategies across the state. Florida also updated FACTS.org, an advising website, to guide former students through the Florida reenrollment process (http://www.fldoe.org/cc/osas/newsletters/pdf/completionmarch12.pdf).

Kentucky State University Project Graduate

The Kentucky State University Project Graduate targets adult students who have earned 90 college credits but have not yet completed a degree. Students at Kentucky State University who have dropped out and are eligible for reenrollment are offered a streamlined readmission process, priority enrollment in classes, and a personal counselor to see them through the program. Started in 2007, this fast-track program offers tuition assistance, application fee waivers, tuition payment plans, and credit for prior learning and work experience. To date, 900 adult learners have returned to college and completed a degree (http://www.cpe.ky.gov/committees/collegeaccess/projgraduate).

Palmetto College

In 2013, the University of South Carolina created Palmetto College, an accelerated liberal arts program geared toward adult students 25 years and older who have taken 60 hours of college credit and would like to finish their 4-year degree. Offered entirely online, this program includes courses from across the South Carolina College System and provides adult learners with the opportunity to complete degrees in business, criminal justice, elementary education, nursing, and organizational leadership. The program, designed to increase access to 4-year degree programs in areas where access is not readily available, is cost controlled and competitive with regional campuses (http://www.palmettocollege.sc.edu).

THE ROAD AHEAD

Cocurricular support services are essential to the success of adult learners, whether those learners are student parents, student veterans, adult learners with disabilities, or adult learners of color. Student affairs practitioners have valuable knowledge and skills sets that colleges and universities must leverage to sharpen their understanding of adult learners and to build institutional cultures and support systems that meet the needs of this population. In turn, student affairs professionals must strengthen their knowledge of adult learner theory and research as well as their ability to use the CAS (2013) *Self-Assessment Guides*, the ALFI Toolkit (Flint, 2005), and the exercises suggested in this module to identify institutional barriers and reduce gaps in support services that could have an impact on adult learner access and success. Institutions must turn their attention to adult learners, without neglecting traditional learners, and design and implement support services that are REAL (relevant, engaging, assessment-oriented, and learner-centered). Student affairs professionals must use their skills and knowledge to build new (or contribute to existing) internal and external partnerships that are essential to the success of undergraduate adults. Finally, our collective mission is to demonstrate in a more tangible manner that student affairs matters to adult learners who need intelligent connections, direction, and support; to faculty members who need partners in designing experienced-based, learner-centered approaches that extend beyond the real or virtual classroom; and to their colleges and universities that need assistance in responding proactively and effectively to the economic, demographic, and technology shifts that are reshaping both the country and the higher education landscape.

APPLY THE CONCEPTS

Exercise 4.1— Institutional Diagnostic

Directions: Invite a group of faculty members, student affairs professionals, administrators, and students to independently complete the following worksheet.

1. Share and compare everyone's responses.
2. Identify and describe the present practices for each category.
3. Brainstorm additional steps the area/office could take.
4. Identify the top three priorities the institution needs to consider implementing in order to increase access, improve navigation, and retain adult students.
5. Present recommendations.

Area/office	Present policies and practices that assist adult students	Additional steps the area/office could take to attract adult students	Top Priorities
Admissions			
Advising			
Financial assistance			
Orientation			
Outreach/recruitment			
Prior learning assessment			
Printed material/ publications			
Registration			
Scheduling (when, where, and in what format courses are offered)			
Technology (e.g., electronic mailing lists, portals, dedicated websites)			
Other (please describe)			

APPLY THE CONCEPTS

Exercise 4.2— Assisting Adult Students to Succeed

Directions: Invite a group of faculty members, student affairs professionals, administrators, and students to think about how the institution assists adult students to succeed once they are enrolled. Each member of the group should complete the following worksheet independently.

1. Share and compare everyone's responses.
2. Identify and describe the present practices for each category.
3. Brainstorm additional steps the institution could take.
4. Identify the top three priorities the institution needs to consider implementing in order to increase success for adult students.
5. Present recommendations.

Adult learner needs	Present practices that assist adult students transitioning to the academy	Additional steps the institution could take to increase persistence and completion rates for adult students	Top Priorities
Accurate skills assessment and course placement			
Career counseling			
Child care/sitter service during events			
College success courses/seminars for adult students			

Adult learner needs	Present practices that assist adult students transitioning to the academy	Additional steps the institution could take to increase persistence and completion rates for adult students	Top Priorities
Faculty and staff skilled at working with adult students			
Financial literacy workshops or seminars			
Personal counseling			
Targeted support services and events for student parents			
Targeted support services and events for transfer students			
Targeted support services and events for student veterans			
Tutoring			
Other (please describe)			

REFERENCES

Bean, J. P., & Metzner, B. S. (1985). A conceptual model of nontraditional undergraduate student attrition. *Review of Educational Research*, 55(4), 485–540.

Betts, K., Welsh, B., Hermann, K., Pruitt, C., Dietrich, G., Trevino, J., Watson, T., Brooks, M., Cohen, A., & Coombs, N. (2013). Understanding disabilities & online student success. *Journal of Asynchronous Learning Networks, 17*(3), 15–47.

Bresciani, D. (2012, Fall). Time for an honest look in the mirror. *Leadership Exchange, 10*(3), 40.

California Postsecondary Education Commission. (2009). *Access and equity for all students: Meeting the needs of students with disabilities* (Report 09-15). Retrieved from http://www.cpec.ca.gov/completereports/2009reports/09-15.pdf

Council for the Advancement of Standards in Higher Education (CAS). (2012). *CAS professional standards for higher education.* Washington, DC: Author.

Council for the Advancement of Standards in Higher Education. (2013). *CAS self-assessment guides (version 5.2).* Washington, DC: Author.

Cross, K. P. (1981). *Adults as learners: Increasing participation and facilitating learning.* San Francisco, CA: Jossey-Bass.

Flint, T. (2000). *Serving adult learners in higher education.* Chicago, IL: Council for Adult and Experiential Learning.

Flint, T. (2005). *How well are we serving our adult learners? Investigating the impact of institutions on success and retention.* Chicago, IL: Council for Adult and Experiential Learning.

Graham, S. W., & Gisi, S. L. (2000). Adult undergraduate students: What role does college involvement play? *NASPA Journal, 38*(1), 99–121.

Hamrick, F. A., & Rumann, C. B. (Eds.). (2013). *Called to serve: A handbook on student veterans in higher education.* San Francisco, CA: Jossey-Bass.

Hanover Research. (2012). *Trends in online and adult education.* Washington, DC: Author.

Knowles, M. (1978). *The adult learner: A neglected species.* Houston, TX: Gulf Publishing.

Merriam, S. B. (2001). Androgyny and self-directed learning: Pillars of adult learning theory. In S. Merriam (Ed.), *The new update on adult learning theory* (New directions for adult and continuing education, No. 89, pp. 3–13). San Francisco, CA: Jossey-Bass.

Moneta, L., & Jackson, M. L. (2011). The new world of student affairs. In G. J. Dungy & S. E. Ellis (Eds.), *Exceptional senior student affairs administrators' leadership: Strategies and competencies for success* (pp. 1–14). Washington, DC: National Association of Student Personnel Administrators.

National Center for Education Statistics. (2011). *Projections of education statistics to 2017* (Publication No. NCES 2008-078). Washington, DC: Author.

Rocco, T. (2001). Helping adult educators understand disability disclosure. *Adult Learning, 12*(2), 10–12.

Ross-Gordon, J. M. (2003). Adult learners in the classroom. In D. Kilgore & P. J. Rice (Eds.), *Meeting the special needs of adult students* (New directions for adult and continuing education, No. 102, pp. 43–52). San Francisco, CA: Jossey-Bass.

Ross-Gordon, J. M. (2005). The adult learner of color: An overlooked college student population. *The Journal of Continuing Higher Education, 53*(2), 2–11.

Schlossberg, N., Lynch, A., & Chickering, A. (1989). *Improving higher education environments for adults.* San Francisco, CA: Jossey-Bass.

Schumacher, R. (2013). *Prepping colleges for parents: Strategies for supporting student parent success in postsecondary education.* Retrieved from http://www.iwpr.org/publications/pubs/prepping-colleges-for-parents-strategies-for-supporting-student-parent-success-in-postsecondary-education

Sissel, P. A., Hansman, C. A., & Kasworm, C. E. (2001). The politics of neglect: Adult learners in higher education. In C. A. Hansman & P. A. Sissel (Eds.), *Understanding and negotiating the political landscape of adult education* (New directions for adult and continuing education, No. 91, pp. 17–27). San Francisco, CA: Jossey-Bass.

Tinto, V. (1993). *Leaving college: Rethinking the causes and cures of student attrition* (2nd ed.). Chicago, IL: University of Chicago Press.

University of California, Berkeley. (n.d.). *Students who are parents at Cal.* Retrieved from http://trsp.berkeley.edu/studentparents.shtml

Watson, H. (2012). *Promoting adult student success at four-year higher education institutions* (Doctoral dissertation, Indiana University of Pennsylvania). Retrieved from http://dspace.iup.edu/handle/2069/1947

MODULE 5

Adult Learners, the Internet, and the Support Service Challenge

Lawrence V. Gould, Tisa A. Mason, and Kindra D. Degenhardt

ABSTRACT

Technology-enabled support services are beginning to play a critical role in the effort to increase retention, persistence, and completion rates among adult learners. Because 70% of the students enrolled in higher education today fall into this category, it has become essential for postsecondary institutions to develop and adopt creative support strategies to serve this growing and unique segment of the learning population. Student affairs practitioners charged with the implementation of these strategies must be knowledgeable about the tactics, tools, and technologies that will facilitate the success of online adult learners. Without this knowledge, an institution can lose its competitive edge in attracting this distinctive grouping of students that is likely to dominate the higher education marketplace for years to come.

THE PROBLEM DEFINED: TECHNOLOGY-ENABLED SUPPORT SYSTEMS

The purpose of this module is to explore the role that technology-enabled support services can play in increasing retention, persistence, and completion rates for adult learners. The past 15 years have seen an incredible growth in adult enrollment, much of it fueled by the expansion of online learning and enhanced accessibility, so it has become essential for postsecondary institutions to develop and adopt creative adult learner strategies to stand out from the competition. These strategies, however, must be organic and flexible because of the unique lifestyles and experiences that adult students bring to the learning experience. In addition, adult learners tend to be more female and minority than the general student population (Eduventures, 2013). In a competitive world, the academic and student affairs practitioners charged with the implementation of these strategies must be knowledgeable about the tactics and tools that will facilitate the success of online adult learners.

In 2008, Eduventures predicted that the distance education market would be evolving from an "age of competition" to an "age of brands." Convenience, flexibility, and price were the essential elements characterizing the competition among online education providers in the first years of the 21st century. By 2008, the basis for competition had changed. Today, the ingredients of reputational capital increasingly consist of a compelling learning experience, greater differentiation, stronger brand development, and an extensive menu of online support services. The world of online education continues to move into an "age of brands" where the promise of a quality learning experience and an extensively supported academic environment can position both the student and the institution for success. In other words, adult student support services enabled by technology will become more important than ever in transforming the student learning experience and building brand equity that can make one institution stand out from others in the clutter and clamor of the distance education marketplace. According to Hanover Research (2012), high-quality support services are becoming increasingly important differentiators in marketing and branding initiatives for higher education institutions. Supporting online, not just on-campus, students has been a growing responsibility for student and academic affairs staff for many years. Adding a *branding responsibility*, however, goes beyond the traditional support role and is a new but essential duty for today's student affairs professional. Understanding how to design, develop, and apply technology-enabled support services to build reputational capital is central to this responsibility (Kolowich, 2013).

TECHNOLOGY: A MANY-SPLENDORED THING

To say technology is transforming American higher education is an understatement. Although most observers would be correct in arguing that powerful demands for accountability, affordability, access, and a focus on learning outcomes coupled with the decline of state funding are driving this transformation, it would be hard to deny that technology has not played a predominant role in the process. From an academic perspective, there is no doubt that technology is changing the way faculty carry out their teaching and students learn on campus. It has become increasingly clear that technology-enabled support services for adult learners are equally significant and likely to be key differentiators for students "shopping" for the best value among a diverse array of educational providers. It is important, though, for student affairs professionals to understand that technology is more of a "strategic support and transformative resource rather than an answer in and of itself" (Bitner, Ostrom, & Burkhard, 2012, p. 38). It can be used to innovate or improve the adult learning experience, but technology by itself is not the solution for meeting the unique needs of adult learners—nor is the simple repurposing of existing or traditional student support services a viable approach. Those intending to leverage services or enhance student success should understand that technology touches the adult learner in a variety of ways and at many points in the support environment. Indeed, not all applications are defined by a student experiencing the technology face-2-face (F2F) or in a direct way. At least six technological touch points can be identified to guide those serving adult learners (Bitner et al., 2012):

1. **Student/F2F technology:** The student physically interfaces with the technology to actualize the support service. For example, the learner may employ a portal entry to complete access to a book in the library. Taking a readiness test would be another example of direct interaction with the technology or software.

2. **Social media technology:** This type of touch point is also based on a physical interface with the technology, but it is distinctively different from a Web 1.0 approach where the locus of value is the information on a Web page or stored in an archive and accessed by the student. With social media, the value of the technological touch point is in the Web 2.0 network of relationships generated by participation and interaction that can become part of the learning experience. Tools like Facebook, YouTube, Twitter, blogs, podcasts, Socrates, and more can be used to facilitate online communities of interest and build networks of engagement and assistance among students, faculty, and student affairs professionals.

3. **Onstage technology:** In this category, the student interacts with the technology to search for support services; not to actualize the service itself. Using a website or kiosk to search for tutoring services would be an illustration of this type of touch point. Drill down another level in this touch point and students become even more empowered with personalized services that allow them to shape their own chances for success (Soares, 2011). For example, a software called SHERPA archives course preferences and allows course choices to be made similar to the way consumers make their choices on Netflix and Amazon. Student preferences, schedules, and previous choices are stored to create profiles. This can be especially helpful for adult learners who may be looking for direction as they develop a sense of confidence about their choices.

4. **Backstage technology:** Use of e-mail, a smartphone, or Excel/SmartDraw to map or facilitate the support service are examples of this technological touch point. Student affairs professionals might use applications in this category to plan a service or assess diagnostics to adjust support levels (e.g., change help desk hours).

5. **Support technology:** This form of technology supports enterprise systems, the registrar's office, advising, admissions, financial assistance, and other activities that make the adult service support environment effective and successful.

6. **Nudge technology:** This technology touch point is multifaceted and prompt-driven. It is intended to provide diagnostic-derived suggestions that produce behavioral changes to solve an array of problems that may mark the student's academic journey, such as class performance, choosing the right courses, seeking out help to improve academic success, coping in life and lifestyle changes, time management, and counseling assistance. Nudge technology can help student affairs professionals increase adult learner engagement and academic success by prodding students into and through college (Wildavsky, 2013).

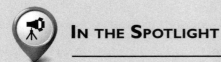

IN THE SPOTLIGHT

"In spite of the power of technology, in spite of the growing belief that technology can provide answers, we must continue to look beyond the tool to the goal. Information technology has made possible many advances, contributing to the globalization, economic development, and democratization of society. Yet technology is neither good nor evil. It is the purposes for which it is used that makes the difference. Technology must be applied to scholarship, preservation, and higher education more broadly by people who have critically considered the purposes for which it can and should be used. . . . Design, rather than disruption, will help us ensure technology lives up to its promise." (Oblinger, 2013, p. 6)

STUDENT DEFICIENCY/INSTITUTIONAL SOLUTION SUPPORT MODEL

Much like Astin's (1991) "talent development view" (p. 6) of academic success, whereby excellence is measured by how much value is added to the learner's intellectual and scholarly potential, student affairs professionals have traditionally developed support services by trying to add value to the whole person. Once a deficiency (academic performance) or need (counseling) is identified, the student affairs professional responds by generating a "solution." Most solutions or support services have a functional basis (fulfilling a perceived need) and have been directed at the on-campus student and traditional learning and living environment. In some cases, the services end up like many of the tools created in the higher education industry—overly transactional and focused on the individual rather than the group or collaborative learning context. Gap analysis represents another way of characterizing this student deficiency/institutional support model (Sener & Baer, 2002).

The traditional on-campus support model has eventually served as the basis for identifying other weaknesses in the virtual learning environment. Most important:

> Serving the off-campus student has not been part of the mainstream campus agenda for most institutions due to a lack of both the resources and the flexibility to meet the unique needs of these students. Where service has been provided, it has most frequently come from the units offering distance courses or programs (e.g., the Division of Continuing Education). On many campuses this has resulted in duplicate systems, one for off-campus and one for on-campus students, supporting such core services as admissions, registration, and student accounts. (Shea & Armitage, 2002, p. 1)

Figure 5.1

Guidelines for Creating Student Services Online

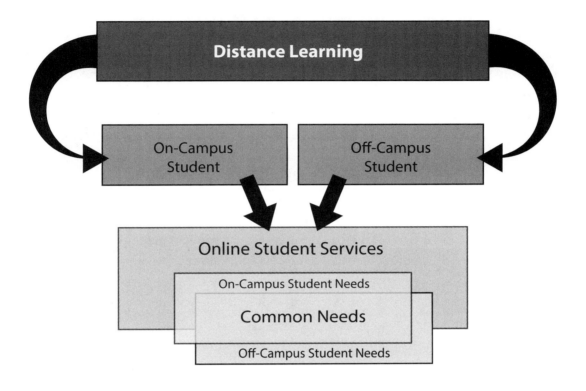

Source: Shea & Armitage (2002, p. 1). Reprinted with permission.

Responsibility for other noncore services, such as advising and technology support, has often fallen to faculty members teaching the courses. The goal should be to implement student services online for as many of the on-campus and off-campus student needs as possible (that is, minimize offline services), as illustrated in Figure 5.1. A lack of comparable services for the off-campus relative to the on-campus learner may even violate accreditation standards in some cases (Shea & Armitage, 2002).

Without an adult learner strategy to provide online support services, many institutions end up with a menu of services that is functionally based and fixed in time. The services may be decentralized and fragmented, complex, inefficient, and difficult to navigate for many students. This is especially troublesome for adult learners who want to focus on a limited array of online services—the big four being financial assistance information, acclimation to the virtual learning environment, prior learning assessment, and a set of success tactics that is proactive, positive, and personalized. Given that support services at many institutions tend to single out students for special attention by "accusing" them of not being prepared or referring to them as "at-risk," a transition to Web-enabled adult support could be the opportune time for student affairs professionals to move away from services that are reactive, accusatory, and un-inviting. If you're a newly enrolled adult learner and your first contact with a university's support services considers you to be a possible "failure," would you be likely to use them again (Jarrat, 2013)? Institutions would be wise to move from a prevent-failure approach to a proactive, success agenda. Few adult students want to be managed as a failed learner in the making.

WHERE ARE WE NOW?

As suggested in the preceding section, the repurposing of traditional on-campus support services to a virtual learning environment or the launching of new online services—unless guided by careful planning and mapping—can produce a decentralized array of services that is likely to be fragmented, complex, inefficient, and difficult to navigate. This has been the case at many institutions where support services have been implemented in an ad hoc fashion, with little cooperation between distance education and student affairs professionals. Instead of including the adult learner/customer's perspective, there is a tendency to simply assume that the service can be added by purchasing a piece of technology or adding another staff position. The prevailing attitude has been to see technology as the easy way out of the service challenge. This additive approach usually fails to consider how services fit together. As Jack Dorsey, the CEO of Twitter, reminds us, "the best technology reminds us of who we are" (Haynie, 2013, p. D1). In other words, as educators and professionals we need to co-design with the customer the actual support service before we launch it. Only when we put our feet up on the desk and look out the window to *think* will we create an adult learner experience that is easy, effective, and enjoyable (IntelliResponse, 2013).

The prevailing approach to planning adult online learner support services needs to go beyond outdated thinking about students as having deficiencies that need to be addressed by the institution. Crawley (2012) described the current design and development of support services as the "phased approach to online student services planning" (pp. 194–198). It consists of seven phases: prelaunch, assessment, planning, design, development, implementation, and evaluation. The ultimate goal of this strategy is to create a "system" of support services that is integrated and aligned; not complex, confusing, or disconnected.

When applying this template for creating support services online, an institution's team can use lessons learned from previous experience. One of the best set of precepts comes from *Guidelines for Creating Student Services Online* (Shea & Armitage, 2002). These precepts are derived from the results of the Learning Anytime Anyplace Partnership (LAAP) project described by Shea and Armitage (2002) and consist of 10 philosophical principles to be considered in each of the seven phases. Taken together, these principles create a context for planning and provide cautionary notes on the use of technology in the planning process.

Big-picture Principles

- **It's about people, not technology.** Moving student services to the online environment is primarily a challenge of leading people in a new direction. Dealing with politics, policies, practices, and culture are human, not technical, issues.
- **It's time to end the silos.** Student services have developed over time as the need for them arose on campus. Many have separate policies, practices, and technical infrastructures. New technologies make it possible to integrate services into a cohesive system of student support. This

requires reengineering student services—designing new policies and practices—and takes a cross-functional campus team to make it happen.

- **The user is king.** Web-based services should be designed from the user's perspective. Students are primarily task-oriented—they want to pay a bill, run a degree audit, schedule an appointment—and they don't want to think about which department provides what service. They prefer a single sign-on to integrated, customized services and the options of self-service, general help, and personalized assistance. The full range of optimized services includes online and real-person/real-time resources.

- **Internal consistency and integrity are vital.** The extent to which an institution puts its student services online should be consistent with its mission, culture, and priorities. If an institution is enrolling distance students in online courses, it must provide those students with accessible services of equal quality to those for campus-based students. Otherwise, these students cannot be expected to succeed at the same rate and it calls into question the institution's commitment to learning for all of its students—not just those privileged to come to campus.

- **Technology should enable new services, not define them.** New technologies and software updates arrive on the market at a rapid pace. In envisioning new services, the focus should not be limited by what is possible today. By defining the ideal and then phasing in the solutions as the technology becomes available, the best service will result.

- **Outside experts move projects forward.** Outside experts bring a broader perspective and objectivity that can help transcend campus politics. Scheduled visits from a consultant in organizational change or best practices in online student services also provide motivation for project teams to accomplish goals. In some cases, the expert may not bring new expertise, but rather validate what the campus is doing—and this can be equally important to project progress. The LAAP project partners identified site visits as one of the most important influences in their success.

- **Distance education staff and student affairs professionals should take a joint leadership role.** On many campuses, staff members in the distance education or other outreach unit have provided both the courses and the services for distance students for many years. They have tremendous expertise in providing remote services that are convenient and just-in-time. As today's campus population looks increasingly like the distance population, it is important that this experienced staff work with student affairs professionals in the redesign of services to support all students. On some campuses, student affairs professionals have not felt the need to become involved in designing support services for both the traditional and virtual learning environments. This will not work in an "age of brands" where adult student support services become part of the value proposition in building reputational capital.

- **Developing decentralized services means focusing on commonalities while respecting differences.** Perhaps as much as 80% of a service is the same across campus, but the last 20% can vary significantly. The trick is to design a system that builds on commonalities with the flexibility to accommodate differences via customization. That means understanding the needs, processes, and policies of each college/department/program in enough detail to make the system work for them.

- **First things first.** It is ideal to put the administrative core services—admissions, registration, financial aid, student accounts—online first as a foundation. These centralized services have many established rules, regulations, and operating procedures so it is easier to achieve consensus about what the new services should be like. Then you can move on to the decentralized ones where each department may have its unique needs.

- **There will never be enough time or money.** Redesigning student services with technology applications costs money and takes time, particularly in the startup phase. Projects will expand to fill both limits so it is better to get started than wait for the perfect combination of time and money, which may never come.

The logic of the phased approach, shaped and conditioned by these big-picture principles, moves the planning and design of adult learner support services another step toward creating a systemic, integrated, and aligned menu of online services enabled by a variety of technologies. Adding the element of collaboration between distance education unit leaders and student affairs professionals represents another key to developing the deep engagement and responsiveness needed for adult online enrollment success.

WHERE SHOULD WE BE GOING?

Without doubt, progress has been made on the way in which student affairs professionals use a "process model" to develop student support services in the virtual learning environment. Moving from the earlier student deficiency/institutional solution model to a more comprehensive phased process informed by big-picture principles represents notable improvement. There remains ample room, however, for innovation and movement toward meeting adult learner expectations of student services. In an age of branded competition, adult student services are already becoming a critical part of how students choose which institution to attend (Hanover Research, 2013b). If nothing else, excellence in online student support services can be a powerful marketing tool in an age where brand equity is the differentiator.

For some innovators, technology is the key to leveraging student support services, but Crawley's (2012) rendition of the phased planning model indicates clearly that technology is a facilitator and implementation tool. It's the people in the process that matter the most—and the most important people are the adult learners using these services. Much of the literature on online services recognizes that there is a perception that services are "delivered" to the student by the resources put in place by the institution and students are led to the service. This is accurate to a point. Yet, there is a need to continuously improve the support infrastructure and processes. Constantly evolving integration and a cohesive system of student support (as noted in the big-picture principles) is essential for advancing student success and satisfaction over the long-term to adult learners scattered throughout the virtual learning environment. This is unlikely to occur unless another big-picture principle is actualized—the user is king. A technique that accommodates the continuous improvement imperative and puts the user in the mix as a perpetual cocreator of the support service is important. One of the most underutilized techniques for accomplishing both objectives is service blueprinting. Supplementing the phased approach with this powerful technique would serve as one more advancement in the quest for excellence in creating adult student support services.

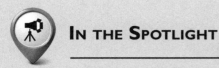

IN THE SPOTLIGHT

"Regardless of your current level of success, a basic SWOT analysis, or Center for Transforming Student Services (CENTSS) Audit (http://www.centss.org), is a great way to create a strategic road map for continuous improvement for the delivery of effective and efficient support services for adult learners. At Fort Hays State University, our SWOT analysis focused on the following questions: (1) In which areas are our current online student support services in alignment with current best practices and innovation? (2) Where can we make the strongest and most immediate contribution to improve the delivery of online student services? Key aspects of our process included a blended team of student and academic affairs staff and a report prepared by an external consultant (Hanover Research) to inform our analysis.

"The exercise both enabled us to better articulate our current robust student service menu benchmarked against best practices and acquire new resources for the 'next step' projects identified as high priority by our SWOT analysis. The exercise further served as a powerful motivator for continued interdisciplinary staff engagement teams, senior management's understanding of both the needs of adult learners and the desire of staff to address those needs, and ultimately increased benefits for adult distance learners that should lead to increased retention and graduation rates." —Brad Goebel, director of strategic communication and marketing, Fort Hays State University (personal communication, September 7, 2013)

STRATEGIES AND APPROACHES: CURRENT PRACTICES FOR ASSESSING 'READINESS' TO TAKE DISTANCE EDUCATION COURSEWORK

Learning style, technical skills, and personal workload are major factors in determining degree completion for adult online learners. Educators can assess a student's level of readiness for online learning with a variety of screening tools, including exams, questionnaires, and primer courses. In addition to assessing readiness, these screening tools can identify a student's learning strengths and weaknesses, therefore illuminating potential problems before they become major issues. Just as students must be ready for online learning, instructors have to be prepared to teach them. Because online teaching involves significantly different instructional design and pedagogical delivery, faculty should also assess their level of readiness for teaching in this new platform.

With the demographics of adult online learners being so diverse, institutions must be able to assess a student's level of readiness. According to Hanover Research (2013b), gauging a student's level of preparedness is the first and most beneficial *pre-intervention* measure for ensuring student success. Therefore, an instrument or screening tool should be used to assess a student's "learning style, computer skills, self-reliance, time management abilities, and cognitive skills" (Hanover Research, 2013b, p. 11).

Assessment of Readiness Exam

The readiness assessment exam is one of the most popular testing methods for institutions that offer distance education. This self-exam asks a variety of questions regarding a student's class necessity, preconceived ideas about online learning, cognitive learning abilities, technology usage, studying habits, and level of commitment. Students whose scores fall below an acceptable rating are usually advised to investigate their level of readiness further or provided with strategies to increase their chances of success. Table 5.1 provides a sample assessment of the readiness tool used by The Community College of Baltimore County in Maryland.

One vendor-produced readiness tool that has revolutionized testing is called SmarterMeasure (http://www.smartermeasure.com). According to Crawley (2012), most students tend to overestimate their technical skills in regard to online learning. In order to combat this self-inflation, SmarterMeasure assesses crucial technical skills, such as screen reading, typing accuracy, and speed. By adding the feature of skill efficiency, SmarterMeasure provides a more accurate and thorough assessment of readiness.

Table 5.1

Self-assessment Test for Online Distance Learning, The Community College of Baltimore County

Question	Choices
1. My need to take this course now is:	A. High—I need it this semester. B. Moderate—I could take it on campus later, or substitute another course. C. Low—It's a personal interest that could be postponed.
2. Feeling that I am part of the class is:	A. Not important to me. B. Somewhat important to me. C. Very important to me.
3. I would classify myself as someone who:	A. Often gets things done ahead of time. B. Needs reminding to get things done. C. Puts things off until the last minute.
4. Classroom discussions are:	A. Rarely helpful to me. B. Sometimes helpful to me. C. Almost always helpful to me.
5. When an instructor hands out instructions for an assignment, I prefer:	A. Figuring out the instructions on my own. B. Trying to follow directions on my own, then asking for help as needed.
6. I need faculty comments on my assignments:	A. Within a few weeks, so I can review what I did. B. Within a few days, or I forget what I did. C. Right away, or I get very anxious.

Source: Community College of Baltimore County (n.d.). Reprinted with permission.

Learning Styles Questionnaire

The learning styles questionnaire, an extension of the assessment of readiness exam, focuses on cognitive learning abilities. Because the online learning environment is predominantly in a written format, students who are visual learners, rather than auditory or kinesthetic, may be at an advantage. Most people use all three learning styles, but one tends to be dominant. If the dominant style is not conducive to online learning, and the student is unable to adapt to another learning style, the traditional classroom setting may be in his or her best interest.

Primer Course

For adult online learners who demonstrate a lack of readiness, an orientation or primer course may be a viable solution. A student who has never experienced online education may be unaware of the extensive time commitment and frequency of interactions (Hanover Research, 2013b). However, a primer course, usually 1 week long, allows first-time online learners to become familiar with important topics and issues related to distance education: time management, student accountability, online communication skills and communities, research and resources, technology considerations, and study habits (Alford & Lawson, 2009).

Faculty Evaluation

Because online education requires an adaptable and unique kind of instruction, some institutions are starting to use assessment of readiness exams for faculty. The University of Central Florida is currently using a faculty readiness form that evaluates prior online teaching experience, practices, and teaching philosophy (Cavanagh, 2011). If faculty members demonstrate that they meet university standards for online instruction, they can be exempt from taking the university's 8-week online course design and instruction workshop (Cavanagh, 2011). Because the workshop is comprehensive, instructors with an abundance of online teaching experience may not find the extensive seminar advantageous.

Early Adopters and Re-active Innovators: Successful Examples From Colleges and Universities With Effective Support Services for Adult Learners

In an attempt to better serve online adult learners, some institutions have adopted new support systems, centralized their old processes, or taken special initiative to discover and meet the needs of these students. Table 5.2 provides examples of benchmark institutions that have successfully developed a support system geared toward online adult learners.

Table 5.2

Benchmark Institutions: Support Services for Adult Learners

Type of Support Service	University	Description
Online tutoring	Oregon State University (2013)	Oregon State University uses a program called Ask Ecampus, which allows users to ask questions from a regularly updated knowledge base. Through the Ecampus portal, students also have access to 24/7 tutoring services in math, science, writing, etc.
Academic advising	St. Joseph's College of Maine (Cochrane, n.d.)	St. Joseph's College has nine academic advisors whose sole mission is to develop supportive relationships with students, provide course schedule counseling and motivational support, advocate for the students, provide a single point of contact to other departments, and contact the students via e-mail or phone at least once every 3 to 4 weeks.
Orientation	Stark State College (Lampner, n.d.)	Stark State College requires all online learners to submit an "Online Student Agreement" that outlines necessary information to be successful in the distance learning environment. Prior to accessing their online courses, students are prompted with a variety of statements that remind them of the best practices and expectations of successfully completing an online course.
Library services	University of Alabama (2013)	The University of Alabama offers library services and databases specifically designed for distance learners. The university provides a succinct yet beneficial list of services, tools, and technical support available to online learners. Additionally, the technology allows students to submit questions to a librarian.
Student affairs and academic affairs advising	Long Beach City Community College (2013)	Long Beach City Community College created a site titled "Online Counseling" that encourages students to ask the counselors detailed questions on records, educational goals, academic history, and resources.
Peer network counseling	Montgomery College (Hanover Research, 2013a)	Montgomery College created a platform for academic and social support called the Germantown Options for Adult Learners. It allows students to interact with each other to discuss a variety of topics, such as how to overcome test anxiety and how to register for classes.

Type of Support Service	University	Description
Faculty and staff engagement techniques	University of Central Florida (2013)	The University of Central Florida (UCF) offers 30-minute stand-alone seminars that provide collegial dialogue and best practice procedures for online teaching. Copresented with the Center for Distribution Learning and UCF faculty, these sessions are highly focused with take-away resources. The sessions are also filmed so faculty can review them at a later date.
Financial aid	University of Wisconsin–Eau Claire (Hanover Research, 2013a)	Two primary entities were developed to meet the needs of adult students: the Nontraditional Student Services Office and the Educational Opportunity Center (EOC). The EOC focuses on providing pre-enrollment services by conducting personalized information sessions that focus primarily on admissions and financial aid.
Technology for retention and persistence	Fort Hays State University (2009)	TigerConnect by ConnectEDU is a fully hosted, Web-based communications system with portals for incorporating interactive resources and social networking tools to enhance peer-to-peer relationships and provide learners with support communities to foster success.

 IN THE SPOTLIGHT

"The National Society of Leadership and Success was founded with the sole purpose of creating lasting positive change. Beginning with a handful of chapters, the society now reaches tens of thousands of students at hundreds of chapters around the world. We encourage community action, volunteerism, personal growth, and strong leadership from our chapters and members worldwide. The National Society of Leadership and Success is an organization that helps people discover and achieve their goals. It offers life-changing lectures from the nation's leading presenters and a community where like-minded, success-oriented individuals come together and help one another succeed. The society also serves as a powerful force of good in the greater community by encouraging and organizing action to better the world.

"The guiding question we established to shape all the important decisions the organization makes is: 'Are we helping the greatest number of people in the greatest way?' The society's online chapter was created to provide our leadership program to students unable to travel to campus frequently enough to complete the requirements toward becoming an inducted member. Since its inception, the online chapter has given thousands of students the opportunity to participate in our life-altering leadership program from the comfort of their own home." —Matthew Sarlo, chapter support coordinator, The National Society of Leadership and Success (personal communication, September 16, 2013)

SERVICE BLUEPRINTING: A 'TRANSFORMATIONAL' SUPPORT SERVICE STRATEGY FOR SERVING ADULT ONLINE LEARNERS

"Servicing your customer" is a truism in the world of business and in many other types of organizations. In terms of success strategies, "top performing businesses have long understood the financial ramifications of a satisfied and engaged customer . . . customer-centricity continues to be a theme for success" (Aberdeen Group, 2013, p. 1). But even in the business world, it is often difficult to change the mindset of an organization to make customer service initiatives a high priority. Simple inattention is often the culprit. At other times, it is intentionally ignored because an organization's leaders are skeptical that profits and a service orientation are in any way correlated.

In the world of higher education, even less credence is given to the idea that good customer service could be related to student and enrollment success. Philosophically, many in higher education resent the introduction of business concepts and terminology into the academic environment (Raisman, 2002).

Increasingly, however, this proscription is beginning to change. More institutions and academic professionals have had to face the realization that "customer service is treating students as if they counted. It places students, their need for being valued as individuals and their learning at the center of the enterprise . . . customer service is simply fulfilling the real expectations of students—'expectations.' Not wants. Not desires, but expectations" (Raisman, 2002, pp. 19, 67). Like most anyone else, students, and adult students even more so, want support services that deliver what they need, consistency of experience, a quick resolution of their problem, and an encounter that makes it clear that someone cares. As Steffensen Pauls (2013) noted:

> Students really care about the experiences they're having. . . . A lot of institutions focus solely on academic quality. That's certainly important, but the other piece is ensuring students receive

QUICK TIP

To ensure online learners have access to needed services:

✪ Put yourself in your students' shoes. Go online and try to do everything that any student would have to do, from registering for classes to accessing tutoring. That process will show you where the real barriers are.

✪ Create a map of everything students must do from the day they apply to the day they graduate. Provide links along that map to direct students to each place they must go for services. Make sure all students get a copy of the map and links.

✪ Make sure students know about "hidden" resources. Those are any resources that aren't necessarily widely publicized but that could help them along the way.

✪ Identify the students who need the most support. Develop an advisement model that works more proactively with them. If you have a very limited support staff, make sure staff members are working intensively with high-need students. Support staff can work reactively with students who are skilled at finding the services they need.

✪ Plan for periodic evaluation. Wrinkles can appear along the way, so be sure you're taking time occasionally to survey online learners to find out how satisfied they are with the support available to them. Adjust services and systems according to their feedback. (Amato & Burns, 2013)

great customer service from the people they interact with across the institution. I know we don't like the words *customer service* in academia, but the reality is that adult students expect good customer service. (p. 12)

In other words, customer service is both a student success tool and a marketing strategy. Satisfied students tell other potential students about their experiences.

As Ostrom, Bitner, and Burkhard (2011) argued, it is essential to view higher education as a service centered on the student, the support service experience as a constant source of information, and the student as a cocreator of value. From their perspective, the student experience is the focus; not just the fact that a student has a need, for example, for financial assistance. What follows is a set of excerpts from Ostrom et al. (2011) that provides the reader with the essential elements of service blueprinting as a process modeling technique. More detail about this mapping and modeling process is available in the resource literature at the end of this module.

Essential Elements of Service Blueprinting as a Process Model

- **Higher education should be seen as a system of "services."** Higher education is a service, or a service system, and transformative issues aiming to address problems like adult student support will benefit from being viewed through a service lens. This puts the customer at the center of improvement and innovation initiatives, considers the customer experience to be a foundation for analyzing and making enhancements, and assumes the customer is a cocreator of value.

- **The student is the center of service in higher education.** In the context of higher education, this means that the student is the center, the student's experience is the foundation for analysis, and the student is the cocreator of his or her educational experience and ultimately the value received. Viewing students as customers has a charged history in higher education, but as the economy has become more service-dominated, it can be beneficial to apply lessons from other businesses to help improve higher education.

- **Customer-centered improvement techniques should be focused on the student experience.** Students need to be at the core of higher education reform. To move in this direction, tools and techniques shown to facilitate customer-focused improvement and innovation should be applied in higher education in order to successfully develop and implement positive change in the student experience and outcomes.

- **Service blueprinting can be used to visualize and detail Internet-enabled adult student support services.** Service blueprinting is a simple-to-learn process-modeling approach that facilitates collaboration among key contributors and stakeholders across a broad customer experience to create a visual depiction, or blueprint, of a service. The service blueprint highlights the steps in the process, the points of contact that take place, and the physical evidence from the customer's point of view. In Figure 5.2, the steps involved in the student experience are shown chronologically from left to right across the top of the blueprint in the customer actions row. The role of technology in delivering and supporting the service is clearly apparent in the row labeled "Onstage Technology Actions" and in the row labeled "Support Processes." Whether the technique is being used to examine existing services or to develop new ones, the discussions that occur during the blueprinting process have the potential to improve or conceptualize services in important ways.

- **Service blueprinting and the re-imagination of online adult student support services.** Beyond detailing support services, service blueprinting can help university leaders and employees redesign, reinvent, and reimagine their educational offerings and service processes from the student's point of view. It is important to ask whether the changes proposed will improve or worsen the student experience and outcomes. Do the changes eliminate "pain points," moments during the service that customers or university employees perceive to be annoying, challenging, or dissatisfying, or do they create new ones? Do the changes lead to innovative and sustainable educational models or just reinforce existing ones? Do multiple or new initiatives work at cross purposes and not align with the student experience?

- **Blueprinting, technology, and new and emerging applications.** Using a service lens to view higher education allows you to put the student at the center and to consider higher education as a cocreated set of activities and initiatives that have value only in their use over time. Service blueprinting is valuable for illustrating the student experience and for bringing the right parties together to support the innovation and improve the existing services that can transform higher education. Blueprinting is easily learned and is applicable across all types of services in higher education. It makes the strategic importance of technology immediately apparent. Technology (both Web 1.0 and 2.0) is as an innovative way to deliver and also support the student experience. As a tool for encouraging high tech/high touch, technology can help with process orientation, decision making, personal recommendations, proactive communications, and real-time interaction with the institution (Venable, 2011). Using service blueprinting to strategically integrate technology into institutional processes and offerings will, ultimately, transform the student experience. Equally important, service blueprinting is a powerful technique that can add value to the current phased approach to designing and developing online student services by defining each phase with greater precision, clarifying the processes involved, and revealing the parts of the support service that may need modification or replacement. Blueprinting each of these support tools can only improve their use and enhance the possibilities of academic success for the adult learner.

CONCLUSION

Increasingly, an institution's competitive position depends on the availability of compelling learning experiences, greater differentiation between itself and its peers, a more powerful brand promise, and the provision of a comprehensive array of services for the online learner. This module has emphasized the potential of technology-enabled support services as tools, tactics, and techniques for enhancing the retention, persistence, and completion rates of adult learners. Knowing about these support methods is important to the 21st century student services professional. But being aware of these approaches is not sufficient. Student services professionals must become skilled at designing, developing, and applying technology-enabled applications. Repurposing existing campus support services is not enough. In fact, designing technology-enabled support services for e-learners and off-campus students offers student affairs professionals unique opportunities to assess and strengthen their current support service model for all students. However, student affairs professionals will not make the jump from good to great until they routinely employ strategies like service blueprinting to refine technology-enabled processes, programs, and services. In the final analysis, technology is a tool that student affairs professionals must use effectively and intentionally to increase access and success for all students, whether they are attending classes on campus, at off-campus sites, or online.

QUICK TIP

Service blueprinting has strong application for defining and refining new and emerging adult learner support tools like coaching, mentoring, prior learning assessment (PLA), and massive open online courses (MOOCs).

IN THE SPOTLIGHT

"Recently, the University of Maryland University College (UMUC) has received press for granting college credit for several MOOCs. I want to clarify, we're not granting credit for the simple completion of all MOOCs. Very specifically, right now, it's six MOOCs that have been evaluated by the American Council on Education. This is really just part of what we've been doing for 40 years.

"I realize that this makes headlines because everybody is very interested in MOOCs, but, honestly, we see it as just one more way to respect and honor adults' ability to learn outside of the traditional college classroom. We have quality processes to measure the learning so that we are sure the student meets the standard that a student would meet if he or she takes the course with us. This means that whether through a MOOC, a college class, or on the job—if a student can demonstrate that he or she has achieved the learning standard of a UMUC course, we grant them the credit.

"So this makes it interesting to bring student affairs professionals into the conversation with traditional-age students. Students learn a great deal in the extracurricular, residence-hall programming, student leadership portions of their experience in college. Why don't we consider ways to help students translate that learning so students can earn college credit in topics such as diversity studies, leadership and management, political science, or education? Some colleges have a cocurricular transcript for students to list their outside activities while in college, but this is still not the same as college credit. Think of it as a local internship for credit.

"Student affairs professionals I have worked with are quite knowledgeable of learning outcomes and how SA [student affairs] activities can support the learning environment. The more we can broaden how students learn and receive credit for college-level learning, the richer will be students' experience and accessibility will be expanded." Marie Cini, provost, University of Maryland University College (personal communication, September 11, 2013)

Figure 5.2

Essential Elements of Service Blueprinting as a Process Model

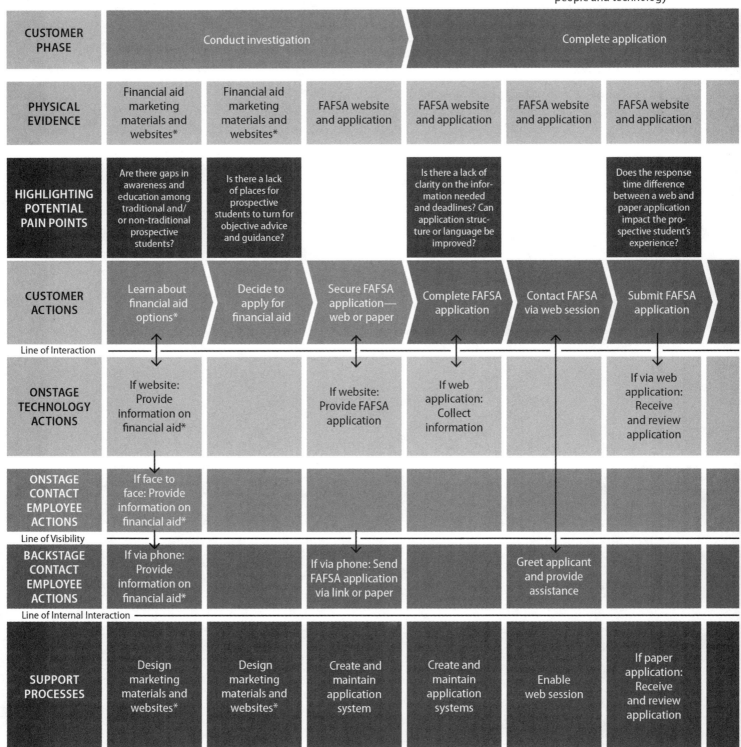

*From high schools, universities, and other sources.

Note: Various support processes span the blueprint, including human resource and training management and database creation and maintenance. To minimize complexity, vertical arrows are not included for support processes.

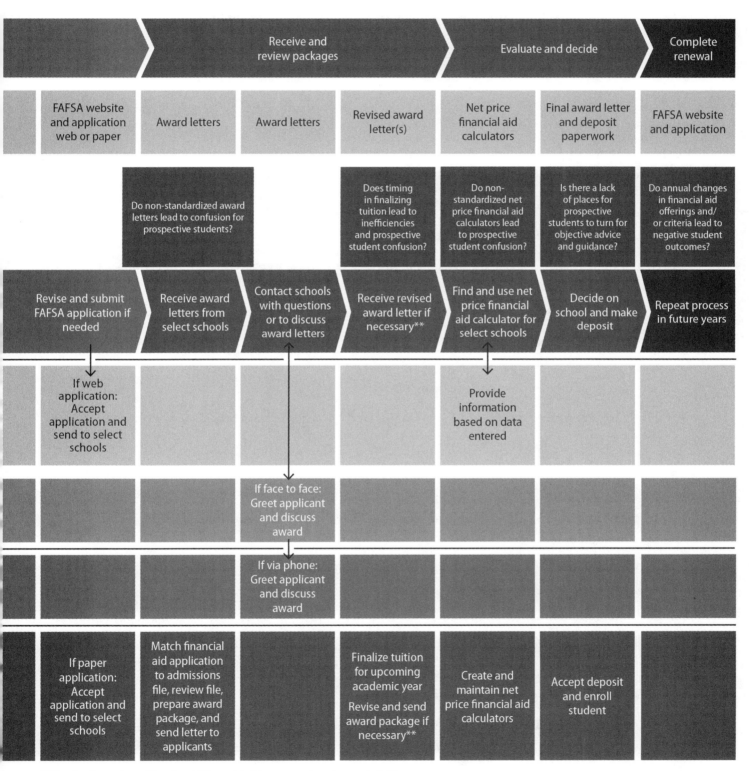

	Receive and review packages			Evaluate and decide		Complete renewal
FAFSA website and application web or paper	Award letters	Award letters	Revised award letter(s)	Net price financial aid calculators	Final award letter and deposit paperwork	FAFSA website and application
	Do non-standardized award letters lead to confusion for prospective students?		Does timing in finalizing tuition lead to inefficiencies and prospective student confusion?	Do non-standardized net price financial aid calculators lead to prospective student confusion?	Is there a lack of places for prospective students to turn for objective advice and guidance?	Do annual changes in financial aid offerings and/ or criteria lead to negative student outcomes?
Revise and submit FAFSA application if needed	Receive award letters from select schools	Contact schools with questions or to discuss award letters	Receive revised award letter if necessary**	Find and use net price financial aid calculator for select schools	Decide on school and make deposit	Repeat process in future years
If web application: Accept application and send to select schools				Provide information based on data entered		
		If face to face: Greet applicant and discuss award				
		If via phone: Greet applicant and discuss award				
If paper application: Accept application and send to select schools	Match financial aid application to admissions file, review file, prepare award package, and send letter to applicants		Finalize tuition for upcoming academic year Revise and send award package if necessary**	Create and maintain net price financial aid calculators	Accept deposit and enroll student	

**Due to discussion with schools' financial aid personnel or change in tuition after the original award letters were sent.

Source: This material was published by the Center for American Progress (http://www.americanprogress.org). Ostrom et al., 2011, pp. 60-61. Reprinted with permission.

RESOURCES

Britto, M., & Rush, S. (2013). Developing and implementing comprehensive student support services for online students. *Journal of Asynchronous Learning Networks, 17*(1), 29–42.

Central Methodist University. (2013). *Online course readiness assessment.* Retrieved from http://www.centralmethodist.edu/cges/online_readiness.php

Eduventures. (2013). *Choice, change, and continuity: Perspectives on five critical issues facing higher education leaders in 2013 and beyond.* Boston, MA: Author.

Kovac, M., Chernoff, J., Denneen, J., & Pratap, M. (2008, December). Strike the right balance between service efficiency and customer satisfaction. *Harvard Business Publishing, 13*(12), 1–4.

Sloan Consortium. (2013). Retrieved from http://sloanconsortium.org

Supporting Students On Line. (2012). Retrieved from http://anitacrawley.net/resources

University of Houston. (2013). *Tools: Test of online learning success.* Retrieved from http://distance.uh.edu/online_learning.html

University of Miami. (2013). *Online readiness assessment quiz.* Retrieved from http://www.miami.edu/dcie/index.php/asap/online_credit_courses/Quiz

University of North Carolina at Chapel Hill. (2010). *Online learning readiness questionnaire.* Retrieved from http://www.unc.edu/tlim/ser

WICHE Cooperative for Educational Technologies. (n.d.). Retrieved from http://wcet.wiche.edu

REFERENCES

Aberdeen Group. (2013, May). *The right financial impact of customer service.* Retrieved from http://www.aberdeen.com

Alford, P., & Lawson, A. (2009). *Distance education student primer: Skills for being a successful online learner.* Retrieved from http://ittraining.iu.edu/free/despr.pdf

Amato, C., & Burns, E. (2013, October). Use these tips to ensure online learners have access to needed services. *Recruiting & Retaining Adult Learners, 16*(1), 5. doi: 10.1002/nsr.20070

Astin, A. W. (1991). *Assessment for excellence: The philosophy and practice of assessment and evaluation in higher education.* New York, NY: Macmillan.

Bitner, M. J., Ostrom, A. L., & Burkhard, K. A. (2012, November/December). Service blueprinting: Transforming the student experience. *Educause Review, 47*(6), 38–50.

Cavanagh, T. (2011). *UCF's online faculty readiness assessment.* Retrieved from http://sloanconsortium.org/effective_practices/ucfs-online-faculty-readiness-assessment

Cochrane, P. (n.d.). *Proactive academic advising for distance students.* Retrieved from http://sloanconsortium.org/effective_practices/proactive-academic-advising-distance-students

Community College of Baltimore County. (n.d.). Distance learning self-assessment test. Retrieved from http://www.ccbcmd.edu/distance/assess.html

Crawley, A. (2012). *Supporting online students: A guide to planning, implementing, and evaluating services.* San Francisco, CA: Jossey-Bass.

Eduventures. (2008). *Understanding the national online higher education market.* Boston, MA: Author.

Eduventures. (2013). *Adult student trends: Selected data from Eduventures.* Boston, MA: Author.

Hanover Research. (2012, August). *Trends in online and adult education.* Washington, DC: Author.

Hanover Research. (2013a, February). *Academic advising for adult students.* Washington, DC: Author.

Hanover Research. (2013b, February). *Promoting the success of underprepared students in online education.* Washington, DC: Author.

Haynie, D. (2013, July 12). How to compare online, on-campus graduate programs. *U.S. News & World Report.* Retrieved from http://www.usnews.com/education/online-education/articles/2013/07/12/how-to-compare-online-on-campus-graduate-programs

IntelliResponse Systems Inc. (2013). *Achieving excellence in online student services.* Retrieved from http://info.intelliresponse.com/rs/intelliresponse/images/5Checkpoints.pdf

Jarrat, D. (2013, August 23). "Success creation" versus "failure prevention": Alternative paradigms in student support. *Inside Track.* Retrieved from http://www.insidetrack.com/success-creation-versus-failure-prevention-alternative-paradigms-in-student-support

Kolowich, S. (2013, August 9). Tech savvy is essential to student affairs, survey finds. *The Chronicle of Higher Education.* Retrieved from http://chronicle.com/blogs/wiredcampus/tech-savvy-is-essential-to-student-affairs-survey-finds/45345

Lampner, W. (n.d). *Online student agreement.* Retrieved from http://sloanconsortium.org/effective_practices/online-student-agreement

Long Beach Community College. (2013). *Online counseling.* Retrieved from http://onlinecounseling.lbcc.edu/counselinghome/counselinghome.cfm

Oblinger, D. G. (2013, July/August). Disrupted or designed? *Educause Review, 47*(6), 4–6.

Oregon State University. (2013). *Ecampus.* Retrieved from http://ecampus.oregonstate.edu/ask-ecampus

Ostrom, A. L., Bitner, M. J., & Burkhard, K. A. (2011, October). *Leveraging service blueprinting to rethink higher education: When students become 'value customers,' everybody wins.* Retrieved from http://www.americanprogress.org/issues/2011/10/pdf/service_blueprinting.pdf

Raisman, N. (2002). *Embrace the oxymoron: Customer service in higher education.* Horsham, PA: LRP Publications.

Sener, J., & Baer, B. (2002, December). *A gap analysis of online student services: Report on administrative and student survey.* Retrieved from http://www.marylandonline.org/about/ sponsored_research_/gap_analysis

Shea, P., & Armitage, S. (2002). *Guidelines for creating student services online.* Retrieved from http://www.wcet.wiche.edu/wcet/docs/beyond/overview.pdf

Soares, L. (2011, October). *The "personalization" of higher education: Using technology to enhance the college experience.* Retrieved from http://www.americanprogress.org/issues/labor/ report/2011/10/04/10484/the-personalization-of-higher-education

Steffensen Pauls, T. (2013, October). Growing programs requires focus on customer service, sharing assessment data. *Recruiting & Retaining Adult Learners, 16*(1), 12. doi: 10.1002/nsr.20070

University of Alabama. (2013). *Library services for distance learners.* Retrieved from http://www.lib. ua.edu/distanceed

University of Central Florida. (2013). *Teaching online.* Retrieved from http://teach.ucf.edu/ professional-development/faculty-seminars

Venable, M. (2011, August). *Providing critical support to online students.* Retrieved from http://www.onlinecollege.org/whitepapers/2011-08.pdf

Wildavsky, B. (2013, September 10). Nudge nation: A new way to prod students into and through college. *Education Sector.* Retrieved from http://www.educationsector.org/publications/ nudge-nation-new-way-prod-students-and-through-college

MODULE 6

Student Veterans as Adult Learners in the Post-9/11 Era

David Vacchi

ABSTRACT

Student veterans have served our nation in various ways, many in combat, and they come to college with the goal of rejoining the civilian population and contributing to society in a meaningful way. Student affairs professionals have a key role in facilitating student veteran success, and that role need not be complicated or difficult. This module identifies innovative practices and programs in working with veterans and describes the types of on- and off-campus partnerships that institutions should build to increase the persistence and completion rates of veterans. Finally, this module offers a conceptual model for facilitating the success of veterans in college and outlines the role that student affairs professionals have in veteran success

STUDENT VETERANS: A DIVERSE AND UNIQUE ADULT LEARNER POPULATION

Student veterans go to college with aspirations of rejoining and contributing to civilian society in meaningful ways. Post-9/11-era veterans come to college with a great educational benefit package that virtually eliminates the obstacle of the cost of higher education. However, student veterans do need help navigating campus structures, building personal support systems, and participating

QUICK TIP

Veteran-friendly is an underdeveloped concept often used without a definition. One comprehensive definition refers to a campus that "identifies and removes barriers to the educational goals of veterans, creates a smooth transition from military life to college life, provides information to veterans about available benefits and services, creates campus awareness of the student veteran population, and creates proactive support programs for student veterans based on their needs" (Vacchi & Berger, 2014, p. 125).

in positive academic experiences. Student affairs professionals are one of the keys to helping student veterans obtain the support they need. They can help institutions create a culture that advocates for veterans and that values and builds on the diversity and unique perspectives student veterans bring to campus. Student affairs professionals can lead the way in helping support staff and faculty acquire the knowledge and develop the skills needed to support veterans effectively. Finally, student affairs professionals can collaborate with their faculty colleagues to assist the student body in embracing student veterans as a positive addition to the campus, thus creating a campus culture that focuses on the success of veterans and is *veteran-friendly*. This module provides an overview of theory, research, and best practices for student veterans that can help student affairs professionals, faculty, staff, and nonveteran students build a veteran-friendly environment.

This module offers an understanding of the inclusive definition of the term *student veteran,* which helps to frame this unique population, since it is their immersion in the military culture that makes student veterans different from traditional students (Vacchi, 2012). This module also discusses the distinctive needs of student veterans entering or returning to college and describes this population for the reader. Although the student veteran literature still lacks a clear leading voice, this module assesses the strengths and limitations of recent research (e.g., DiRamio, Ackerman, & Mitchell, 2008; DiRamio & Jarvis; 2011; Livingston, Havice, Cawthon, & Fleming, 2011; Rumann & Hamrick, 2010); describes innovative practices in working with veterans; and provides examples from institutions that have implemented one or more of these innovative practices. This module also describes on- and off-campus partnerships that institutions can build to increase the persistence and completion rates of veterans and outlines the student affairs professional's role in building these partnerships. This module concludes with a conceptual model for facilitating the success of veterans in college.

American society treats post-9/11-era veterans much better than society treated Vietnam War-era veterans. Even with this progress, anecdotal conversations at conferences and in meetings across the nation reveal uncertainty about how to work with student veterans to facilitate their success. Further, veteran sentiment in the empirical literature consistently offers a description of veterans who feel isolated on college campuses. Although this module is not all-inclusive, it offers a brief orientation and some tools to begin serving our nation's veterans in college. With this orientation and a collaborative approach that includes the student veteran perspective, institutions will see their veteran population grow into a robust and productive student population that is a source of great pride for all members of the campus community.

DEFINING AND DESCRIBING STUDENT VETERANS

Student veterans are among the most unique and least understood populations on the 21ˢᵗ century college campus. Unfortunately, much of what campus community members do know about student veterans is based on misinformation or dated information from past veteran generations, particularly the Vietnam War era. This module frames the population based on the comprehensive description of the student veteran population in Volume 29 of the *Higher Education Handbook of Theory and Research* (Vacchi & Berger, 2014). However, before describing this population, it is important to discuss the logic for using the term *student veteran* as opposed to *veteran student,* or *military student.* First, *student veteran* is the most common term used for the student population comprised of current or former military members. Second, *veteran student* suggests a label for students who have been on campus for a long time without leaving. Finally, *military students* may more accurately describe the students of our military academies or colleges (Vacchi & Berger, 2014). Hence, the term used in this module is *student veteran.*

Regardless of the term used on any particular campus, it is important to use that term to describe an inclusive student population of all current or former service members. Vacchi (2012) defined the inclusive population for student veterans as "any student who is a current or former member of the Active Duty Military, the National Guard, or Reserves regardless of deployment status, combat experience, legal veteran status, or GI Bill use" (p. 17).

QUICK TIP

Student veteran is the most common and logical term for the student population consisting of veterans and currently serving military members. The NASPA Veterans Knowledge Community (n.d.) recommends using this term to minimize confusion between campuses about this population.

The National Clearinghouse for Educational Statistics (NCES) term *independent undergraduate* most closely represents the student veteran population, with more than 60 percent of student veterans being married, married with children, or single parents (Radford, 2011). Perhaps the most obvious distinction between student veterans and traditional students is age, with less than 16 percent of student veterans being under age 24 and roughly 60 percent being between ages 24 and 39 (Radford, 2011). A less tangible difference, but perhaps more important, is that student veteran experiences differ considerably from those of traditional students, aligning even the youngest student veterans with adult learners. It is important to understand that student veterans have been powerfully and positively socialized to the military culture (Vacchi, 2012), which means traditional approaches to student development, and sometimes classroom instruction, may alienate them.

Student veterans are as demographically diverse as the general college-going population (Radford, 2011), with the exception of women, who comprise roughly 35 percent of the student veteran population (Holder, 2011), but approximately 57 percent of all college students (U.S. Census Bureau, 2013). However, only 15 percent of military service members are women (U.S. Census Bureau, 2013), confirming that women use their GI Bill benefits at greater rates than men do (Holder, 2011). Hispanic and Black student veteran populations are generally similar to the general population,

QUICK TIP

Not all veterans were *Soldiers*: This is an Army term. The Navy has *Sailors*, the Air Force has *Airmen*, the Coast Guard has *Coastguardsmen*, and the Marine Corps has *Marines*. In recent years, the U.S. government formally acknowledged all of these words as proper nouns that should be capitalized for internal communication (U.S. Army, 2013). Members of multiple services are *military* or *service members*.

whereas Asians are underrepresented both in the military and among student veterans (Radford, 2011).

Veterans may seem like a homogenous culture, given the pervasive uniformity of training and socialization that instills a level of respect for all military members, despite traditional demographic differences. Therefore, in order to acknowledge the diversity of veterans, it may be more useful for student affairs practitioners to think of military branch (e.g., Army, Navy), service component (i.e., Active Duty, National Guard, or Reserves), or combat experience as the most relevant aspects of diversity within the student veteran population. The positive effect of embracing this seemingly complex array of military service backgrounds is that it may be the best way to demonstrate respect for a veteran. One need only refer to certain Marines as *Soldiers* to hear the impassioned response, "I'm a Marine," indicating that the Marine Corps culture instills a permanent status as a Marine, while the rest of the military refers to service in the past tense, such as, "when I was a Soldier . . ."

Contemporary student veterans, unlike their veteran predecessors, all volunteered for military service and are not primarily from the poorest families (Vacchi & Berger, 2014) as were many of their drafted predecessors. A comprehensive analysis of the background of student veterans does not exist, but first-generation status may be a prevalent factor for student veterans. Finally, until the wars connected with the Global War on Terror are over, it is highly likely that contemporary student veterans have combat experience or overseas deployments. This differentiates post-9/11 student veterans from their immediate predecessors of the Montgomery GI Bill era who served between 1975 and 2001 and are largely not combat veterans. These distinctions should compel the higher education community to seek a specific understanding of post-9/11-era student veterans.

CONSIDERING THE STUDENT VETERAN LITERATURE

The post-9/11-era student veteran literature is the most concentrated effort to explore veterans on campus since World War II, but it is insufficient in quality and quantity. Much of the recent literature on student veterans (e.g., DiRamio et al., 2008; Livingston et al., 2011; Rumann & Hamrick, 2010) uses qualitative methods with uncertain success. Still, because of a general lack of empirical knowledge about student veterans, qualitative approaches may be the best method to explore and explain the experiences of veterans in college. However, the combined sample of these qualitative studies is less than 50 student veterans, and the methods may not be grounded in adequate theory and methodology, resulting in questionable application for other campuses. Further, the exploration of these studies largely involves the transition from the military to campus culture and overlooks the rest of the college experience. Finally, these studies connect with traditional student literature through Tinto's (1993) theory rather than nontraditional student theory (e.g., Bean & Metzner, 1985), or they use Schlossberg's (1981) counseling framework.

Both of these approaches appear problematic for framing and conceptualizing the experiences of student veterans. Table 6.1 depicts a brief summary of recent studies on student veterans.

Table 6.1

Student Veteran Literature Summary

Citation	Sample size	Connection to literature	Notes
DiRamio et al. (2008)	25 (Qualitative)	Tinto's (1993) Theory of Student Departure; approach veterans as traditional students	Transition coach (peer-to-peer mentor); little evidence of transition difficulty
Ackerman & DiRamio (2009)	n/a (Collection of practices on select campuses)	Summary of early approaches in serving post-9/11-era student veterans	Useful broad brush of what was being done in 2008; little theory or research
Cook & Kim (2009)	Quantitative	Study of veteran-friendly services provided by institutions that documented the low number of institutions providing targeted services to veterans	Not empirically grounded; no definition for veteran-friendly; questionable methods
Rumann & Hamrick (2010)	6 (Qualitative)	Minor adaptation of Schlossberg's (1981) 4S Model; connects to college impact literature through DiRamio et al. (2008)	Little evidence veterans have transition difficulties
Holder (2009, 2011)	Quantitative (secondary data analysis)	Not connected to the literature; based on U.S. Census data	Female veterans use benefits at greater rates than male veterans; veterans earn a higher percentage of advanced degrees than nonveterans
Radford (2009, 2011)	Quantitative (secondary data analysis)	Not connected to the literature; based on NCES data	Basic statistical description of student veterans
Livingston et al. (2011)	15 (Qualitative)	Substantial adaptation of Schlossberg's (1981) 4S Model; connects to college impact literature through DiRamio et al. (2008)	Veterans transition to campus relatively easily
DiRamio & Jarvis (2011)	Secondary data analysis of Cook & Kim (2009); theoretical summary	Tinto (1993); Schlossberg (1981); Cook & Kim (2009)—deficit model for veterans	Faulty secondary data analysis of Cook & Kim (2009); acknowledges insufficiency of using Tinto's (1993) approach for student veterans
Lang & Powers (2011)	Quantitative	Not connected to the literature; based on data from Tillman Scholar and Operation College Promise partnership institutions	Veterans on campuses with supportive programming do as well or better than nonveterans
McBain, Kim, Cook, & Snead (2012)	Quantitative	Follow-up to Cook & Kim (2009); documents the disturbingly low number of institutions providing dedicated services to veterans	Fixed some methodological flaws of prior study, but no significant change in findings
Steele, Salcedo, & Coley (2010)	Quantitative	Not connected to the literature; based on Rand Corp. data (Radford, 2011)	Focuses on transition; challenges the institutional perspective

Similarly, a recent series of quantitative reports attempt to explain the background, experiences, and services for veterans on college and university campuses. These studies (i.e., Cook & Kim, 2009; Holder, 2009, 2011; Lang & Powers, 2011; McBain et al., 2012; Radford, 2009, 2011; Steele et al., 2010) do not connect with any higher education literature or theory and offer few comprehensive insights into the experiences of veterans and few ways to serve student veterans better.

QUICK TIP

Benchmarking may be the best way to take constructive first steps to tailor programs, services, and policies to individual campuses. Create a veterans task force and develop a diverse team, including student veterans, to establish a guiding philosophy, specific goals, and an initial menu of programs and support services for veterans.

Although useful for starting a national conversation about student veterans, these studies demonstrate the inefficacy of trying to apply Tinto's (1993) theory and Schlossberg's (1981) 4S Model to understanding the college experiences, and even the transitions, of veterans. Throughout this literature, the subject of identity negotiation recurs as a central component of transition challenges, yet the literature insufficiently explains how Schlossberg's model or Tinto's theory helps us frame identity issues. This has caused this body of student veteran literature to be obscured by a debate over the applicability of conceptual models or theoretical frameworks.

Beyond these studies, there is an absence of research or scholarly publications on the entire college experiences, identity, or complete transition from military to civilian life of student veterans. Until a more robust body of literature and empirical studies emerge, individual campuses are best served by researching and tracking their own student veteran population and benchmarking services and programs with peer institutions. Exploring the approaches offered in this module can help a campus create the structures needed to facilitate student veteran success.

SELECT APPROACHES TO STUDENT VETERAN SERVICES

Many veterans may not need any help whatsoever when they come to college, but this does not absolve campuses of the need to be prepared to work with veterans who need some, or even substantial, help to succeed. The following approaches represent some of the most effective strategies for translating theories and research into processes, programs, and services for student veterans.

Navigating the Campus

Many freshmen feel lost when arriving on a college campus, and this can be disconcerting for veterans who are used to advocating for themselves and resolving their own issues but who cannot, because of the stark differences in campus structures compared with military organizations. Perhaps a difference between the typical veteran and the typical traditional-aged student is that veterans are likely to need help navigating the various campus bureaucracies only once, while younger students may need help multiple times.

Education Benefits Processing

Virtually all student veterans in the near future will need assistance processing benefits. Federal law requires each college or university to maintain a certifying official trained in the processing of GI Bill benefits through the VA Once system. The magnitude of this responsibility will vary according to the size of the institution and the number of student veterans on campus, but timely and accurate processing of educational benefits appears to be the most important need that a higher education institution can address for student veterans (Radford, 2011; Steele et al., 2010; Vacchi, 2013).

Peer-to-Peer Support

Most student veterans enjoy the camaraderie of being around other veterans. Veterans can thrive on regular contact with other veterans and may benefit from frequenting a student veteran lounge or joining a student veteran organization. Still, while most veteran-to-veteran contact can be healthy, student affairs professionals connected with student veteran organizations should mitigate the potentially isolating effects of a homogenous veteran group (Rendón, Jalomo, & Nora, 2000). With less than 10% of the U.S. population as military veterans, it is unlikely that the typical student veteran will work in an organization dominated by veterans after graduation. Part of a healthy transition to civilian life should be some degree of interaction with nonveterans during college. Although empirical evidence demonstrates that social integration with a campus culture does not influence nontraditional student retention rates (Bean & Metzner, 1985), this evidence does not suggest that intentional isolation from traditional students in academic or social settings is appropriate. Veterans should develop comfort interacting with nonveterans in academic settings and should become comfortable as veterans in a nonveteran world. Still, the ability to reach back to other student veterans for support from time to time can facilitate transitions for student veterans.

QUICK TIP

One area on which existing research agrees is that the timely and accurate processing of education benefits is the most important veteran-related administrative task for any institution.

Learning Resource Center/Tutoring Center

Many students benefit from peer tutoring, and veterans do, too. Their reasons for needing academic assistance may be different from traditional students, however. For example, unlike traditional students, veterans are likely to have had 3 or more years since their last formal education setting other than military training. Many student veterans benefit from activities designed to refresh their skills related to note taking, study strategies, library skills, writing, math, and time management.

Disability Services

Veterans may need an array of services from the office of disability services, including physical disability accommodation, special testing accommodations (e.g., quiet or solitary rooms, extra test time), and note-taking accommodations (e.g., smart pens, digital recorders, personal note-takers).

These accommodations are available at all colleges and universities and need not isolate a veteran; in fact, some campuses striving for veteran-friendliness offer these special test and note-taking accommodations to all veterans to preclude any disability stigma for veterans.

Veteran Health Care

Some veterans may need psychological counseling to cope with the dramatic transition from the military to civilian life. Although the number requiring these services is much smaller than recent false reports and poorly informed studies would suggest (Vacchi & Berger, 2014), institutions must be prepared to offer this support. This counseling may involve the signature wounds of the Global War on Terror: post-traumatic stress disorder (PTSD) and traumatic brain injury (TBI). Although PTSD is a psychological response to traumatic events most frequently occurring in combat, this condition can also be found among other students who are survivors of traumatic nonmilitary incidents. Still, the prevalence of PTSD among student veterans is likely to be higher than among nonveteran students; recognizing the signs and symptoms of PTSD can be critical to early intervention for some student veterans.

Traumatic brain injury is a physical injury, also appearing among athletes in contact sports, in which a concussive event causes the brain to move around inside the skull, bruising the brain lining. It is unlikely that many campuses have medical professionals well versed on TBI or PTSD, but being able to identify these injuries from known symptoms may help campus health staff to make an appropriate reference to a Department of Veterans Affairs (VA) medical facility near campus. Information about PTSD and TBI can be found at the VA website (http://www.ptsd.va.gov and http://www.polytrauma.va.gov).

The One-Stop Shop

This is one of two primary concepts for student veteran services, and both depend on campus physical space, staffing, and budgetary resources. The one-stop-shop concept may seem ideal, but it works well only when the institution provides a large enough space and staffs it with professionals who have the correct level of training and expertise. The idea behind the one-stop shop is to provide veterans with the opportunity to access an array of services without walking all around campus, similar to the way many veterans experienced services while in the military. Services such as college enrollment, registrar, bursar, benefits certification, financial aid, academic advising, disability services, and peer-to-peer advising could all be included in a one-stop shop. For many campuses, this concept is unrealistic due to space and staffing restrictions, or simply because there are not enough student veterans to warrant such a space. These colleges and universities have another option, which is better than having no special support for veterans at all: the warm handoff.

The Warm Handoff Approach

The warm handoff is not unique to veteran services, but is common among organizations with a *customer first* philosophy. The concept is simple and suggests that from a central location, typically a veteran services office, a dedicated staff member or VA work-study student will bring a student veteran needing assistance to the office capable of resolving the issue. Critical to the success of the warm handoff approach is having a person in each of these offices designated as a regular point of contact for all veterans. For example, the bursar, registrar, financial aid, disability services, and health services might all benefit from assigning the responsibility of helping veterans to a single (or selected) staff member(s). This accomplishes two things: (1) If veterans know that the person in a specific office is a well-trained ally, this increases their trust and comfort level in seeking and accepting services; and (2) rather than burden all staff members with the unique circumstances and nuances of working with veterans, having a dedicated staff member learn the systems, language, and culture of veterans can significantly reduce the potential for errors.

QUICK TIP

Faculty and staff training to create veteran allies in specific locations on campus is a growing trend on college campuses. Numerous free and fee-based programs or webinars are available to get any campus started, and a comprehensive resource is the American Council on Education veteran-friendly toolkit found at https://vetfriendlytoolkit.acenet.edu/Pages/default.aspx.

INNOVATIVE APPROACHES FOR SERVING STUDENT VETERANS

Many colleges and universities do superb work in assisting student veterans; others do little more than perform the federally mandated benefits certification function (McBain et al., 2012; Steele et al., 2010). The following approaches offer ideas for student affairs professionals to assist their institutions in effectively supporting the success of veterans.

Alumni and Institutional Involvement

Some campuses may be able to support the success of student veterans without the support of the institution overall, but having the support of an institution's senior leadership is critical to creating a sustainable veteran-friendly campus climate. Further, funding for programs and supplemental scholarships can be difficult to come by, particularly as campuses are developing new programs and services for student veterans. The University of Massachusetts Lowell (UMass Lowell) is a prime example of both enthusiastic support from the chancellor and the entire top-level administration to the execution of superb programming and active involvement of an alumni organization, the Pershing Rifles, who made a generous donation of $250,000 to support programming and scholarships for student veterans. Donations from alumni and grants, such as the FIPSE and Wal-Mart grants, are rare and should not be planned for by any campus, but support from the central administration is free. The symbolic support from senior leaders of any campus can go a long way to creating a supportive culture in which student veterans not only succeed, but thrive. More information about UMass Lowell veteran services is available at http://www.uml.edu/student-services/veterans/default.aspx.

Bridge Programs

Bridge programs provide opportunities for academically underprepared students to brush up on needed skills before starting formal coursework. Eastern Kentucky University (EKU) is not geographically close to a Veterans Upward Bound (VUB) program, so in order to increase the likelihood that underprepared student veterans will succeed, EKU created the Veterans Bridge to College Success program. A cohort-based model, the Veterans Bridge program brings small groups of entering veterans together in veteran-only classes to boost confidence through peer support and reduce the stigma of being older and unable to keep up in class with traditional students. Assessment of a recent pilot study of this program suggests that participants develop the skills necessary to succeed in entry-level college courses and also that the cohort model increases persistence at rates greater than those of academically prepared veterans (Morris, 2013). Additional information about EKU's broader Operation Veteran Success program is available at http://va.eku.edu/insidelook/operation-veteran-success.

Perhaps the most important consideration for bridge programs is the effect these programs can have on degree attainment and GI Bill benefit use. Although many veterans do not need all 10 semesters of benefits available to them under the post-9/11 GI Bill to complete their degrees, those veterans who are academically underprepared may need all of those semesters to earn a degree. Tension develops when introductory courses required in bridge programs may not count toward a college degree. Therefore, it is essential that bridge programs contain as many useable credit-bearing courses as possible.

Orientation and Transition Support Programs

Although the small body of research does not make it clear whether veterans are likely to experience difficulty transitioning to college, anecdotal observations show that some veterans benefit from regular support during their first year on campus. One approach is to provide an orientation for veterans that focuses on their unique needs and considers the cultural and developmental differences between student veterans and traditional first-year students. A more comprehensive approach, offered by Suffolk University, is a 2-week boot camp designed for veterans who either have not been on a campus as students in a long time or have never been students. The goal of the boot camp is to ensure that the stark differences between the military and higher education do not become an obstacle for entering veterans. Affiliated with the VUB program, this creative approach for veteran orientations presents a substantive alternative for schools looking to do more than just a few hours of supplementary orientation for veterans and can serve to identify veterans with potential transition issues early in the college-going process. Detailed information about the Suffolk Boot Camp program is located at http://www.suffolk.edu/academics/20556.php.

Still another approach to supporting veteran transitions is the first-year cohort model, such as offered at Salem State University. This voluntary program evolved through the veterans collaborating with university staff to help prepare first-year student veterans by addressing an evolving menu of academic concerns. For example, the program began when a group of veterans approached university staff with reservations about public speaking. The core of the original program consisted of a first-year seminar, a general education history course, and a public speaking course designed exclusively for veterans. These three courses provided a safe space for veterans to learn, while the remaining courses integrate veterans into the regular student body. Detailed information about the Salem State first-year cohort program is available at http://www.salemstate.edu/5927.php.

Student Veteran Organizations

Many campuses across the nation have seen the emergence of student veteran organizations (SVOs) for social interaction and peer-to-peer support. The benefits of having an SVO far outweigh potential drawbacks, but student affairs professionals should know four things about them. First, the creation of an SVO should not appear to be conceived by university officials; student organizations that do not develop organically are likely to disband due to lack of interest. Second, SVOs have a dynamic life cycle because of the turnover of student veterans, and the peaks and valleys may be extreme. Therefore, continuity and committed advising of SVOs can be critical to their sustainability over time. Third, SVOs can enjoy enthusiastic initial support from institutional leaders willing to make some rapid changes, but advisors should ensure veterans do not pursue change the same way on campus that they may have while serving in the military. The military process is necessarily a rapid top-down process, whereas change on campus often rises up from the bottom over a longer period. Finally, the greatest potential downside of SVOs is isolating veterans as a student affinity group (Rendón et al., 2000), thereby detracting from transitions to civilian life. Other than nurturing the sustainability of the SVO, the most important responsibility for student affairs professionals overseeing SVOs may be monitoring for members having particular difficulty adjusting to campus life and referring them for the appropriate support or counseling.

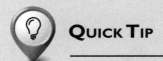

QUICK TIP

The Student Veterans of America is the largest network of SVOs, with roughly 850 affiliated SVOs around the world. Additional information is available at http://www.studentveterans.org.

VA Work Study Program

The VA provides colleges and universities with funds to hire one work-study student for every 100 certified students using VA educational benefits. For those campuses with fewer than 100 students using benefits, the VA authorizes one work-study student. These work-study students have two primary purposes: to assist the certifying officials in benefits certification and to advocate for veterans and veterans programming on campus. Many campuses know about the VA Work Study program, but few realize that the program rarely, if ever, exhausts the allocated budget at the federal level. Campuses seeking to create, increase, or improve veteran services and programs may be able to request additional work-study students through the VA Work Study program. There are precedents for these requests, but the VA can honor them only if some institutions do not use their allocated funds. Additional information about the VA Work Study program is available at http://www.gibill.va.gov/resources/education_resources/programs/work_study_program.html.

Veterans Upward Bound

There are 47 free VUB programs across the nation that help underprepared student veterans acquire the academic or life skills required to begin a degree program. Participation in a VUB program does not reduce a student veteran's GI Bill benefit potential. If a VUB program is available, veterans with below-average academic backgrounds should use it to strengthen writing and math skills before attempting mainstream college courses. More detailed information is available at http://www.navub.org.

Warm Handoffs

In 2009, the University of Mississippi embraced the need to strengthen its programming for veterans but they did not have a large enough space to support a one-stop shop. As a veteran-friendly institution in a veteran-friendly state, taking care of student veterans has always been a priority for Ole Miss. Determined to ensure that no veteran was overlooked, the university implemented a warm handoff approach to serving student veterans in the offices of the bursar, registrar, academic advising, disability services, and tutoring. Additional information about the way Ole Miss delivers services to student veterans is available at http://www.olemiss.edu/depts/registrar/va.html.

Off-Campus Partnerships

Student affairs professionals must be knowledgeable about the off-campus resources available to student veterans, such as VA medical facilities that provide returning combat veterans with 5 years of free health care. These facilities, which include hospitals and outpatient clinics, are staffed with experts in the most complicated medical conditions that student veterans experience: PTSD and TBI. To find medical facilities near any college or university, use the following search engine from the VA website: http://www.va.gov/directory/guide/home/asp.

There is an array of veteran affiliation and support organizations and representatives, most of which are available near any college campus. First, each town or municipality in the nation is funded to maintain a veterans services officer. The purpose of these officers is to facilitate VA disabilities claims and to connect veterans with local programs and services. To find a local veterans services officer, the best place to start is at the town hall or city government office. There are also numerous nongovernmental veteran support programs and services funded by grants and charitable donations. These vary by area, but many are veteran-run and can offer good and confidential support to veterans in need of such services.

Many local communities have Veterans of Foreign Wars (VFW) and American Legion organizations. Although participation in these organizations by the post-9/11-era veterans is not as prevalent as it was with Vietnam-era veterans, the VFW is open to veterans who served in any combat zone; the American Legion is open to all veterans. Both organizations are an excellent source of potential support for student veterans. In addition, when space is limited on campuses, Legion and VFW halls may serve as surrogate safe places for student veterans to gather.

A MODEL FOR STUDENT VETERAN SUPPORT

An important component of any campus's approach to serving veterans is to develop a philosophy that guides the design and implementation of effective programs and services. Although most of the recent literature focuses on conceptual models dealing with transitioning out of the military (e.g., DiRamio et al., 2008) or into college (e.g., Livingston et al., 2011; Rumann & Hamrick, 2010), these approaches do not address the entire college experience or the entire transition from military to civilian life by student veterans. An alternative conceptual model more appropriately focuses on the success of student veterans as individuals, for whom the transition to college is only a small component, but one in which academic and personal support are of equal importance.

A Student Veteran-Centered Model

Recent literature on student veterans, based largely on Schlossberg's (1981) 4S Model, struggles to convince readers of the soundness of taking a transitions-based approach to understanding student veterans holistically. The weaknesses of models based on the 4S Model and Tinto's (1993) theory are that they are linear, offer inflexible prescriptions for success that ignore the unique nature of individual students, and are institution-centric—these are essentially deficit models. Table 6.2 provides a brief overview of these theories.

Table 6.2

Snapshot of Student Veteran Theories and Models

Scholar/Theory/Model	Challenges in applying to veterans
Tinto's (1993) Theory of Student Departure	Traditional student-based deficit model
Schlossberg's (1981) 4S Model	Linear counseling model; not adaptable for veterans
DiRamio et al. (2008)	Adaptation of Tinto (deficit model)
DiRamio & Jarvis (2011)	Adaptations of Tinto/Schlossberg's 4S (deficit model)
Livingston et al. (2011)	Adaptation of Schlossberg's 4S Model (deficit model)
Rumann & Hamrick (2010)	Adaptation of Schlossberg's 4S Model (deficit model)

Perhaps most telling is that this literature offers little evidence that veterans as a population have a uniform problem with their transitions to college. Concerned professionals may see anecdotal evidence of transition difficulties on individual campuses, but these are not unique to veterans and may simply be evidence of a bad fit with an institution, lack of preparedness for college, or other issues unrelated to being a veteran. Placing the individual student veteran at the center of a conceptual model appropriately places the focus on the student, rather than on institutional processes and policies (Hurtado, Alvarez, Guillermo-Wann, Cuellar, & Arellano, 2012). This focus invites institutions to think about the impact of what they do for all student populations, including student veterans.

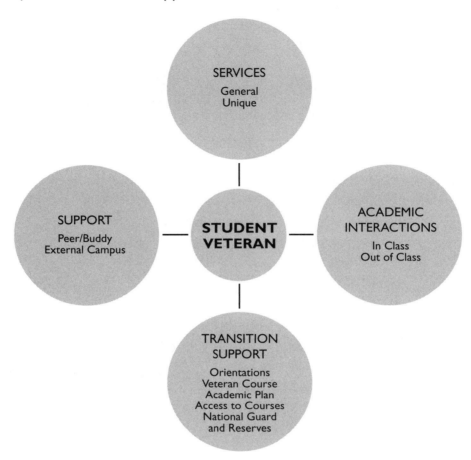

Figure 6.1

Vacchi's Model for Student Veteran Support

Four Key Areas to Support Student Veteran Success

Emerging and existing research and theory intersect to suggest four key areas in which to explore student veteran experiences in college (see Figure 6.1). First, the most logical starting point when considering strategies to increase the success of student veterans is services designed to assist veterans with GI Bill benefits, credits for military service, health insurance waivers covered by VA health care, and access to specific services they require (e.g., disability services).

A second component of student veteran success involves the veteran's transition into college, which represents only a piece of the college experience. A reexamination of using a transitions lens to view veteran success suggests that college may be a lengthy and complex macro-transition from the military to civilian life, perhaps a more appropriate application of Schlossberg's (1981) theory. *Moving In, Moving Through, and Moving Out* (Schlossberg, 1981) provides an effective theoretical framework to consider the entire collegiate experience as the *moving through* phase of a transition from the military to the civilian workplace. The recent literature presumes a relationship between the transition to college and retention, which may overestimate the influence of this transition, particularly for a resilient population such as veterans. However, transitions can influence success, and the literature does offer many thoughtful approaches for assisting veteran transitions to college including orientations, veteran-only courses, academic plans, access to courses, and working with National Guard and Reserves organizations to allow student veterans the flexibility of serving their nation and community while going to college.

While transitions are important to the success of student veterans, a third aspect of the college experience may more directly influence a veteran's chances of success. Bean and Metzner

QUICK TIP

Evidence suggests that an overwhelming majority of student veterans (85%) choose not to participate in existing student veteran organizations (Student Veterans of America, 2011). This may indicate that student veterans tend to seek relationships with nonveterans or are focused only on the academic aspects of college.

(1985) demonstrated that in order for nontraditional commuter students to succeed, social integration with a campus is not required; veterans generally do not live on campus and align closely with commuter populations. Bean and Metzner noted that while the social integration factors of Tinto's (1993) model appear insignificant for nontraditional students, the academic integration aspects of Tinto's model are more pronounced for nontraditional students than for traditional students. Simply put, what goes on in the classroom is critically important to the success of adult learners such as student veterans. Although this is not a primary aspect of what student affairs professionals do on campus, being aware of this reality can encourage them to take a leading role in collaborating with faculty on initiatives to support student veteran success.

A fourth key area for supporting the success of student veterans is the effect personal support has on student veterans. This has two components. A critical first component of *support* is peer advising, frequently called peer mentorship, and may not be a function of formal structures such as a student veteran organization or formal peer sponsorship relationships. Peers can have a strong influence on student persistence and success (Pascarella & Terenzini, 2005; Tinto, 1993; Weidman, 1989) and represent an important pathway for veterans to learn to navigate campus independently. However, scholars should not overstate the significance of peer influence for student veterans, particularly because they are nontraditional students (Bean & Metzner, 1985), and evidence suggests that many such students may not seek or need connections with peers in order to succeed in college. Still, providing veterans with opportunities for peer support and advice through formal or informal mechanisms may be advisable on campuses with enough veterans to support such endeavors. Some contemporary literature asserts that a student veteran organization is important to the success of student veterans (DiRamio et al., 2008; DiRamio & Jarvis, 2011; Livingston et al., 2011; Rumann & Hamrick, 2010), despite evidence to the contrary (Woosley, Kock, & Lipnicki, 2011). The benefits of an effective student veteran organization are primarily healthy peer relationships, which may result in beneficial informal advice to student veterans but do not need to come from formal structures and organizations.

A second component of support is *general campus support,* which may vary according to the needs of individual student veterans. The transparency of campus policies, such as transfer credit for military experiences, may influence student veteran perceptions about a campus. Seeking veteran-friendly recognition can be a double-edged sword: Once institutions earn that label, there is an obligation to back it with a supportive environment. The most unfortunate circumstance for veterans would be to believe an institution's claim of veteran-friendliness, only to arrive on campus to find little substance to that claim and that the general environment on campus creates obstacles to success, rather than supporting success.

Conclusions

Concerned institutions are not so far behind that they cannot catch up and join the ranks of innovative, veteran-friendly colleges and universities. Benchmarking is a useful tool for adapting ideas to support the success of student veterans, but any program or support should be used with a full understanding of the unique context surrounding each campus's student veteran population. Simply adopting some of the best practices highlighted in this module without sustaining those efforts or assessing their effectiveness on an individual campus can exacerbate problems and create a negative reputation for an institution.

Understanding that academic experiences, supportive relationships, and support services and systems significantly influence the success of student veterans reinforces the importance of student affairs professionals taking the lead to provide faculty and staff with the conceptual tools to support the success of student veterans. A safe space and a veterans' organization can be important to student veterans, but student affairs professionals must ensure these do not become isolating structures and obstacles to completing a healthy transition to civilian life. Moreover, student affairs professionals must remember the most important lesson in working with student veterans: In the final analysis, the ability to focus on academics without any major distractions is what generates the most success. One of the most important distractions to eliminate is improper education benefits processing. Finally, approaching veterans with a customer-first mentality will go a long way to demonstrating that the college or university is veteran-friendly and supports successful transitions from military to civilian life.

QUICK TIP

Receiving proper transfer credit for prior education and military experience is a significant issue for many student veterans. Working with the registrar and individual degree programs to help veterans earn appropriate credits for experience can demonstrate good faith efforts by an institution and demonstrate veteran-friendliness while helping student veterans get a fair start to a successful college career.

While institutions talk about student retention, student persistence is far more important in the big picture for determining whether veterans achieve their educational goals: This may involve multiple institutions. A fair critique of recent scholarly literature on student veterans is that it offers inflexible institution-centric models that do not account for differences among student veterans. Veterans are a unique but diverse student population and understanding these students can go a long way toward facilitating their success. Until definitive scholarly works emerge in the literature, seeking the voice of an experienced veteran-scholar, a veteran with several years of service in the military, or someone with a long-term recurring and intimate professional interaction with veterans may be the best resource for student affairs professionals seeking to help student veterans succeed.

The conceptual model offered in this module is a starting point for campuses as they develop programming and services for student veterans. Unlike previous models, the one highlighted in this module considers the entire college experience of student veterans. NASPA–Student Affairs Administrators in Higher Education is actively engaged in productive dialogue and scholarly activity through its Veterans Knowledge Community and through the NASPA Research and Policy Institute and is a leader on student veteran issues and best practices. As the literature continues to develop, it is important that institutions share their innovative practices and internal research and assessments through professional organizations such as NASPA.

REFERENCES

Ackerman, R., & DiRamio, D. (Eds.). (2009). *Creating a veteran-friendly campus: Strategies for transition and success* (New direction for student services, No. 126). San Francisco, CA: Jossey-Bass.

Bean, J., & Metzner, B. (1985). A conceptual model of nontraditional undergraduate student attrition. *Review of Educational Research, 55*(4), 485–540.

Cook, B., & Kim, Y. (2009). *From soldier to student: Transition programs for service members on campus.* Santa Monica, CA: Rand.

DiRamio, D., Ackerman, R., & Mitchell, R. (2008). From combat to campus: Voices of student-veterans. *NASPA Journal, 45*(1), 73–102.

DiRamio, D., & Jarvis, K. (2011). Veterans in higher education: When Johnny and Jane come marching to campus. *ASHE Higher Education Report, 37*(3).

Holder, K. (2009). *Profile of veterans: 2009. Data from the American community survey.* Washington, DC: U.S. Department of Veterans Affairs National Center for Veterans Analysis and Statistics.

Holder, K. (2011). *Educational attainment of veterans: 2000 to 2009.* Washington, DC: U.S. Department of Veterans Affairs National Center for Veterans Analysis and Statistics.

Hurtado, S., Alvarez, C., Guillermo-Wann, C., Cuellar, M., & Arellano, L. (2012). A model for diverse learning environments. In J. Smart & M. Paulsen (Eds.), *Higher education: Handbook of theory and research* (Vol. 27, pp. 41–122). New York, NY: Springer.

Lang, W., & Powers, J. (2011). *Completing the mission*: *A pilot study of veteran students' progress toward degree attainment in the post 9/11 era.* Trenton, NJ: Operation College Promise and the Pat Tillman Foundation.

Livingston, W., Havice, P., Cawthon, T., & Fleming, D. (2011). Coming home: Student veterans' articulation of college re-enrollment. *Journal of Student Affairs Research and Practice, 48*(3), 315–331.

McBain, L., Kim, Y., Cook, B., & Snead, K. (2012). *From soldier to student II: Assessing campus programs for veterans and service members.* Washington, DC: American Council on Education.

Morris, B. (2013). *A bridge program's effect on non-college ready student veterans* (Unpublished doctoral dissertation). Eastern Kentucky University, Richmond, KY.

NASPA Veterans Knowledge Community. (n.d.). *Veterans.* Retrieved from http://www.naspa.org/constituent-groups/kcs/veterans

Pascarella, E., & Terenzini, P. (2005). *How college affects students: A third decade of research.* Indianapolis, IN: Jossey-Bass.

Radford, A. (2009). *Military service members and veterans in higher education: What the new GI Bill may mean for postsecondary institutions.* Santa Monica, CA: Rand.

Radford, A. (2011). *Military service members and veterans: A profile of those enrolled in undergraduate and graduate education in 2007–08* (Document NCES-163). Washington, DC: U.S. Department of Education.

Rendón, L., Jalomo, R., & Nora, A. (2000). Theoretical considerations in the study of minority student retention in higher education. In J. Braxton (Ed.), *Reworking the student departure puzzle* (pp. 127–156). Nashville, TN: Vanderbilt University Press.

Rumann, C., & Hamrick, F. (2010). Student veterans in transition: Re-enrolling after war zone deployments. *Journal of Higher Education, 81*(4), 431–458.

Schlossberg, N. (1981). A model for analyzing human adaptation to transitions. *Counseling Psychologist, 9*(2), 2–18.

Steele, J., Salcedo, N., & Coley, J. (2010). *Service members in school: Military veterans' experiences using the post-9/11 GI Bill and pursuing postsecondary education.* Santa Monica, CA: Rand.

Student Veterans of America. (2011). *The dissection of an SVA chapter.* Retrieved from http://www.studentveterans.org/?p=1259

Tinto, V. (1993). *Leaving college: Rethinking the causes and cures of student attrition* (2nd ed.). Chicago, IL: University of Chicago Press.

U.S. Army. (2013). Preparing and managing correspondence (Army Regulation 25-50). Retrieved from http://www.apd.army.mil/pdffiles/r25_50.pdf

U.S. Census Bureau. (2013). *Profile America: Facts for features.* Retrieved from http://www.census.gov/newsroom/releases/archives/facts_for_features_special_editions/cb13-ff04.html

Vacchi, D. (2012). Considering student veterans on the twenty-first century college campus. *About Campus, 17*(2), 15–21.

Vacchi, D. (2013, April). *Perceptions of veteran-friendliness: Giving student veterans a voice.* Research paper presented at the annual conference of the New England Educational Research Organization (NEERO), Portsmouth, NH.

Vacchi, D., & Berger, J. (2014). Student veterans in higher education. In M. Paulsen (Ed.), *Higher education: Handbook of theory and research* (Vol. 29, pp. 93–151). New York, NY: Springer.

Weidman, J. (1989). Undergraduate socialization: A conceptual approach. In J. C. Smart (Ed.), *Higher education: Handbook of theory and research* (Vol. 5, pp. 289–322). New York, NY: Agathon.

Woosley, S., Kock, J., & Lipnicki, S. (2011, March). *Supporting student success for active military and veterans.* Presentation at the NASPA Annual Conference, Philadelphia, PA.

MODULE 7

Seamless Learning Requires Partnerships between Academic and Student Affairs

Marguerite McGann Culp and James Morales

ABSTRACT

Critics and supporters agree: The current higher education model is unsustainable. Emerging research indicates that a "best process" approach that involves the entire college community in improving student completion rates is more effective than an isolated "best practices" approach. Students accustomed to seamless, customized, 24/7 experiences with online retailers expect the same level of service from higher education. In response, college and university leaders promise to dismantle silos and build institutional cultures that value—and reward—collaboration. This module explores the importance of partnerships between academic and student affairs in creating seamless learning environments, describes what higher education professionals can learn from partnerships developed to support adult learners, and provides opportunities for readers to assess both their institution's partnership climate and the skills they bring to any partnership.

DEFINITIONS MATTER

Partnerships between student affairs and academic affairs that directly benefit adult learners may be few and far between, but good examples of these partnerships within higher education do exist. These partnerships are important for three reasons: (1) They support the institution's mission, (2) they

Quick Tip

"Adult learners need clear, coherent, expeditious paths to achievement of their educational goals. Clear pathways through the curriculum, to completion of certificates and degrees, require intensive collaboration. That collaboration must extend to work to embed academic and student support into course syllabi." —Kay McKlenney, director, Center for Community College Student Engagement, The University of Texas at Austin (personal communication, July 10, 2013)

increase student persistence and completion rates, and (3) they generate shared definitions, beliefs, and goals. Because shared definitions also are important when talking about partnerships, this module starts with a brief introduction to the essential terms used here.

Adult learner is a term relatively new to higher education. Educators have used a series of terms to describe the older college student population: older students, nontypical students, and nontraditional students. Eventually, each of these terms encountered limitations as this segment of the population changed. The term *older students* was too vague: Its utility and appropriateness depended entirely on the age cutoff used to define this group. The term *nontypical student* met a similar fate: Proponents struggled to distinguish between *typical* and *nontypical* on the basis of a variety of factors (enrollment status, gender, ethnicity, geographic origin, or some other attribute). The term *nontraditional student* had, and still enjoys, some staying power; but it gradually has morphed into or been replaced with the term *adult learner*.

In 1965, Johnstone and Rivera published the first profile of an adult learner based on their extensive Carnegie Corporation-funded study of this population. They defined an adult learner as "a person under 40 with a high school education who earns above-average income, is married with children, and lives in an urban area" (p. 8). Over the years, this definition has been updated, most notably by the National Center for Education Statistics (NCES) and the American Council on Education (ACE). In 1996, NCES defined an adult learner as someone who displays many of the following characteristics: did not enroll in postsecondary education immediately after high school, attends part time, works 35 or more hours a week while enrolled, is considered independent for financial aid purposes, has dependents, is a single parent, or does not have a high school diploma. ACE (n.d.) defined adult learners as students 25 or older and noted that "for almost two decades, adult learners have comprised close to 40 percent of the college-going population, spanning a range of backgrounds and experiences, from Iraq and Afghanistan war veterans and GED credential holders to 55-year-old professionals and skilled workers in career transition" (para. 1).

Posttraditional learners recently emerged as a term to describe undergraduates who are not typical 18- to 22-year-old college students. Soares (2013) defined posttraditional learners as "individuals already in the work force who lack a postsecondary credential yet are determined to pursue further knowledge and skills while balancing work, life, and education responsibilities" (pp. 1–2). As indicated in Module 1, the term *posttraditional learner* is gaining traction for two reasons: (1) It encourages educators to view adults who do not enter college immediately after graduating from high school as the "new normal" rather than viewing them as deviations from the traditional undergraduate norm, and (2) it helps institutions think twice before asking adults to fit into existing administrative, instructional, and support service models that may not meet their needs.

Student affairs focuses on all things related to the student and the student's life outside the classroom. It has a body of knowledge, a professional literature, a set of commonly recognized jobs and functions, and an established professional philosophy outlined in *The Student Personnel Point of View*, first published in 1937 (ACE, 1994a) and updated in 1949 (ACE,

QUICK TIP

"We need a new mental model of college that suits post-traditional learner realities. Embracing post-traditional learners as innovation partners and not excluding them as aberrations is the key." (Soares, 2013, p. 15)

1994b). *The Student Personnel Point of View* eloquently articulated three core beliefs that anchor the profession:

- One of the basic purposes of higher education is to preserve, transmit, and enrich the important elements of culture: the products of scholarship, research, creative imagination, and human experience.
- Colleges and universities have an obligation to assist students in developing to the limits of their potential and contributing to the betterment of society.
- Colleges and universities must develop the student as a whole person. This means focusing on emotional, social, spiritual, physical, and aesthetic growth as well as intellectual and economic development.

Academic affairs, in its most basic form, is the label applied to the instructional enterprise of higher education that deals with the delivery and dissemination of knowledge from source to student via various established pedagogical methods. The Council of Independent Colleges offers a more formal definition that describes academic affairs as the area with responsibility for "the core functions of higher education—teaching students, conducting scholarly research, and service to the academic community" (Hartley & Godin, 2010, p. 1).

Partnerships are broadly defined as "a relationship . . . usually involving close cooperation between parties having specified and joint rights and responsibilities" (Partnerships, n.d.). John-Steiner, Weber, and Minnis (1998) described partnership relationships more specifically: "They plan, decide, and act jointly; they also think together, combining independent conceptual themes to create original frameworks" (p. 776). In the context of student affairs and adult learning, *The Student Learning Imperative* (American College Personnel Association [ACPA], 1994) held that the term *partnership* is best defined as a collaboration that "maximizes academic and student affairs' ability to have a positive impact on the lives of their students" (p. 3). There are two types of partnerships: those that involve cooperation and those that require collaboration. Partnerships based on cooperation are typically short-term ventures with limited objectives and commitment between the partners (Stein & Short, 2001). Partnerships based on collaboration involve joint decision making and risk taking, the development of a shared philosophy, and a significant commitment of time and talent from everyone involved (Engstrom & Tinto, 2000).

Learning-centered institutions "place learning and the learner first" (O'Banion, 1997, p. 21). Learning is defined as "a comprehensive, holistic, transformative activity that integrates academic learning and student development" (Keeling, 2004, p. 4). Learning-centered institutions require learner-centered instruction and learning-centered support services. As Weimer (2013) observed, learner-centered teaching:

1. Engages students in the hard, messy work of learning.
2. Motivates and empowers students by giving them some control over the learning process.
3. Encourages collaboration, acknowledging the classroom (be it virtual or real) as a community where everyone shares the learning agenda.
4. Promotes students' reflection about what they are learning and how they are learning it.
5. Includes explicit learning skills instruction. (p. 15)

QUICK TIP

"Student affairs and academic affairs are two halves of the mission; both provide important learning opportunities for students. To build partnerships, student affairs professionals must do what is essential in any partnership: listen and learn what is important to colleagues, and then find ways to support those important initiatives. Think data (qualitative and quantitative). Ask questions and find answers to show the ways student affairs programs support the initiatives of the university in general and academic affairs in particular."
—Gage Paine, vice president of student affairs, The University of Texas at Austin (personal communication, June 28, 2013)

Well-developed learning-centered institutions send clear messages to the college or university community that collaboration is important: competition, divisions, and silos are not.

Learning outcomes are discussed in detail by Culp and Dungy (2012). In relation to non-classroom support services, the term refers to learning that occurs as a result of participating in an outside-the-classroom activity, program, or service. Identifying and assessing learning outcomes presents student affairs with unique opportunities to (1) demonstrate its contributions to the institution's mission and (2) create partnerships with academic affairs that increase student persistence and completion rates. As Table 7.1 demonstrates, the learning outcomes developed by the Association of American Colleges and Universities (n.d.) as part of its Liberal Education and America's Promise (LEAP) campaign provide a natural starting point for partnerships between academic and student affairs, partnerships between student affairs and other areas within the higher education community, and discussions about integrating knowledge and skills across the institution.

Table 7.1

LEAP Learning Outcomes

Beginning in school, and continuing at successively higher levels across their college studies, students should prepare for 21st century challenges by gaining:
Knowledge of Human Cultures and the Physical and Natural World • Through study in the sciences and mathematics, social sciences, humanities, histories, languages, and the arts *Focused by engagement with big questions, both contemporary and enduring*
Intellectual and Practical Skills, including • Inquiry and analysis • Critical and creative thinking • Written and oral communication • Quantitative literacy • Information literacy • Teamwork and problem solving *Practiced extensively, across the curriculum, in the context of progressively more challenging problems, projects, and standards for performance*
Personal and Social Responsibility, including • Civic knowledge and engagement—local and global • Intercultural knowledge and competence • Ethical reasoning and action • Foundations and skills for lifelong learning *Anchored through active involvement with diverse communities and real-world challenges*
Integrative and Applied Learning, including • Synthesis and advanced accomplishment across general and specialized studies *Demonstrated through the application of knowledge, skills, and responsibilities to new settings and complex problems*

Source: Reprinted with permission from College Learning for the New Global Century. Copyright © 2007 by the Association of American Colleges and Universities.

TODAY'S HIGHER EDUCATION CLIMATE

Fundamental change is viewed as both necessary and inevitable in higher education (Christiansen & Eyring, 2011; Levine & Dean, 2012). There is clear consensus on what will drive change: online learning, technology, shifting student demographics, and state and federal mandates. Agreement on how and when change will occur is less clear. In the best-case scenario, change will be driven from within by faculty, staff, and administrators working together; in the worst-case scenario, colleges and universities will become the victims of disruptive innovations launched by the private sector (Christiansen & Eyring, 2011). The impact of this changing climate on student affairs remains unknown; it is clear, however, that the ability to collaborate with a variety of on- and off-campus partners is becoming increasingly important.

Higher education literature is full of information about the benefits of and need for partnerships. In their landmark study, Kuh, Kinzie, Schuh, and Whitt (2005) discovered that one of the distinguishing features of high-performing institutions was their commitment to and ability to nurture partnerships and cross-functional collaborations. The Task Force on the Future of Student Affairs, appointed jointly by ACPA and NASPA–Student Affairs Administrators in Higher Education, extolled the value of partnerships and cautioned against building "metaphorical fences between 'student affairs professionals' and others who also are engaged in fostering student success" (ACPA & NASPA, 2010, p. 7). Cherrey and Allen (2011) urged student affairs to "develop new ways of relating, influencing change,

IN THE SPOTLIGHT

Jim Fatzinger, associate vice president for student affairs, and Jo Galle, associate vice president for academic affairs, both at Georgia Gwinnett College, a public 4-year institution that includes the integration of academic and student affairs as part of its mission, share their perspective on building partnerships.

✿ Presidents can initiate partnerships between academic and student affairs by asking three questions: (1) Are there institutional-level outcomes that support the institution's mission and vision? (2) Are there opportunities for academic and student affairs to provide evidence of meeting the institutional-level outcomes that bridge the divide between academic and student affairs? (3) Are there institutional rewards in place that emphasize the importance of academic and student affairs partnerships beyond traditional teaching, research, and service measures?

✿ Faculty and student affairs professionals who wish to build or strengthen partnerships between their areas need to:

- o Identify key faculty/student affairs team members open to collaboration.

- o Create an environment that values academic and student affairs collaboration.

- o Identify goals and outcomes spanning academic and student affairs.

- o Demonstrate linkages between the collaboration and the institution's mission and vision.

- o Celebrate collaborative initiatives.

✿ Georgia Gwinnett College has eight institutional-level student learning outcomes. All degree programs (academic affairs) and all units within student affairs are required to align some of their student outcomes with the eight student institutional-level learning outcomes. As a result, all areas within student affairs assess student learning. (personal communication, June 28, 2013)

learning, and leading" (p. 56) in a networked knowledge era. Arcelus (2011) warned colleges and universities that they could no longer afford to tolerate the separation of student and academic affairs and urged them to replace competition and isolation with conversations and partnerships.

PARTNERSHIPS IN TODAY'S HIGHER EDUCATION CLIMATE

Partnerships between academic and student affairs benefit higher education institutions in three significant ways. First, as Kezar and Lester (2009) noted, these partnerships are typically strongly aligned with and provide direct support to the mission of a college or university by increasing student satisfaction, persistence, and completion rates; strengthening institutional communication and decision making; and improving campus relationships and organizational functioning. Second, partnerships between academic and student affairs help develop trust and understanding across the college or university community, thereby reducing unproductive tension, isolation, and competition for resources. The literature in this area identifies "the primary reasons for collaboration [between student affairs and academic affairs] as improving student learning and the environment for learning, as well as providing opportunities to enhance institutional efficiency and effectiveness and eliminate waste and redundancy" (O'Halloran, 2007, p. 44). Partnerships also reduce the tendency to silo services for students, thus improving the effectiveness and efficiency of operations (Kezar & Lester, 2009). Third, these types of partnerships do much to create a shared campus culture that is learning-centered, characterized by seamless learning environments, and concerned about the learning that takes place outside the classroom. Finally, research demonstrates that partnerships between academic and student affairs increase student engagement and the institution's impact on students (Kezar & Lester, 2009).

Right now, partnerships that increase adult learner completion rates are getting significant attention for several reasons. In an address to a joint session of Congress on February 24, 2009, U.S. President Barack Obama outlined what has become known as the College Completion Agenda: By 2020, the United States will have the highest proportion of college graduates in the world. To achieve this goal, the United States must graduate 10 million additional Americans ages 25–34 with an associate or baccalaureate degree—3.7 million more traditional-age students and 6.3 million adult learners (Kanter, Ochoa, Nassif, & Chong, 2011). The College Completion Agenda cannot be achieved solely by increasing the number of traditional-age college graduates; the adult population must generate a substantial number of degree earners if our country is to achieve the objectives outlined by the president. For institutions faced with reduced state appropriations, adult learners have always represented attractive alternative revenue; however, the phenomenal growth of online and distance education offerings has allowed competing institutions to target and enroll previously inaccessible, place-bound adults. Institutions that want to continue to attract adult learners must do a better job of supporting them, whether their courses are online, on campus, or at distant sites. Finally, building partnerships is simply the right thing to do for two reasons:

1. **Philosophy.** At the heart of the student affairs profession is the belief that every type of student and their success matters. Colleges and universities—the very institutions that bear responsi-

bility for creating models that support the widest range of student types possible—have an obligation to serve the adult learner population and serve it well.

2. **Demographics.** As Module 1 demonstrates, adult learners are the new majority in higher education. The future of many colleges and universities may depend on their ability to intelligently educate, learn from, and support this growing population.

Partnerships: A Force-field Analysis

Numerous factors play a role in building partnerships. One of the most important is knowledge of partnership theory and research. Exercise 7.1 presents readers with an opportunity to assess their knowledge of theories and research related to higher education partnerships.

Partnerships typically involve change, and theory suggests that change is more likely to occur when the dynamics favoring change are stronger than the dynamics inhibiting it (Lewin, 1936). Therefore, it is important that student affairs professionals develop a clear picture of the institutional forces that influence partnership development, and then use that knowledge to lessen the influence of inhibiting forces. Exercise 7.2 identifies the factors that create supportive partnership environments as well as forces that produce less favorable ones. The exercise also invites readers to identify significant limiting forces at their institutions. Because these forces typically reflect the institution's culture, their identification helps readers pinpoint the climate changes needed to support partnerships and to prepare the institution to address the many challenges facing higher education today. How readers use this information depends on variables only they can assess. Exercise 7.3 suggests one approach for using the knowledge gained in Exercise 7.2 to bring about needed climate shifts.

Partnerships: Respect the Past, Embrace the Future

Numerous book chapters and journal articles offer advice on creating seamless learning environments (e.g., Kuh, 1996), organizing student affairs to support cooperation and collaboration (e.g., Manning, Kinzie, & Schuh, 2006), or building partnerships between academic and student affairs (e.g., Arcelus, 2011). Seven of the nine principles for effectively serving adult learners developed by the Council for Adult and Experiential Learning require partnerships between academic and student affairs (Klein-Collins, 2011). Partnerships between academic and student affairs get a lot of attention, as they should, but there is a growing belief that such partnerships represent only a portion of the partnership picture. Momentum is building for student affairs professionals to focus more on delivering quality programs and services that support the institution's mission, using quantitative and qualitative data to demonstrate their contributions to student success, and expanding their

QUICK TIP

"Stop thinking about deliberately building bridges and start thinking about aligning the didactic and the experiential in a coherent and predictable way. Everything we do is a form of academic support. Make the cocurricular relevant to the institution's academic objectives."
—Larry Moneta, vice president for student affairs, Duke University (personal communication, June 3, 2013)

search for partners beyond their colleagues in academic affairs.

There are many reasons for the shift, but one of the most important is the growing awareness within higher education that institutions cannot succeed in a seamless, networked, learning-centered world unless the offices responsible for institutional research, instruction, support services, and technology collaborate with, support, and influence one another.

Figure 7.1 illustrates the relationship that must exist among these four areas in a learning-centered institution. Table 7.2 outlines the skills and abilities that student affairs professionals bring to any partnership; it also lists the skills that student affairs professionals must strengthen if they want others in the higher education community to continue to value them as partners.

QUICK TIP

"There are three reasons why research and technology are emerging as essential partners to both student and academic affairs: (1) The ability to understand and use predictive analytics is becoming essential to student learning and institutional effectiveness; (2) students, no matter what their age, expect the same seamless services from colleges and universities that they receive from online vendors—and seamless services require collaboration; and (3) higher education institutions are moving to a 24/7 existence that focuses on learning (not teaching) and outcomes (not processes)."
—William Carter, vice chancellor for information technology, Houston Community College (personal communication, August 22, 2013)

Figure 7.1

Partnership-driven Circle of Learning

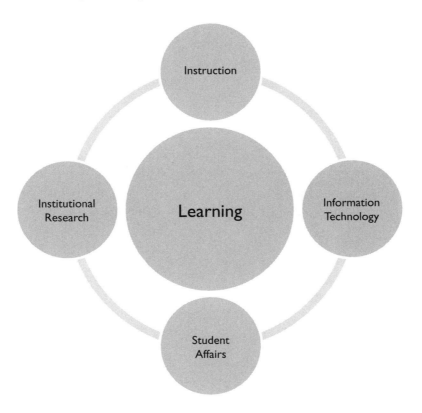

Table 7.2

Student Affairs and Partnerships: Strengths and Areas Needing Improvement

Strengths	Areas needing improvement
Long-standing commitment to shared learning, communication, and collaboration	Increase capacity to recognize, shape, and adapt to changing conditions
Established commitment to developing the whole student	Become more outcomes-oriented and data-driven
Adept at using "soft power" (influence rather than control)	Leverage technology to design processes, programs, and services that meet the needs of today's students
Skilled at decoding, adapting to, and influencing group dynamics	Increase ability to translate theories and research into processes, programs, and services
Proficient in helping students integrate their learning experiences and apply what they have learned	View the institution as a system; help members of the system make decisions that support learning and benefit students
Experienced in working with posttraditional students, higher education's new majority	Update skill sets, especially in technology; commit to continuous lifelong learning

Partnerships Start at the Top

Presidents play a significant role in creating learning-centered institutions (O'Banion, 1997), reducing fragmentation and increasing collaboration (Kezar & Lester, 2009), and providing leadership during times of change that "views the university idealistically, as something more than a business and something better than a slave to the logic of economic competition" (Lewis, 2006, p. xii). The ability of chief student affairs officers (CSAOs) to earn respect, influence the college community, and effectively manage and lead (Culp, 2011) also is essential in building partnerships, as is the CSAO's ability to guide student affairs through a rapidly changing networked knowledge era (Cherrey & Allen, 2011). What else matters? Exercise 7.4 provides readers with an opportunity to review the conditions that encourage partnerships, while Exercise 7.5 allows readers to examine strategies that produce effective partnership. Both exercises invite readers to identify the partnership strategies and conditions currently in place, in the planning stages, or worth implementing at their institution.

QUICK TIP

"Presidents need to legitimize collaboration, talk about its potential value, and recognize partnerships in the institution's reward system. Presidents need to help everyone understand that partnerships enable the college or university to achieve its desired outcome more effectively." —Arthur W. Chickering, former professor of educational development and human leadership, George Mason University; coauthor of *Education and Identity* (Jossey-Bass, 1993) (personal communication, June 5, 2013)

Fresh Ideas: Partnerships to Support Adult Learners and Student Parents

Colleges and universities that serve significant adult learner populations are developing innovative on- and off-campus partnerships. Some of these partnerships began as efforts to improve the climate for all students but had a direct impact on the higher education experiences of adult learners (Table 7.3). Other partnerships grew out of the desire to improve the climate for specific adult learner subpopulations such as student parents or veterans. Because Module 8 focuses on external partnerships and Module 6 describes partnerships that benefit veterans, this module explores internal partnerships that benefit adult learners in general and student parents in particular.

QUICK TIP

"Presidents need to create a culture in which there is mutual respect and value between academic affairs and student affairs. Collegiality and respect should be the core values of the executive leadership team." —Brian Hemphill, president, West Virginia State University (personal communication, June 5, 2013)

Table 7.3

Partnerships Designed for All Students That Benefit Undergraduate Adult Learners

Strategies to increase access (In place at many institutions)	Strategies to increase success (Emerging at selected institutions)
Leverage technology by building dedicated websites; offer online admissions, advising, orientation, and registration services; and use social media to communicate and connect with students.	Implement flexibility in scheduling by supporting a Block Calendar System with multiple start dates (Rio Salado College, Arizona, http://maricopa.edu/rio_salado.php) or implementing incremental credentialing or "stacking" that allows students to drop out and return without running into entry delays or processing barriers (University of Minnesota Fast TRAC, http://www.mnfast-trac.org/docs).
Appoint process improvement teams to analyze and streamline both the campus-based and Web-based systems that students use.	Design Web-based early alert systems (Sinclair Community College, Ohio, http://www.sinclair.edu/support/success/ea; University of Arizona, http://www.studentaffairs.arizona.edu/faculty).
Add evening and weekend office hours for essential services.	Strengthen partnerships between academic and student affairs that benefit career exploration programs, career services, and students (California University System, http://www.fullerton.edu/Crew/projects/docs/PurposefulPartnerships.pdf).
Provide front-line staff with additional training in working with adult learners.	Strengthen online career services (San Jose State University, California, http://www.careercenter.sjsu.edu; Valencia College, Florida, http://www.valenciacollege.edu/lifemap).

Strategies to increase access (In place at many institutions)	Strategies to increase success (Emerging at selected institutions)
Cross-train all staff to work effectively with online, on-campus, and distance learning students.	Use logic regression to identify first-year students at risk of dropping out and provide appropriate interventions (e.g., University of South Florida) (Thomas E. Miller, personal communication, June 28, 2013).
Put more emphasis on academic advising: build cohorts; provide career counseling, especially for undecided students; and create community for both online and on-campus students.	Provide faculty and staff who advise adult learners with up-to-date resources and training (http://www.nacada.ksu.edu/resources/Clearinghouse/View-Articles/Adult-Learner-Resources.aspx).
Use a data-based approach to identify and eliminate unnecessary online and on-campus barriers to student access.	Reenvision support services for distance learners (e.g., North Carolina State University) (Dare, Zapata, & Thomas, 2005).

Partnerships With Counseling and Financial Aid. Programs and services to support adult learners and student parents take many forms. Some institutions have well-established, stand-alone programs; others identify contacts within existing offices. Some programs are housed in student affairs; others in academic affairs. Some involve dedicated space and staff; others share these. The budget for some programs is part of the institution's operating budget; others rely on external funding. Whatever the location, reporting structure, or funding source, the effectiveness of these programs frequently depends on partnerships with counselors and financial aid staff. Table 7.4 offers a few examples of these partnerships.

Table 7.4

Partnerships With Counseling and Financial Aid That Benefit Adult Learners and Student Parents

College or University	Partnership
Norwalk Community College (Connecticut)	Provides scholarships for adult learners and/or student parents (Kristina Testa-Buzzee, personal communication, February 24, 2014).
Portland Community College (Oregon)	Project Independence helps single mothers and nontraditional adult students prepare for college by offering a free credit course that includes career and life planning, values clarification, an introduction to assertiveness, and strategies to overcome math anxiety (http://www.pcc.edu/resources/women/cascade/project-independence.html).
Rockland Community College (New York)	Provides scholarships for adult learners and/or student parents (http://www.sunyrockland.edu/prospective-students/adult-learners).
St. Catherine University (Minnesota)	Works with the financial aid office to identify students with dependents who might benefit from the university's Access and Success Program (Carissa Morris, personal communication, September 3, 2013).

College or University	Partnership
University of Minnesota–Twin Cities	During a required intake interview, the Student Parent HELP Center (SPHC) at the University of Minnesota–Twin Cities helps student parents evaluate their academic and career goals and understand how to access the university support services they need. SPHC also partners with a financial aid staff member who helps SPHC students understand the changing financial aid landscape and access scholarship and grant money (Susan Warfield, personal communication, September 12, 2013).
University of Toledo (Ohio)	College of Adult and Lifelong Learning provides adult learners with assistance in clarifying career goals, defining educational goals, and meeting personal goals. The university also offers career and life coaching (http://www.utoledo.edu/call).
University of Wisconsin–Milwaukee	Provides life coaches for disadvantaged parents on scholarship (http://www4.uwm.edu/lifeimpact).

Partnerships With Students. Adult learners bring a variety of dreams, expectations, fears, and skills to college. The partnerships that colleges and universities establish with these students and the partnerships these students establish with one another are vital to their success. At DePaul University (Illinois), the University of Minnesota–Twin Cities, and the University of California (UC), Berkeley, adult students worked with a variety of on- and off-campus partners to design and implement family-friendly events to help student parents learn about and access resources, network with other student parents, and develop support systems.

Adult learners at the University of California, San Diego, launched advocacy initiatives that led to child-friendly study rooms in campus libraries, family access to recreational facilities, a student-parent e-mail list, and a pilot project that allows student parents to apply for early registration (http://students.ucsd.edu/well-being/wellness-resources/student-parents/index.html). Advocacy initiatives at the University of Minnesota–Twin Cities produced a change in university attendance policies to include "the illness of students or the student's dependents" as an allowed absence (Susan Warfield, personal communication, August 26, 2013). When renovating an existing facility, St. Catherine University (Minnesota) created a space where parents can both study and supervise their children playing in an adjacent area, visible through a glass wall (Carissa Morris, personal communication, September 17, 2013).

Because student parents benefit when the general student population supports the use of activity fee revenue to assist with child care expenses or when the student government association allocates a portion of its budget to support child care initiatives, adult learner groups partnered with other students to gather support for using student activity fee revenue to support child care centers at the University of Wisconsin–Madison ($750,000 a year) and to fund child care discounts at Western Oregon University and Indiana University Bloomington. At Stony Brook University (New York) and at the Community Colleges of Spokane (Washington), student government associations agreed to contribute part of their annual budgets to support child care services for student parents (http://www.iwpr.org/publications).

Partnerships With Academic Affairs. As Table 7.3 demonstrates, advising presents an obvious opportunity for partnerships between academic and student affairs. Student parent programs spend a lot of effort helping faculty members understand, value, and work effectively with adults in general and student parents in particular. Programs employ a variety of strategies. For example, DePaul

University offers presentations at faculty meetings (Haydee Nunez, personal communication, August 22, 2013). The University of Minnesota–Twin Cities cosponsors Single Parent Visibility Day, provides a PowerPoint presentation to include in a support service thumb drive developed by the student affairs division for faculty use, collaborates with the Center for Teaching and Learning to help faculty develop syllabi sensitive to the needs of parents with children, and works with various graduate programs to use interns in student parent programs (Susan Warfield, personal communication, August 26, 2013).

Involving academic affairs in preparing adult learners to succeed in college has produced partnerships that offer undergraduate adult learners a free semester-length Self Sufficiency Program before starting college to strengthen critical thinking, math, and computer skills; learn how to apply for admission and financial aid; and develop educational goals, all at the University of Wisconsin–La Crosse (http://www.uwlax.edu/ssp). Partnerships at Endicott College (Massachusetts) produced APL 100, a three credit course that assists adult learners to create a proficiency portfolio that documents learning as a result of significant work and life experiences (http://www.endicott.edu/assessmentofpriorlearning). Partnerships at UC Berkeley (http://trsp.berkeley.edu/studentparents.shtml) produced two pass/fail courses: One is designed to meet the needs of re-entry students 25 years of age or older; the other is an orientation course for student parents. At Portland Community College (Oregon) (http://www.pcc.edu/resources/women/cascade/project-independence.html), partnerships created a free, credit-bearing course to prepare single mothers and other nontraditional adult students for college. The University of Akron (Ohio) developed a program titled Express to Success (http://www.uakron.edu/express) that allows adult learners to review their knowledge of specific subjects and then assess their chances of passing a for-credit exam in the subject.

Involving the wider college or university community in supporting undergraduate adult learners and student parents has resulted in innovative partnerships with the Colleges of Education, Health, and Public Policy at DePaul University, including an annual conference called Students with Children. The partnership also produced the Take a Professor to Lunch program that invites adult learners to apply to have lunch with a faculty member (Haydee Nunez, personal communication, August 22, 2013). UC Berkeley's School of Social Welfare (http://www.trsp.berkeley.edu/studentparents.shtml) provides service-learning internships for student parents. The School of Medicine and Public Health and the Teaching Assistant Association at the University of Wisconsin–Madison provide annual financial gifts to the university's child care centers (Boressoff, 2013).

Partnerships With Information Technology and Institutional Research. Few institutions routinely disaggregate data to study adult learners, but many programs designed to support student parents work with their institution's information technology (IT) office to collect data required for state, federal, and foundation reports; design easy-to-navigate websites for current or potential students; and develop early warning systems for students in their programs. The Access and Success Program at St. Catherine University–Minneapolis Campus, for example, worked with the IT office to build a stand-alone system that allowed students, faculty, and staff associated with the Access and Success Program to download documents related to the programs and link to information and websites on the Internet (Carissa Morris, personal communication, September 17, 2013).

Few institutions consistently conduct longitudinal research on the impact of nonclassroom support services on the success rates of undergraduate adult learners or student parents. However, the

Student Parent HELP Center (SPHC) at the University of Minnesota–Twin Cities has compiled a comprehensive literature review on adult learners and students with children, developed an internal database that tracks all contacts with student parents and the services received, and collaborates with IT and the Office for Institutional Review to track student parent graduation rates and other academic outcomes. The SPHC also has an internal student group identifier that allows the university to track all SPHC student parents from 1994 to the present in order to assess outcomes and to compare the performance of SPHC students to university benchmarks and to the performance of student parents not participating in SPHC (Susan Warfield, personal communication, August 26, 2013).

LESSONS LEARNED

Partnerships that benefit adult learners are as different as the institutions that produce them, but the people who build them seem to share a fundamental set of beliefs: (1) The power of people working together toward a common goal is exponentially stronger than the power of one person or a group of people working in isolation; (2) culture matters: hiring talented people is a waste of money if the institution's culture holds them back; (3) intelligent leadership at all levels is essential: if leaders do not create a culture that expects, values, and rewards partnerships, partnerships will not happen; (4) technology is useless if educators simply use it to replace physical barriers with digital barriers; and (5) people represent the most valuable "software" an institution has: they must be respected, periodically updated, and linked to other "software" with the potential to increase their effectiveness.

Although partnerships that benefit adult learners involve many types of collaborators, effective partnerships share four characteristics. They are: (1) mission-driven, learner-focused, and outcomes-oriented; (2) grounded in theory and a firm sense of what adult learners need; (3) committed to respecting, listening to, and engaging adult learners; and (4) doing work that will benefit all students because their focus is both learning- and student-centered. Diana Doyle, president of Arapahoe Community College, identified the most vital lesson that higher education can learn from partnerships that benefit adult learners: "Not one of us is as smart as all of us together. Active and continued teamwork among all sectors of the college community makes the greatest impact on student success" (personal communication, July 1, 2013).

 IN THE SPOTLIGHT

Research indicates that adult learner success rates depend on the type of institution attended. The gap between completion rates of adults and traditional students at 4-year private colleges is 22%; the gap at public colleges is 18.5%. Only 2-year colleges post comparable success rates for adult and traditional learners. "These findings suggest that the different postsecondary sectors can learn from one another" (National Student Clearinghouse Research Center, 2012, p. 50).

THE ROAD AHEAD

More than a decade ago, the Student Learning Project Work Group developed six mental models that approximated the views of students, faculty, student affairs professionals, and external stakeholders about what matters most in student learning and personal development. In sharing the models, Arnold and Kuh (1999) offered three findings that resonate today:

1. Students were so diverse that they required three models: one for traditional students living in residence halls, one for traditional students who commuted, and one for undergraduates over the age of 25. The mental models of undergraduates over 25 and the mental models of commuter students had much in common.
2. "No group frames its primary purpose in terms of learning outcomes" (p. 29).
3. "Each group's notion of what matters in undergraduate education is unique; no single vision is shared across constituencies. Each appears locked into mental models that define goals in terms of existing functional areas and preferred activities" (p. 33).

Fourteen years later, colleges and universities are still struggling to develop a shared view of learning, build partnerships that promote learning, and understand the needs of and create seamless educational experiences for students, the majority of whom no longer enter college directly after graduating from high school and live in residence halls.

The emergence of adult learners as higher education's new majority may present educators with their best opportunity to implement the recommendations that emerged from the findings of the work group (Arnold & Kuh, 1999), recommendations that urged academic and student affairs to:

- Identify and acknowledge their differing assumptions, values, and beliefs.
- Build a shared vision of student learning, including indices of success.
- Develop a shared definition of what matters in undergraduate education.
- Rethink old roles and traditional spheres of influence.
- Tighten the connection between in-class and out-of-class learning.
- Establish student learning as an institutional imperative.

If educators use the current focus on adult learners to revisit these recommendations, they will be taking a significant step toward building that seamless, data-driven, learning-centered model that higher education needs to meet the needs of 21st century students.

APPLY THE CONCEPTS

Exercise 7.1—Research Related to Partnerships

Directions: Assess your knowledge of partnership research. Match the "Finding" with the associated "Researcher(s)."

	Finding		Researcher(s)
I	Out-of-class experiences are more important to the cognitive development of students than faculty believe.	A	Baxter Magolda (1996, p. 21)
2	The most important thing institutions can do to increase student learning is "to get students to think more often about what they are doing—in classes and other areas of their lives—and to apply what they are learning to both." Faculty and student affairs must work together "to couple more tightly the connections between the curriculum and out of class life."	B	Love & Love (1995, p. 6)
3	Partnerships increase student involvement, success, and graduation rates.	C	Kuh et al. (2005)
4	"Our current approach to bifurcating the cognitive and affective dimensions of learning does not work."	D	Kuh, Branch, Lund, & Ramin-Gyurnek (1994, pp. 84, 95)
5	"Intellectual development does not happen exclusively in a class and ... social and emotional development does not happen exclusively out of class."	E	Pascarella & Terenzini (2005, p. 603)
6	"Students change in holistic ways and ... these changes have their origins in multiple influences in both the academic and nonacademic domains of students' lives."	F	Kinzie & Kuh (2004)
7	Partnerships increase student agency, success, and graduation rates.	G	Terenzini, Pascarella, & Blimling (1996)

Answer key on page 157.

APPLY THE CONCEPTS

Exercise 7.2—Analysis of Partnership Climates

Directions: Identify the partnership challenges at your institution.

Forces moving institutions toward partnerships	Forces with the potential to limit partnerships
Emerging research that questions the ability of existing practices, programs, and processes to meet the needs of posttraditional students	Institutional culture 1. 2.
Pressure from government agencies to become more seamless, transparent, and outcomes-oriented	Institutional history 1. 2.
Public policy initiatives at the federal and state levels whose goals are to change how public colleges and universities are funded and evaluated	Limited exposure to research on high performance organizations, partnerships, and public policy initiatives 1. 2.
Changing student demographics, enrollment patterns, and needs	Resistance to change 1. 2.
Student demands for seamless, personalized learning experiences and support services	Absence of leadership 1. 2.
Technology	Limited capacity within the student affairs staff 1. 2.
Online learning	Additional limiting factors at your institution 1. 2.

APPLY THE CONCEPTS

Exercise 7.3—Eliminate or Reduce Partnership Barriers

Directions: Use your analysis of the partnership climate at your institution (Exercise 7.2) to reduce or eliminate partnership barriers.

What did you learn from Exercise 7.2 about the most significant barriers to building partnerships at your institution?
Which of these barriers can student affairs directly influence?
What strategies are most likely to produce the desired change (reduction or elimination of one or more partnership barriers)?
What are the steps needed to carry out the strategy? Who will be responsible for executing each step?
How will you know when change has occurred?
When change occurs, how do you plan to leverage it to produce one or more partnerships?

APPLY THE CONCEPTS

Exercise 7.4—Conditions That Support Partnerships at Your Institution

Directions: Identify the conditions currently in place, in the planning stages, or worth considering at your institution that either support or have the potential to support partnerships.

	In place	Planned	Worth a look
Institution's mission clearly states that it is committed to educating the whole person			
Institutional culture and organizational structure support collaboration and partnerships			
Barriers to communication, collaboration, and partnerships have been identified and either removed or significantly reduced			
Incentives to communication, collaboration, and partnerships are built into the institution's culture and organizational structure			
The institution's leadership team sends clear messages that: • Learning is everyone's business • Student success is a significant institutional value • Partnerships based on true collaboration are important • Mutual understanding and respect are essential • Data-driven decisions are expected • Building capacity is an important institutional value			

APPLY THE CONCEPTS

Exercise 7.5—Effective Partnership-Building Strategies at Your Institution

Directions: Identify the strategies currently in place, in the planning stages, or worth considering at your institution that either support or have the potential to support partnerships between academic and student affairs.

	In place	Planned	Worth a look
Partnerships based on collaboration are incorporated into the institution's: • Annual goals and outcome measures • Budget-building and resource-allocation processes • Faculty and staff goal-setting and evaluation procedures • Faculty and staff search and selection procedures • Strategic and operational plans • Vision and values statements			
New faculty and staff orientation activities emphasize the value that the institution places on communication, collaboration, and partnerships			
The institution creates opportunities for, supports, and rewards cross-functional communication, data sharing, and problem solving			
The institution earmarks funds for professional development of faculty, staff, and administrators and links all development activities to its mission and strategic plan			
With support from Information Technology and Institutional Research, academic and student affairs share responsibility for the following areas: • Academic advising • Assessment and course placement • Early warning systems • Process improvement activities • Student persistence and completion model			

REFERENCES

American College Personnel Association. (1994). *The student learning imperative: Implications for student affairs.* Washington, DC: Author.

American College Personnel Association & National Association of Student Personnel Administrators. (2010). *Envisioning the future of student affairs: Final report of the Task Force on the Future of Student Affairs.* Retrieved from http://www.naspa.org/images/uploads/main/Task_Force_Student_Affairs_2010_Report.pdf

American Council on Education. (n.d.). *Adult learners.* Retrieved from http://www.acenet.edu/higher-education/topics/Pages/Adult-Learners.aspx

American Council on Education. (1994a). The student personnel point of view. In A. L. Rentz (Ed.), *Student affairs: A profession's heritage* (2nd ed., American College Personnel Association Media Publication No. 40, pp. 66–77). Lanham, MD: University Press of America.

American Council on Education. (1994b). The student personnel point of view. In A. L. Rentz (Ed.), *Student affairs: A profession's heritage* (2nd ed., American College Personnel Association Media Publication No. 40, pp. 108–123). Lanham, MD: University Press of America.

Association of American Colleges and Universities. (n.d.). The essential learning outcomes. Retrieved from https://www.aacu.org/leap/documents/EssentialOutcomes_Chart.pdf

Arcelus, V. J. (2011). If student affairs-academic affairs collaboration is such a good idea, why are there so few examples of these partnerships in American higher education? In P. M. Magolda and M. B. Baxter Magolda (Eds.), *Contested ideas in student affairs: Diverse perspectives and respectful dialogue* (pp. 61–74). Sterling, VA: Stylus Publishing.

Arnold, K., & Kuh, G. D. (1999). What matters in undergraduate education? Mental models, student learning, and student affairs. In E. J. Whitt (Ed.), *Student learning as student affairs work: Responding to our imperative* (pp. 11–34). Washington, DC: National Association of Student Personnel Administrators.

Baxter Magolda, M. B. (1996). Cognitive learning and personal development: A false dichotomy. *About Campus, 1*(3), 16–21.

Boressoff, T. (2013). *Financing child care for college student success.* Washington, DC: The Institute for Women's Policy Research at George Washington University.

Cherrey, C., & Allen, K. E. (2011). Student affairs leadership in a networked knowledge era. In G. J. Dungy & S. E. Ellis (Eds.), *Exceptional student affairs administrators' leadership: Strategies and competencies for success* (pp. 41–58). Washington, DC: National Association of Student Personnel Administrators.

Christiansen, C. M., & Eyring, H. J. (2011). *The innovative university: Changing the DNA of higher education from the inside out.* San Francisco, CA: Jossey-Bass.

Culp, M. M. (2011). Don't fence me in: The senior student affairs officer in the 21ˢᵗ century community college. In G. J. Dungy & S. E. Ellis (Eds.), *Exceptional student affairs administrators' leadership: Strategies and competencies for success* (pp. 15–40). Washington, DC: National Association of Student Personnel Administrators.

Culp, M. M., & Dungy, G. J. (2012*). Building a culture of evidence in student affairs: A guide for leaders and practitioners.* Washington, DC: National Association of Student Personnel Administrators.

Dare, L. A., Zapata, L. P., & Thomas, A. G. (2005). Assessing the needs of distance learners: A student affairs perspective. In K. Kruger (Ed.), *Technology in student affairs: Supporting student learning and services* (New directions for student services, No. 112, pp. 39–54). San Francisco, CA: Jossey-Bass.

Engstrom, C., & Tinto, V. (2000). Developing partnerships with academic affairs to enhance student learning. In M. J. Barr & M. K. Desler (Eds.), *The handbook of student affairs administration* (2ⁿᵈ ed., pp. 425–452). San Francisco, CA: Jossey-Bass.

Hartley, V. H., & Godin, E. E. (2010). *A study of chief academic officers of independent colleges and universities.* Washington, DC: Council of Independent Colleges.

John-Steiner, V., Weber, R., & Minnisis, M. (1998). The challenge of studying collaboration. *American Educational Research Journal, 35*(4), 773–783.

Johnstone, J., & Rivera, R. (1965). *Volunteers for learning: A study of the educational pursuits of American adults.* Chicago, IL: Aldine.

Kanter, M., Ochoa, E., Nassif, R., & Chong, F. (2011). *Meeting president Obama's 2010 college completion goal* [PowerPoint Slides]. Retrieved from http://www.ed.gov/sites/default/files/winning-the-future.ppt

Keeling, R. P. (Ed.). (2004). *Learning reconsidered: A campus-wide focus on the student experience.* Washington, DC: American College Personnel Association and National Association of Student Personnel Administrators.

Kezar, A. J., & Lester, J. (2009). *Organizing higher education for collaboration: A guide for campus leaders.* San Francisco, CA: Jossey-Bass.

Kinzie, J., & Kuh, G. D. (2004). Going DEEP: Learning from campuses that share responsibility for student success. *About Campus, 9*(5), 2–8.

Klein-Collins, R. (2011). Strategies for becoming adult-learning-focused institutions. *Peer Review, 13*(1), 4–7.

Kuh, G. D. (1996). Guiding principles for creating seamless learning environments for undergraduates. *Journal of College Student Development, 37*(2), 135–148.

Kuh, G. D., Branch, D., Lund, J. P., & Ramin-Gyurnek, J. (1994). *Student learning outside the classroom: Transcending artificial boundaries* (ASHE-ERIC Higher Education Report, No. 8). Washington, DC: The George Washington University.

Kuh, G. D., Kinzie, J., Schuh, J. H., & Whitt, E. J. (Eds.). (2005). *Student success in college: Creating conditions that matter.* San Francisco, CA: Jossey-Bass.

Levine, A., & Dean, D. R. (2012). *Generation on a tightrope: A portrait of today's college student.* San Francisco: CA: Jossey-Bass.

Lewin, K. (1936). *Principles of topological psychology.* New York, NY: McGraw-Hill.

Lewis, H. (2006). *Excellence without a soul: How a great university forgot education.* New York, NY: Public Affairs.

Love, P. G., & Love, A. G. (1995). *Enhancing student learning: Intellectual, social, and emotional integration* (ASHE-ERIC Higher Education Report No. 4). Washington, DC: The George Washington University, Graduate School of Education and Human Development.

Manning, K., Kinzie, J., & Schuh, J. (2006). *One size does not fit all: Traditional and innovative models of student affairs practice.* New York, NY: Routledge.

National Center for Education Statistics. (1996). *Nontraditional undergraduates: Trends in enrollment from 1986 to 1992 and persistence and attainment among 1989–90 beginning postsecondary students* (NCES 97-578). Retrieved from http://nces.ed.gov/pubs/97578.pdf

National Student Clearinghouse Research Center. (2012, November). *Completing college: A national view of student attainment rates.* Retrieved from http://nscresearchcenter.org/wp-content/uploads/NSC_Signature_Report_4.pdf

O'Banion, T. (1997). *A learning college for the 21st century.* Westport, CT: American Council on Education and Oryx Press.

O'Halloran, K.C. (2007). The state of student and academic affairs partnerships: A national perspective. In J. H. Cook & C. Lewis (Eds.), *Student and academic affairs collaboration: The divine comity* (pp. 33–52). Washington, DC: National Association of Student Personnel Administrators.

Partnerships. (n.d.). In *Merriam-Webster's online dictionary.* Retrieved from http://www.merriam-webster.com/dictionary/partnership

Pascarella, E. T., & Terenzini, P. T. (2005). *How college affects students: A third decade of research.* San Francisco, CA: Jossey-Bass.

Soares, L. (2013). *Post-traditional learners and the transformation of postsecondary education: A manifesto for college leaders.* Retrieved from http://www.acenet.edu/news-room/Documents/Post-traditional-Learners.pdf

Stein, R. B., & Short, P. M. (2001). Collaboration in delivering higher education programs: Barriers and challenges. *Review of Higher Education, 24*(4), 417–436.

Terenzini, P. T., Pascarella, E. T., & Blimling, G. S. (1996). Students' out-of-class experiences and their influence on learning and cognitive development: A literature review. *Journal of College Student Development, 37,* 149–162.

Weimer, M. (2013). *Learner-centered teaching: Five key changes to practice.* San Francisco, CA: Jossey-Bass.

Answer Key for Exercise 7.1: 1-G, 2-D, 3-F, 4-A, 5-B, 6-E, and 7-C.

MODULE 8

Meaningful Community Partnerships for Adult Learners

Elizabeth Baldizan and Pamela J. Schreiber

ABSTRACT

Institutions of higher education today see a population of adult learners growing throughout their academic communities. It is critical to pursue and establish partnerships with external entities that are equally committed to the success of these students. Meaningful partnerships create bridges that span the divide often experienced by these individuals because of the multitude of roles and responsibilities they fulfill in addition to that of being a student. Establishing these partnerships requires an intimate understanding of adult student needs, knowledge of local and national resources, and a willingness to identify common goals and mutually beneficial results.

PARTNERSHIPS THAT MATTER

Of the many strategies for supporting the retention and persistence of adult learners, developing partnerships with external entities is recognized as a key component to a comprehensive effort. In fact, using strategic partnerships is identified by the Council for Adult and Experiential Learning (CAEL, n.d.) as one of nine Principles of Effectiveness for Serving Adult Learners. CAEL describes institutions that operate by this principle as those that "engage in strategic relationships, partnerships, and collaborations with employers and other organizations in order to develop and improve educational opportunities for adult learners" (p. 2).

These partnerships can support a number of areas deemed important for adult learner success. For example, many institutions partner with employers to develop curricula that allow graduates to make a smooth and successful transition into the world of work, a promotion, or an advanced position because their skills and knowledge specifically and directly meet the needs of those employers. Institutions partner with community agencies to provide adult learners with services and resources (e.g., child care services, financial aid, scholarship application guidance), while others develop partnerships with entities to enhance the adult learner's out-of-classroom development through networking opportunities, life skills development (e.g., financial planning), and career guidance.

There is no doubt that establishing partnerships with external organizations to serve adult learners makes good sense. "In a number of communities across the country, nonprofit organizations are working with the same adult learners who are showing up on community college campuses. And, many of these nonprofits are teaming up with community colleges, aligning their resources and investments in order to help more adult learners succeed in the classroom and the labor market" (Aspen Institute Workforce Strategies Initiative, 2013, p. 2). The benefits of such partnerships can be far reaching, positively affecting not only the learner and respective external partners, but also the community at large. One example is the Community College/Career Collaboration initiative (http://www.aacc.nche.edu/Resources/aaccprograms/cwed/Pages/goodwill.aspx) through Goodwill Industries International, Inc., and the American Association of Community Colleges. This program documents and replicates education models that expand skills and lead to meaningful employment and credentials.

Higher education has a proud history and has adapted to changing conditions, albeit archaically slowly at times. Today, America is in dire need of a greater talent pool, one that will meet the needs of jobs now and in the future, and American higher education finds itself at a crossroad. Shall we seek new ways to provide higher rates of college graduation or ignore an issue that is too important to ignore? American universities remain the model for the world and yet new ideas and delivery methods must emerge (Moore & Sorge, 2011). One such idea may be found in unprecedented collaborations across major enterprises of government, education, and business. According to the National Leagues of Cities (2012):

> Recognizing the economic necessity of building a highly skilled and educated workforce, more city, education, and business leaders are joining a growing national movement to achieve a 60 percent postsecondary attainment level over the next decade. In order to achieve this goal, individuals pursuing higher education—including both young people moving from high school to college and adults without a postsecondary degree—will need a variety of services and supports. These services must address a range of needs that span the educational pipeline: college readiness, access and financing, transition into postsecondary studies, persistence toward credentials, and the push to completion and attainment of multiple types of diplomas and certificates. (p. 1)

In general, developing effective partnerships with external organizations should start as any other initiative intended to serve students. Careful consideration of the needs of adult learners will likely lead to a model for student services that is different from one designed to meet the needs of traditional students. Student affairs professionals must develop an intimate understanding of the characteristics, needs, and experiences of adult learners in order to identify partnerships that will result in the greatest benefit. This module provides specific strategies for identifying, cultivating, and supporting partnerships that benefit adult learners.

THE ROLE OF THE STUDENT AFFAIRS PROFESSIONAL IN ESTABLISHING EXTERNAL PARTNERSHIPS

Student affairs professionals are well positioned to be the drivers in identifying and establishing beneficial relationships with external entities. Their fundamental role is student advocacy and supporting student success; removing barriers and unearthing resources aimed at this mission are almost second nature. Student affairs professionals have experience facilitating relationships that bring partners together when there is a common goal and opportunity for mutual benefit. They also connect students to resources and demonstrate how to organize programs and services for easy access. Finally, because of the nature of their work, student affairs professionals routinely work across organizational lines and know how to navigate the institutional landscape to get things accomplished.

QUICK TIP

"This is about serving the whole individual, just as schools and colleges must contend with the baggage students bring from their personal lives that can stand in the way of their ability to learn. No one entity is to blame for these problems, nor do they bear the sole responsibility of solving them. Only by working together is this possible." —Lamar Mitchell, director, Catawba Valley Champions of Education, an initiative of Catawba Valley Community College, Hickory, North Carolina (personal communication, August 19, 2013)

Every institution of higher learning that engages adult learners is obligated to provide support for successful completion, but often student support programs and services are designed for "traditional" students, 18- to 21-year-old individuals with no dependents, with part-time or no employment obligations, who reside on or near the campus, and rely, at least to some extent, on parents or other family for assistance (e.g., financial, social, transportation, health care). If adult students are to be sufficiently supported, student affairs professionals must first raise awareness of the needs of this student population, and then take action toward creating and sustaining the necessary programs and services.

The first step for any student affairs professional may be to assess his or her level of understanding of this student population. Rachel Brighton, coordinator for Nontraditional/Multicultural Programs at Utah State University, reinforced this when she said:

> Know your students. When I attend monthly community council meetings with an understanding of the daily challenges my students face, it equips me to uncover "golden nuggets" as I interact and network with my community partners. My understanding of students is

my guide on what to watch and listen for as I learn about community offerings. (personal communication, August 30, 2013)

Consider using self-assessment Exercise 8.1 as a way of identifying strengths and areas for development.

Understanding the needs of adult learners and the challenges they face is critical to serving them. Student affairs professionals must embrace advocacy for these students as one of their fundamental roles but one that can be carried out successfully only with a level of understanding of the characteristics of this student population.

STRATEGIES FOR INITIATING PARTNERSHIPS

So where should you start? This section presumes you are starting with few to no established partnerships with external entities. The key to success is to identify partnerships that meet the needs of adult learners in a meaningful way. Herein lies the importance of knowing the adult learners on your campus and the particular challenges they face; these challenges lead straight to the types of external partners you might pursue, as described in Table 8.1.

Table 8.1

Adult Learners and Potential Partners

Challenges	Potential partners
Access to the physical campus for application, enrollment, and coursework	Partners that can provide physical space in convenient locations
Selection of career path that will lead to employment	Partners that conduct job placement services, community workforce development councils, and employers and employer networks; internship sites
Child care	Partners who provide child care and family support services
Lack of awareness of/access to community resources	Community resource centers; community services networks
Access and familiarity with financial aid, scholarships, and internships	Partners that provide financial planning, hire university students, offer scholarships, and respond to needs in the community
Professional development	Partners that provide recertifications for specific careers, continuing education units, professional organizations, and testing
Preparation after long stints away from the classroom	Partners that can provide space for placement testing, adult high schools, and tutoring experts

Another more specific strategy is to work with municipal officials in conducting a scan of local efforts:

> The purpose of the scan is to take stock of the local landscape of services, supports, and institutions that promote postsecondary success, and then use that scan to develop a comprehensive strategy for helping more students receive the support they need to earn their degree or credential. (National League of Cities, 2012, p. 1)

Institutional resources (e.g., research assistants, funding) may be key to completing such a project, and the relationships developed as a result of conducting the scan could lead seamlessly to formal partnerships. The results of the scan will indicate opportunities for easy connections ("low-hanging fruit"), common goals, and potential partnerships that were not otherwise very obvious. Specific action steps for completing a scan are outlined in National League of Cities (2012).

Student affairs professionals can also reach out to adult learners attending their institution and ask about the associations, organizations, and communities to which they belong. The list of potential partners this may yield is a great place to start. Establishing a student organization for adults, providing student government representation, developing an Adult Learner Advisory Council, or creating an annual adult learner event are examples of engagement options that can bring together adult learners and provide a mechanism for connecting with potential partners.

In pursuing potential partners, student affairs professionals should seek to learn as much as possible about the partner's program, organizational structure, personnel, funding, mission, and events. They can participate in events and activities hosted by the potential partner in an effort to build a relationship and further understand the organization. Lauren Williams, director of the Office of Military and Veterans Services at Marywood University, shared this strategy as key to her work connecting veterans and their families to other available services; she makes an effort to attend programs and events hosted by external organizations as much as her schedule allows (personal communication, August 14, 2013).

Like the institution, external partners are passionate about delivering on their respective missions; opportunities that advance this objective will be welcomed. Identify potential partners whose goals align with the institution's and be able to articulate how a partnership can meet these shared goals (e.g., workforce development, reducing dependency on government services, family stability, reducing unemployment).

According to Patrick Lane, project coordinator at the Western Interstate Commission for Higher Education (WICHE) Adult College

QUICK TIP

When asked about how to initiate partnerships with external organizations, Leodis Scott, research associate and part-time faculty at DePaul University School for New Learning, shared this advice: "By understanding their challenges, problems, and difficulties and explaining how creating a relationship would help the both of us. This means revealing some of our own challenges, but with a sense of building a shared experience of needs and trust. This relationship grows through expanding this shared experience by looking at specific points, such as programs, courses, or policies that affect the organization and by finding ways we could reconsider" (personal communication, August 19, 2013).

Completion Network, there are not many hard and fast rules for seeking partnerships with different types of organizations, but one commonality would be that, "It all starts with an invitation" (personal communication, August 16, 2013). This invitation is the first step in generating awareness of the sincere interest and potential benefits. The discussion that follows must allow all parties to engage together with a collective sensitivity to respective needs, hopes, goals, and opportunities.

Lamar Mitchell directs an initiative in Western North Carolina called the Future Workforce Alliance, made up of 3 Workforce Development Board regions, 15 counties, and 8 community colleges. He recommends targeting the agencies or organizations with whom you want to partner and inviting them to a meeting where you share information about your program and specific, prescriptive ways in which you want them to be involved and resource needs or gaps that you may have in serving your clients (personal communication, August 23, 2013).

Once the invitation has been extended, it is crucial to articulate a vision for how the partnership could impact the adult learner experience. This vision includes practical strategies that, if implemented, could solve a current problem. This is why knowing the vision and mission statement of the external organization is an important step in initiating a relationship, because it allows the space for all parties to align with a single vision and a shared purpose (Leodis Scott, personal communication, August 19, 2013).

Prospective partners might find helpful examples of already functioning partnerships at the institution or at other institutions. The Complete the Degree Program in Chicago was born out of a preexisting relationship among colleagues from several nonprofit organizations who volunteered on an Advisory Council for the Chicago Workforce Investment Council. The partnership grew organically from discussions about the need for workplace adult literacy and college completion. The result was three nonprofit organizations joining together to hone their idea and creating a partnership with the Chicago Workforce Investment Council (Gabi Zolla, personal communication, September 4, 2013).

Finally, communicating the value the institution places on external partnerships could be reinforced by introducing potential partners to CAEL's Principles of Effectiveness for Serving Adult Learners.

 IN THE SPOTLIGHT

Timing and the right situation can create an opportunity, as Brian Knudsen, community resource coordinator for the city of Las Vegas, Nevada, explained. He saw an opportunity in 2009 when the city was making layoffs because of the economic downturn. Two staff members from the city staff development office had resigned. Knudsen reached out to the Workforce Development program at the local College of Southern Nevada (CSN). He needed staff development and CSN needed space for their classes. As it turns out, the new City Hall downtown was being finalized, and there just happened to be extra space—10,000 square feet. The city now has training for its employees, provided by CSN Workforce Development during the day. And the community has education provided for them in the evening and off hours at a campus downtown (personal communication, August 23, 2013).

By pointing out that developing strategic partnerships is a critical function in supporting adult learners and a standard of practice, student affairs professionals can demonstrate their serious commitment to making the partnership a successful one.

ELIMINATING POTENTIAL ROADBLOCKS TO DEVELOPING PARTNERSHIPS

Some external entities may be reluctant to partner with institutions because of misperceptions about mission, access, student needs, and the possible benefits of such a partnership. To many, the typical higher education institution is made up of units and departments with nondescript labels (or acronyms) and is organized in a way that is not always logical to outsiders. In cultivating these partnerships, student affairs professionals may find it necessary to first "translate" the educational environment by using more common labels, focusing less on titles and reporting structure and more on job roles and outcomes. Easy-to-understand graphical depictions of how institutional departments work together to support adult learners can serve as a road map for external partners to understand who at the institution works with these students and in what capacity.

The partnerships themselves involve adults who need to learn. Consider the characteristics of adult learners:

- Autonomous and self-directed
- Accumulated a foundation of experiences and knowledge
- Goal oriented
- Relevancy oriented
- Practical
- Needing to be shown respect (Knowles, 1970)

This "language" issue and the fact that no two institutions look the same in terms of organizational structure contribute to confusion and misperceptions, such as the following:

- The institution is exclusive, inaccessible.
- The educational process is confusing and bureaucratic.

QUICK TIP

The following is a checklist for student affairs professionals for identifying and initiating partnerships that meaningfully support adult learners:

- ✪ Know the challenges your adult students face.

- ✪ Look for common problems to solve at your institutions.

- ✪ Look for common goals that connect the community with the campus and students.

- ✪ Become familiar with external organizations in your local community.

- ✪ Know how to articulate benefits for all involved, especially adult learners, by using a variety of media.

- ✪ Create a vision for the partnership that can be seen, understood, and articulated by others.

- ✪ Be transparent about the institution to ensure consistency and commitment.

- ✪ Extend an invitation to meet and dialogue in a welcoming environment, recognizing strengths and seeking complementing skills.

- The siloed nature of the institution makes communication difficult and inconsistent.
- The institution is not committed to the persistence and retention of adult learners.
- The institution does not provide programs or services aimed at the unique needs of adult learners.

Typically, publicity about the institution tends not to focus on adult learner programs and services, especially when the institution enrolls a predominately traditional undergraduate student population. Student affairs professionals need to make a special effort to provide evidence of the institution's commitment to these students. "Telling your story" takes on a critical role in helping potential partners see the institution in a different light; using student experiences can be the most compelling way to demonstrate the difference resources can make in the retention and persistence of adult learners. Student affairs as a profession is sometimes generalized under the broad heading of "service," but the defined skills and deliverables that can be brought to a partnership are not clearly understood. When asked about advice for student affairs professionals, Steven Moore, from the Degrees Matter! Program, commented, "This is about rethinking the role you play in this work. Once others learn about it, it is powerful" (personal communication, August 27, 2013).

QUICK TIP

"You know you have reached deep engagement when the agency is telling your story to other agencies even better than you ever could and that they are supporting each other with a feedback loop of affirmation and successes." —Lamar Mitchell, director, Catawba Valley Champions of Education, an initiative of Catawba Valley Community College, Hickory, North Carolina (personal communication, August 20, 2013)

An effective strategy for eliminating confusion is to identify a single point of contact, someone who can coordinate and communicate between agencies, claiming the role of nonpartisan champion, and articulating status and progress. Having a constant and clear voice that keeps the focus on the greater cause can unite and ignite collaboration.

Sometimes local businesses and other community resources are approached by institutions of higher education only seeking money or other resources. Often, this serves as an immediate roadblock to establishing a truly robust and long-term relationship. Taking the time to explore and articulate the potential benefits to the external partner outside of any particular event or institutional initiative can open up lines of communication, because there is no pressure to take action within a particular time frame.

While the institution of higher education can be confusing, so can the world of governmental agencies and private-market employers. Student affairs professionals should school themselves on the organizational norms and practices of other organizations with which they have little or no experience as a strategy for eliminating perceived roadblocks. Corporate Voices for Working Families has a series of publications about the benefits of education-friendly policies for employers. For example, their research shows that tuition assistance has a positive return on investment for companies (usually through lowered retention costs). This type of research can help student affairs professionals better understand private sector concerns and perspectives (Patrick Lane, personal communication, August 16, 2013).

Brian Knudsen, community resource coordinator for the city of Las Vegas, Nevada, shared that his experience working with a local college and the city meant navigating two very large bureaucratic organizations with infrastructures that did not necessarily align (personal communication, August 21, 2013). Two different legal counsels were involved in finalizing the agreements. In this case, persistence and patience were keys to resolving those issues that initially were seen as roadblocks.

The inaugural partnership perspective should strive to create a win-win combination. Consider the motivating factors from both perspectives:

Educational Institution	**Business/Organization**
Design relevant curricula	Provide flexible work schedule
Demonstrate value	Identify interested students/include education in employee reviews
Provide follow-up to tuition assistance	Conduct human resources outreach and marketing

INSIGHT FOR SUSTAINING SUCCESSFUL PARTNERSHIPS

Regardless of whether a relationship with an external partner took time or happened serendipitously, sustaining these relationships long term takes attention, trust, creativity, flexibility, and dialogue. Here, the role of student affairs professionals becomes that of advocate, communicator, promoter, and planner; the professional must focus on both sides of the relationship at the same time, ensuring that all involved see that by working together, more will get accomplished. Consider these key actions in sustaining successful partnerships:

- Advocate for and represent the institution to the partner while also advocating for and communicating about the partnership to the campus community. Tools such as public service announcements, profiles of student success stories, letters of recognition and appreciation (copying supervisors), website notices, and personal telephone calls all go a long way in serving as a voice that unilaterally supports the relationship.

- Be visible and present at partner events and initiatives and find opportunities to engage the partner in institutional activities and programs. Not unlike student events that the advisor attends, a physical presence speaks volumes about commitment while cultivating a deeper relationship. It begins with awareness of the partnering organization and identifying timely and appropriate events.

- Introduce the partner to the institutional norms, traditions, and values, and become intimately familiar with the partner's history, priorities, and goals. Higher education is known for creating annual rituals and traditions, whether it is homecoming and a football game, a speakers' series, or a poster session put on by a specific college. A scan of your institution's events provides myriad choices to share with partners.

- Promote the partnership to adult learners and provide the partner with easy opportunities to interact directly with adult learners. Similar to donors wanting to meet with the students who receive their scholarship, partners want to see the results of their work with the institution. Provide an opportunity (possibly your own annual event) that allows for interaction, story sharing, and celebration.

- Keep the partner informed of major institutional issues and changes (e.g., new leadership). As a result of providing ongoing communication about happenings at the institution, transparency and trust are advanced for the partnership. It might be helpful to keep a file where you can "drag and drop" ongoing changes that are not major, but which can be shared in a monthly update.

- Whether formally (e.g., in institutional publications) or informally, take opportunities to share information about external partners. Rachel Brighton, nontraditional/multicultural program coordinator at Utah State University, reinforced this idea when she said:

  > Share what you learn. When you connect with colleagues in the community, share what you learn about their organizations and services. Share what you learn during a staff meeting, better equipping your employees and colleagues to connect students to solutions. Share your knowledge with individual students you serve. Mass communicate your knowledge of community resources through social media, e-mail lists, and office websites. Dormant knowledge is wasted knowledge. (personal communication, August 31, 2013)

- Identify indicators of success and agree on how these will be measured and communicated. The indicators are pivotal in establishing empirical measures of action, commitment, and direction. Consider the options for gauging:

  o Bottom-line dollars
  o Number of students involved
  o Cost per student
  o College- or university-based focus
  o Participation numbers
  o Retention
  o Re-entry
  o Attrition

  It will be important to provide these indicators on a longitudinal basis, connecting the trends and clearly communicating results. Again, this type of accountability only builds on trust.

- Set aside time to talk about the partnership (What is missing? Is communication clear and sufficient? Are meetings too frequent/not frequent enough? Are the needs of all partners being met?). The result of being attuned to the quality and quantity of the communication cannot be underestimated. It is not about striving for perfection, but being honest in the intent to stay true to the purpose of the partnership. This type of "pause" can offer professional regard and, often, additional opportunities.

- Recognize both the students who benefit and the partners who support their success. The Edmonds Community College (n.d.) *Student Resource Guide* provides a good example of how to recognize a key partner. The guide promotes the partner, shares a personal profile of a student, and unifies the services in a single publication. Each individual story could stand on its own and provide a springboard for the specific academic program or partnering organization to "tell more." Consider at the start how you can plan for students, the institution, and the partnering agency to easily capture information so the recognition can flow.

QUICK TIP

"The most important thing to consider for those developing the partnerships is that this is a long-term proposition. Results won't happen overnight, whether it's the partnerships themselves or the outcomes that should derive from the partnerships."
—Lamar Mitchell, director, Catawba Valley Champions of Education, an initiative of Catawba Valley Community College, Hickory, North Carolina (personal communication, August 20, 2013)

ARTICULATING AND UNDERSTANDING BOUNDARIES

Like any healthy relationship, trust is a key ingredient when establishing partnerships with external entities for the benefit of adult learners. The concept of "professional trust," according to Patrick Lane at the WICHE Adult Completion Network,

> is not so much the idea of a ropes course or trust falls, but rather, the idea that partners involved are effective and follow through on their commitments. Akin to accreditation, are we doing what we say we do? Can we document it and show it through consistent and understandable means? (personal communication, August 16, 2013)

The signature characteristics for Complete the Degree Chicago are trust and respect, said Gabi Zolla, vice president and chief operating officer for CAEL. "Now in its second year, this program has partnered with nine institutions, has further established roles between three nonprofit organizations, has secured funding, and has advanced their initiative for degree completion." Zolla pointed out that the growth has led, in large part, to the flexibility and adaptability of the participating partners; a reflection of the trust they have among the organizations (personal communication, September 4, 2013).

Establishing a cooperative agreement or memorandum of understanding (MOU) is highly advisable. It does not necessarily require legal counsel review, but it is a tool for articulating expectations and responsibilities for all involved. It provides for continuity in the case of staff transition, holds both parties to mutually agreed on roles and responsibilities, and institutionalizes the relationship, putting it on record by establishing a start date. An annual or otherwise routine review of the document provides an opportunity to revisit the partnership to make any necessary adjustments without having to declare that something is wrong. Finally, the signing of a cooperative agreement or MOU can be a dynamic and positive celebration of the launch of a new and exciting initiative.

Figure 8.1

Example Memo of Understanding

COOPERATIVE AGREEMENT

This Cooperative Agreement reflects the commitment of each partner to the successful delivery of [_____], including the specific responsibilities and roles each one bears in administering an academic opportunity through the [institution and/or organizations].

Parties desire to engage in an educational collaboration under the following conditions:

Service/Program/Educational Program: _____

Objectives

[_____] and the [_____] agree to [_____].

All courses or programs are subject to [_____] and institutional policies and procedures.

Actions that may be carried out under this Agreement include:

The parties agree that the courses or program developed from this Agreement will be subject to the following protocols:

_____

Roles and Responsibilities

Services provided by [_____]

_____

Responsibility of the [_____]

_____

Responsibility of the [_____]

_____

Fiscal considerations

_____

Duration and Modifications

This Agreement will be in effect for three (3) years, starting on the date the last party signs the agreement.

This Agreement may be modified or extended by written amendment executed by both parties. The modifications or extensions will be effective on the date the amendment is executed by both parties.

Dispute Resolution

This Agreement is entered into by the parties in good faith. The parties will use their best efforts to resolve any conflict or dispute which may arise regarding the interpretation and enforcement of this Agreement.

Any disputes or conflicts which cannot be resolved at the appropriate operating levels shall be referred to the Vice Provost of Educational Outreach and Provost for final resolution.

The parties have executed this Agreement as of the last date set forth below:

Name: _____   _____
           (Printed)   (Signature)

Title: _____   Date: _____

Department: _____   Division: _____

Name: _____   _____
           (Printed)   (Signature)

Title: _____   Date: _____

Department: _____   Division: _____

SUCCESSFUL PARTNERSHIP EXAMPLES

There are as many types of partnerships as there are campuses and communities. Maybe because of this, they can be dynamic and meaningful for the people they serve.

Below are examples of existing partnerships:

Civic and Community Groups

- The Family Economic Security Program at Norwalk Community College works with students who are parents to create strong economic futures by encouraging and supporting their financial, academic, career, and personal success (http://www.ncc.commnet.edu/fesp).
- Greater Louisville, Inc., partners with a variety of local institutions to help increase overall college attainment rates. A specific component of the project focuses on adults (http://www.greaterlouisville.com/hire/default.asp).
- Corporate Voices for Working Families and "Learn and Earn Partnerships" between business and education providers bridge the skills gap for employers while encouraging and supporting current and future employees to attain postsecondary credentials with labor market value (http://www.pge.com/includes/docs/pdfs/about/careers/powerpathway/newseventsmedia/LearnEarn_ExecSumm_web.pdf).
- Goodwill, Inc., has developed numerous partnerships across the country that focus on providing job skills training in addition to credit-bearing courses provided by institutions.

Specialized Organizations

- The Institute for Women's Policy Research, the Student Parent Success Initiative, and the National Coalition for Campus Children's Centers have joined together and developed a toolkit, Financing Child Care for College Student Success. The kit provides a collective body of knowledge and highlights an array of funding opportunities including public funding at the federal, state, and local levels (http://www.iwpr.org/publications/pubs/financing-child-care-for-college-student-success).

 IN THE SPOTLIGHT

With support from the Lumina Foundation, the University of North Carolina, Greensboro, Undergraduate Studies Division is developing a regional discussion of leadership in the corporate, public, and nonprofit sectors. Through dialogue, stakeholders seek to develop innovative solutions for increasing degree attainment among members of the Piedmont Triad workforce. Collaborators envision working with business, civic, and academic leaders to generate new and creative ways to solve the degree attainment crisis locally.

- Degrees Matter! is a shared partnership among educational institutions, local foundations, and nonprofit organizations with the mission to increase the number of residents with college degrees in the Greater Greensboro/High Point area (http://www.degreesmatter.org).

Institutions of Higher Education

- The Graduate Network started in Philadelphia and has expanded to other cities. The program provides intake advising and has relationships with various institutions around the Philadelphia area where they place students. They also provide ongoing support for students by outlining action plans specific to decision making, documentation, comparison, commitment, persistence, and degree completion. (http://www.graduatephiladelphia.org).

- The University Center of Lake County is a consortium of 20 colleges and universities created by the Illinois Board of Higher Education to bring bachelor's completion, graduate, and professional development programs to the region. The target audience is working adults, with programs that are run during the evenings, weekends, and online (http://www.ucenter.org and http://www.uclcconference.org).

- At the University of Toledo, the College of Adult and Lifelong Learning partnered with Toledo Public Schools and the Penta Career Center to help parents and community members lead the way for their children to excel in school. By engaging families to further their education, the children will be influenced toward academic success (http://www.utoledo.edu/call/ut_tps.html).

- The Working Families Grant Program provides funding to single custodial parents and establishes a partnership philosophy that embraces academic advising and support services, career assessment, and community services in administering the funds (http://www.marianuniversity.edu/wfg).

- The Future Workforce Alliance partnership of Catawba Valley Community College in Western North Carolina has two strategies. The first is a messaging campaign, "Get NOT Out of Your Life," and the other is the establishment of Success Coach teams at the community colleges (http://www.getthenotout.com).

 IN THE SPOTLIGHT

The Council for Adult and Experiential Learning (CAEL) developed the Adult Learning Focused Institution (ALFI) Assessment to assist institutions in evaluating the extent to which programs and services reflect the nine principles of effectiveness for serving adult learners. After participating in an ALFI assessment, Marylhurst University determined a need to further foster partnerships with business, community groups, labor unions, and other such external stakeholders. Marylhurst University's strategy for making this improvement was to establish a standing committee whose charge is to build alliances with these external entities. Formalizing this responsibility through the establishment of a committee means that this effort has shared accountability, will survive staff turnover, and has expected outcomes to meet.

External Partnerships to Benefit Adult Learners With Children

- At the University of Alabama, Undergraduate Parent Support (UPS) works with community partners to design and implement family-friendly campus events to help adult learners who are parents become aware of and access college and community resources. UPS sponsors an annual Family Resource Fair, maintains a website with links to community partners, and uses the site to host forums on issues of interest to adult learners with children.

- The Family Child Care Network links adult learners with children to participating independently owned and licensed child care facilities near California State University, Northridge.

- Norwalk Community College operates the Family Economic Security Program in partnership with community foundations. The program provides scholarships, financial education, achievement coaching, and family-friendly activities.

QUICK TIP

"Don't go it alone. No one professional or organization can be all things to all students. Build a network of colleagues, not only on campus but in your community, and then become the 'stepping stone' for your students to those professionals and the opportunities and services they provide. Community organizations can have a significant impact on students' ability to navigate difficult circumstances, making all the difference in their ability excel in academics and persist to degree completion." —Rachel Brighton, coordinator, Nontraditional/Multicultural Program, Utah State University (personal communication, August 30, 2013)

- Angelina College in Texas partnered with a nonprofit called Buckner Children and Family Services and the Women's Shelter of East Texas to build 40 apartments on college land, with a child development center and multiple support services. The apartments house adult women with children, many of them former victims of abuse, who are continuing their education.

- University of California, Berkeley, partners with Whole Foods, The Cheese Board, and Noah's Bagels, among others, to operate The Bear Pantry, a source of emergency food assistance for student parents.

ADVOCACY: A NEEDED VOICE

Up to this point, Module 8 has focused on strategies that student affairs professionals can employ to develop partnerships that support specific adult learners or adult learner subpopulations. There are other types of partnerships, ones that can have broader implications by influencing public policy pertaining to and impacting adult learners. Unlike grassroots efforts in building relationships, this type of initiative takes place at the policy level and requires the engagement of institutional presidents, board members, and other executive leaders.

Public policy has far-reaching influence on posttraditional learners. No longer can we "conflate postsecondary learning and education exclusively with traditional college settings while in a knowledge economy meaningful learning is happening (and required) in many different places, i.e., online, in the workplace, and as part of military service" (Soares, 2013, p. 10).

IN THE SPOTLIGHT

The Cache County Interagency Council in Utah comprises 85 different organizations, including governmental, nonprofit, social service, health care, faith-based, and workforce development agencies. It is an excellent example of the power of association in bringing together multiple groups in search of support, synergy, and resources with minimal investment. The group meets once each month at a local restaurant to network and hear a presentation by a member organization about its programs and services. Partnerships emerge when common goals or needs are identified. The group has an electronic mailing list that is heavily used to share information between meetings and has also been a convenient way to post and respond to unanticipated issues and needs; e-mails have also included offers of free resources, even a donated copy machine.

The adult learner must have policy that supports accessible and meaningful learning. Our workforce demands it and our communities deserve it. When we look at our past, the role public policy played in the 20th century was "remarkably successful in expanding access for millions of Americans and making the United States a human capital driven powerhouse. In a successful 21st century, the literature to be written must point to a bottom-up entrepreneurship in which post-secondary education leaders transform institutional, instructional, credentialing, and financial models based on the learning needs of post-traditional learners" (Soares, 2013, p. 16). Consider the questions in Exercise 8.2 as a way of identifying opportunities for broader advocacy of adult learners.

A CALL TO ACTION

Developing meaningful community partnerships takes specific attention and effort. Creating a plan for pursuing these partnerships along with specific strategies increases the likelihood of success. The following is a list of specific actions student affairs professionals can take to begin the process of initiating and sustaining successful partnerships.

1. Complete the self-assessment included in this module (Exercise 8.1) and discuss your conclusions with a colleague; devise a plan to fill gaps in your awareness of adult learner issues.

2. Initiate a meeting on your campus of staff and faculty whose work or research focuses on adult learners. Create an overview of the programs and services provided to adult learners as a tool to use in talking with prospective partners; consider establishing an institutional electronic mailing list or committee to share information, issues, and resources.

3. Register for the Adult College Completion Network at accn@listserv.wiche.edu.

4. Review CAEL's (n.d.) Principles of Effectiveness for Serving Adult Learners and become familiar with the nine principles, in particular the principle pertaining to developing strategic partnerships with employers and other organizations.

5. Identify all governmental, nonprofit, and community services in your community; identify any associations, meetings, or networks that bring these groups together.

6. Conduct a survey of adult learners at your institution to discover programs and services they already use.

7. Develop an outreach plan to connect with potential partners by identifying special events and activities hosted by the partner, open meetings, and other opportunities for you to participate.

8. Prepare a communications plan and collateral material about your institution that "tells your story." This should include testimonials from current adult learners or recent graduates.

9. Prepare and present to other student affairs professionals on your campus an overview of the characteristics of adult learners, the challenges and barriers they face, and examples of how partnerships with external organizations can be of benefit.

10. Invite external organizations to your campus for a tour, open house, special event, or program. Provide opportunities for the potential partners to meet currently enrolled adult learners.

11. Work with municipal officials to conduct a scan of local programs, services, and institutions that promote postsecondary success.

12. Share with your colleagues, supervisor, and community contacts your efforts to support adult learners and seek information and opportunities as a result of these relationships.

13. Learn about other successful partnerships by visiting the Web links included in the previous section of this module. Use what you learn to create a vision of how potential partners might engage with your institution.

14. Practice explaining institutional structure and roles using easily understood titles and labels and without acronyms. Create materials that demystify institutional processes such as the application and enrollment processes, degree and course selection, and the financial aid application process.

15. Formalize partnerships by drafting a memorandum of understanding, and use this document as a vehicle for clarifying roles, responsibilities, and expectations.

16. Nurture partnerships by engaging them in campus events, bringing attention to the partnerships and the difference they make for students, and celebrating success by recognizing the achievements of adult learners.

17. Ask a colleague at another institution to visit your website and provide feedback on how clear it is that you support adult learners.

18. Review the InsideTrack blog (as noted in the conclusion) that suggests a paradigm shift from "failure prevention" to "success creation." Consider the perspective taken at your institution and whether a shift is needed to better serve adult learners.

19. Look for opportunities to celebrate and create a tradition that recognizes adult learners year after year.

20. Meet with academic advising units at your institution and familiarize them with the profile of adult learners. Ask them for their insight and advice based on their advising experience with adult learners.

21. Join the Association for Non-Traditional Students in Higher Education, an international partnership of students, academic professionals, institutions, and organizations whose mission is to encourage and coordinate support, education, and advocacy for the adult learner (http://www.myantshe.org).

22. Develop an Adult Learner Advisory Council on your campus that has broad representation.

CONCLUSION

Of the many strategies for supporting the retention and completion rates of adult learners, creating partnerships between the academy and external organizations recognizes the relationship in the student's life between school and other responsibilities. Student affairs professionals have a unique opportunity and the right skill set to cultivate, establish, and nourish these partnerships so that all involved find great benefit. In determining the best partnerships, perhaps a helpful paradigm in working with adults is the concept of "success creation versus failure prevention." This concept suggests that partnerships should be aimed at meeting the complex needs of the adult learner but not because he or she is at risk or different from the traditional student. Partnerships built on enabling success rather than simply trying to avert failure are more likely to engage the student in taking full advantage of institutional services (InsideTrack, 2013).

By 2018, an estimated 62 percent of jobs in America will require some form of postsecondary education (Carnevale, Smith, & Strohl, 2010). How the United States responds in producing enough graduates with the requisite knowledge and skills to fulfill employers' needs depends on partnerships and systemic changes that allow adult learners to fully participate in an educational opportunity. Successful partnerships can have a significant impact on adult student retention and completion rates. The primary reason students cite for leaving college is balancing work and school (Sloate, 2009). Adult learners face the challenge of having prior responsibilities integrated into their lifestyle, things as varied as family, career, mortgages, and soccer practice. The reason they return to school might be invigorating and positive or it may be traumatic and daunting. In either case, it is a major disruption in the flow of life. For the profession of student affairs, this is an ideal opportunity to proactively and thoughtfully develop partnerships and engage services that support the adult learner.

Success is measured in many different ways. As university educators, we witness firsthand every day the need for our students of all ages, both traditional and nontraditional, to have something coherent to believe in, some centering values and goals to strive for (Nash & Murray, 2010, p. xiv). Partnerships can strengthen the experience, engage the community, and ultimately deliver for the student.

QUICK TIP

Even graduation rates themselves calculated in the traditional NCAA 4-, 5-, and 6-year method fail to capture the success of part-time or working students or community college transfer students. Part-time and working students may take 7 or 8 years to graduate. These successful students appear as failures in the data, and the standard methodology does not even count transfer students (Lombardi & Capaldi, 1997). Consider a conversation with your Office of Institutional Analysis, and acquaint yourself with how your institution counts (or does not count) the part-time student or transfer student. There is an opportunity to establish a voice for these students.

APPLY THE CONCEPTS

Exercise 8.1—Gauging Your Understanding of Adult Learners: A Self-Assessment

Directions: Invite a group of adult learners, faculty members, student affairs professionals, and administrators to independently complete the following exercise.

1. Who on your campus is considered an expert on adult learning or is currently working with adult students?

2. What do you know about the adult learners that attend your institution in terms of demographics? How do these data compare to other student populations served by your institution?

3. What are the unique needs of adult learners? How have you acquired (or would you acquire) this information?

4. What percentage of adult learners on your campus persists to degree or program completion? What are the reasons cited by adult learners at your institution who stop out or drop out?

5. What student activities, events, and leadership development opportunities are intended for adult learners? Who offers these programs?

6. Evaluate academic and operational policies in regard to the recognition of the needs of adult learners.

7. What is the experience of adult learners in the classroom? To what extent do faculty understand the needs and characteristics of adult learners?

8. What barriers to participation exist for adult learners?

9. How do you stay in touch with the adult learners on your campus?

10. What is the vehicle at your institution that provides a voice for adult learners?

11. How is student affairs represented and involved within your local community?

APPLY THE CONCEPTS

Exercise 8.2—Advocacy and Adult Learners

Directions: Invite a group of faculty members, student affairs professionals, continuing education staff, and administrators to collectively discuss and complete the following exercise.

1. Do you know the funding formula difference for your institution or state between a part-time student and a full-time student?

2. Is the Continuing Education unit represented at the leadership table at your institution?

3. Are you familiar with workforce development organizations in your region?

4. Do you know what the professional certificate programs are delivered by the Continuing Education unit at your institution?

5. Are the adult learners from Continuing Education at your institution invited to become members of the alumni association?

6. How does your institution provide for a representative voice for the adult learner?

REFERENCES

Aspen Institute Workforce Strategies Initiative. (2013, February). *Helping adult learners navigate community college and the labor market.* Retrieved from http://www.aspenwsi.org/wordpress/wp-content/uploads/update_cte_march2013.pdf

Carnevale, A., Smith, N., & Strohl, J. (2010). *Projections of jobs and education requirements through 2018.* Washington, DC: Georgetown University, Center on Education and the Workplace.

Council for Adult and Experiential Learning. (n.d.). *Principles in practice: Assessing adult learning.* Retrieved from http://www.cael.org/alfi/principle.html

Edmonds Community College. (n.d.). *Student resource guide.* Retrieved from http://www.edcc.edu/support/documents/student-resource-guide.pdf

InsideTrack. (2013, August 23). *"Success creation" versus "failure prevention": Alternative paradigms in student support.* Retrieved from http://www.insidetrack.com/success-creation-versus-failure-prevention-alternative-paradigms-in-student-support

Knowles, M. S. (1970). *The modern practice of adult education: Andragogy versus pedagogy.* New York, NY: Association Press.

Lombardi, J. V., & Capaldi, E. D. (1997, March). Students universities and graduation rates: Sometimes simple things don't work. *Ideas in Action, IV*(3), 1–7.

Moore, S., & Sorge, C. (2011, October). *Current issues and trends in expanding American degree attainment with adult learners.* Greensboro, NC: University of North Carolina, Greensboro.

Nash, R. J., & Murray, M. C. (2010). *Helping college students find purpose: The campus guide to meaning making.* San Francisco, CA: Jossey-Bass.

National League of Cities. (2012). *Municipal action guide: Conducting a scan of local efforts to promote postsecondary success.* Washington, DC: Author.

Sloate, T. (2009). Degree completion hindered by work and family responsibilities. *InFocus, 14*(7), 3.

Soares, L. (2013). *Post-traditional learners and the transformation of postsecondary education: A manifesto for college leaders.* Retrieved from http://www.acenet.edu/news-room/documents/soares-post-traditional-v5-011813.pdf

MODULE 9

Building a Culture of Evidence

Using Data to Improve

Adult-Learner-Focused Initiatives

Katie Busby and Adam S. Green

ABSTRACT

This module is designed to help leaders of adult learner initiatives establish and maintain a culture of evidence. It may seem overwhelming for coordinators of adult learner programs to accept the responsibility of advancing a culture of evidence, given the myriad demands competing for their attention and the resource-constrained environment in which many operate. However, an investment in establishing and maintaining a culture of evidence will pay dividends of better decision making, greater program efficiencies, and improved allocation of limited resources. All of these benefits strengthen adult learner programs and initiatives and ultimately lead to student success. A culture of evidence can be developed if faculty and staff focus their efforts on the broader benefits of examining programs and services in addition to concentrating on the necessary details of program planning. Such a culture embraces the ongoing review of data to inform progress toward identified student outcomes and promotes an ethos of effectiveness. It is important to keep in mind that "assessment techniques are of little use unless and until local academic cultures value self-examination, reflection, and continuous improvement" (Angelo, 1999, p. 5).

USING THIS MODULE

This module provides leaders of adult learner initiatives with the information necessary to enhance their understanding of a culture of evidence and its importance, to use data from a variety of sources to improve programs for adult learners, and to ultimately develop such a culture. Adult learning takes place in a variety of settings including 2- and 4-year institutions, as well as workplace settings. Learning assessment can and should exist in workplace, corporate, and nonprofit entities, and many of the techniques presented in this module can be implemented in those settings. However, this module focuses on assessment of learning and development among adult learners in higher education. Specifically, this module:

- Defines culture of evidence.
- Outlines key components in a culture of evidence.
- Emphasizes the importance of a culture of evidence.
- Describes sources of data and technology used to inform decision making.
- Illustrates improvements made to adult learner programs.
- Highlights examples of programs operating within a culture of evidence.

CULTURE OF EVIDENCE

What is a culture of evidence and why is it important? Culp (2012) defined a culture of evidence in the context of student affairs as "a commitment among student affairs professionals to use hard data to show how the programs they offer, the processes they implement, and the services they provide are effective and contribute significantly to an institution's ability to reach its stated goals and fulfill its mission" (p. 5).

Banta (2004) defined a culture of evidence more broadly as "an environment in which important decisions are based on the study of relevant data" (p. 6). Regardless of where adult learner initiatives are structured within an institution, these definitions are applicable to adult learner programs. Several key conditions are necessary to foster a culture of evidence. These conditions include support from the program, unit, or institution leader; involvement of faculty, staff, and students; a collegial environment in which ideas can be shared; an implicit understanding that assessment activities will take place; a belief that assessment and use of assessment results will lead to improvements; and the ability to conduct assessment activities within institutional context and culture (Seagraves & Dean, 2010; Suskie, 2009).

A culture of evidence requires strong leadership at all levels of a unit or institution and involves faculty, staff, and students. Leaders set the tone and vision for all activities, and when those responsible for adult learner programs value and promote a culture of evidence, then others who are involved will follow suit (Suskie, 2009). Banta, Jones, and Black (2009) reminded us that "if individuals in a unit are to embrace the responsibility for taking action they must own the assessment process" (p. 12).

Institutional leadership is also an important factor in student success. In 2004, the Lumina Foundation for Education launched Achieving the Dream: Community Colleges Count (ATD), an

IN THE SPOTLIGHT

Central Washington University (CWU) is located in Ellensburg, Washington, and enrolls 3,100 students, 22% of whom are adult learners. CWU also has eight branch campus locations that serve upper-division students, nearly all of whom are adult learners. Through the Center for Diversity and Social Justice and under the leadership of Diversity Officer Michelle Cyrus, CWU provides robust nontraditional student programming that has evolved through evidence-based decision making.

Successful programs include a nontraditional student welcome carnival, nontraditional student week activities, and a professional development series designed specifically for adult learners. Cyrus has established a culture of evidence that keeps it simple. She conducts quarterly focus groups with diverse groups of nontraditional students, including students of all adult ages, parents, working professionals, and veterans. The results of the focus groups are used primarily to improve the professional development series curriculum, but also to inform the unit strategic plan and other institutional reports. Specifically, the professional development series curriculum has included topics such as time management, team building, and leadership skills, but the delivery of these topics is designed to focus on the needs of adult learners. Student feedback often confirms the direction of student programs, but sometimes students provide interesting and unexpected suggestions. For example, nontraditional students at CWU indicated a desire to continue their education beyond an undergraduate degree and expressed interest in learning more about graduate and professional programs. Subsequently, a workshop series on selecting and applying to graduate and professional schools was developed. Cyrus has worked hard to establish a culture of evidence at CWU and her evidence-based programming is meeting the needs of nontraditional students at all campus locations (Michelle Cyrus, personal communication, October 18, 2013).

initiative designed to increase student success among minority and low-income students. ATD began with 26 community colleges, expanded to include more than 160 community colleges, and 6 years later became an independent, nonprofit group (Ashford, 2011). The first step in ATD's five-step process for improving student success is leadership commitment. A study of the initial 26 ATD institutions found that more than 33% of institutional presidents exemplified a strong commitment to a culture of evidence and student success, and in approximately one-half of the participating institutions, senior administrators led these initiatives. Over the 3-year period of this study, 81% of the participating colleges improved the culture of evidence on campus. In addition to having strong leadership, these colleges implemented or improved many of the components of such a culture by using data to make decisions, engaging stakeholders, and implementing continuous improvement strategies. Attention to all aspects of a culture of evidence is needed, but "what seemed to make the most difference for development at these colleges were strong, visionary leaders at multiple levels of the institution" (Rutschow et al., 2011, p. 113).

Quick Tip

Assessment efforts within adult learner programs and services can be used to demonstrate progress toward broader institutional goals. The assessment efforts within the Learning Resources Center (LRC) at the University of Alaska Anchorage provide an example of evidence-based improvements taking place within an individual unit and contributing to broader university goals. The LRC conducted a robust assessment of its tutoring program and the student learning that took place and used the results to define its unique contributions to institutional goals. The process yielded benefits for the tutoring program, provided evidence in support of universitywide retention goals, and resulted in continuous improvement efforts. (DeFao, 2012)

Another key component of a culture of evidence is the use of relevant data to inform decision making and demonstrate progress toward stated goals. The data used in decision making can come from many sources, including institutional data, peer comparisons, results of quantitative measures, qualitative findings, and direct as well as indirect measures of student learning. Most important, the data gathered are used to inform program and pedagogical decisions (Suskie, 2009). The consistent and appropriate use of assessment results is what truly defines a culture of evidence, and when a culture of evidence is present all individuals involved will make program-related decisions informed by data. For example, community colleges, which often enroll large numbers of adult learners, can use data to understand more specifically the barriers and challenges that adult learners experience, work to remove those barriers, and develop the necessary programs and services that will help students meet their educational goals (McClenney, McClenney, & Peterson, 2007; MDC, 2006).

IMPORTANCE OF A CULTURE OF EVIDENCE

A culture of evidence has many advantages and benefits for adult learners, adult learner programs and initiatives, student affairs divisions, and institutions. Many adult learners tend to be autonomous and self-directed in their pursuit of knowledge. They also desire to understand the relevance of what they are learning and how that knowledge can be leveraged to meet their goals (Knowles, 1980). A culture of evidence fosters an open discussion of expected learning outcomes, involves students in the assessment process, and promotes sharing and using assessment results for improvement. Through this type of involvement, adult learners can gain a deeper understanding of what is expected of them and may also recognize the link between classroom and programmatic activities and the associated learning outcomes. Simply having a culture of evidence may motivate adult learners and subsequently improve student success (Zemke & Zemke, 1995).

Sharing feedback with adult learners about their performance is a particularly helpful technique that contributes to the students' learning and capacity for self-direction (Kasworm & Marineau, 1997). Adult learners benefit from knowing where their performance met expectations, where improvement is needed, and how their performance compares against that of their peers.

Evidence-based decision making is critical to the continuous improvement of adult learner programs, and the hallmark of a culture of evidence is the use of results. Program and curricular decisions based on relevant data related to program goals yield stronger results than decisions based solely on instinct or hunches. The data gathered from institutional databases, surveys, focus groups, exams, and performance assessments must be examined carefully in the context of the adult learner initiatives, the division of student affairs, and the institution. Suggested improvements to programs and initiatives should be based on this information. Robust discussions about program improvement are among the most meaningful consequences of a culture of evidence. Such discussions can lead to the revision of program goals or outcomes, refinement of assessment measures, changes to programs or services, or implementation of new services, just to name a few. Some changes will be easy to implement though others may be more difficult. For example, extending the hours of operation of a learning resource center could be done quickly and with relative ease if the necessary resources are available. However, creating an orientation class specifically designed for adult learners would require involvement from numerous offices and likely could not be implemented in a single semester. When any changes are implemented, the evaluation should continue to determine the effectiveness of those improvements.

QUICK TIP

A Background Knowledge Probe allows students to articulate their understanding of a particular topic. This technique provides data about students' content knowledge and encourages students to think about the forthcoming topics (Angelo & Cross, 1993).

When a culture of evidence exists within adult learner programs and services, they are well positioned to contribute to the larger assessment and improvement efforts within student affairs and the institution. Institutions are often being asked to provide evidence of the effectiveness of their programs and services to many institutional stakeholders, including students, alumni, governing boards, legislators, and accreditors. The culture of evidence within adult learner programs helps meet the broader need to provide evidence of effectiveness for accountability purposes. For example, data produced from the U.S. Census Bureau (2012) clearly demonstrated that college-credentialed individuals have a significantly higher annual median income than individuals with just a high school degree. Additionally, research from the Georgetown Public Policy Institute's Center on Education and the Workforce indicated that 65% of job openings by 2020 will require some form of education and training beyond high school (Carnevale, Smith, & Strohl, 2013). Therefore, it is imperative that student affairs professionals create an environment that fosters, supports, and measures worthwhile interventions that lead to more credentialed adult learners.

Institutions of higher education are called to demonstrate their effectiveness toward meeting established goals and outcomes, and program evaluation results can be used to fulfill regional and professional accrediting requirements. An increasing number of state policymakers are moving away from student enrollment-based funding models. Instead, many are adopting outcomes-based funding models to align the state's financial investment in higher education with the state's higher education goals and priorities. Data produced by the National Conference of State Legislatures (2013) indicated that 12 states have already adopted some form of performance-based funding; 4 are transitioning to it; and 19 states are engaged in formal discussions regarding a potential shift in this direction. For this reason, demonstrating a culture of evidence is vital to the future of student affairs. Professionals must

QUICK TIP

Leaders of adult learner programs should also take time to celebrate positive results and should never use negative results to penalize individual faculty or staff members (Suskie, 2009).

carefully measure the impact each program has on student persistence and completion—including programs aimed at aiding adults.

Educational foundations, such as the Lumina Foundation, as well as the president of the United States have set goals to increase the number of college graduates or number of adults with postsecondary educational credentials (Lumina Foundation, n.d.; U.S. Department of Education, 2011). Many states have set similar goals for their own residents. For instance, the Kentucky Council on Postsecondary Education launched an effort in 2007 to significantly increase the number of degree holders within its state. The Double the Numbers initiative aims to have twice as many state residents with bachelor's degrees by 2020. Much of the emphasis of the initiative focuses on adult learners because officials realized that they could not rely solely on the shrinking number of high school graduates within the education pipeline to meet this goal (Southern Regional Education Board, 2010). To reach these goals, more adult students will need to enroll in college and complete their degrees. A culture of evidence in adult learner programs will work to improve the programs and support students toward completing their degrees.

BEST PRACTICES IN GATHERING AND USING DATA

A culture of evidence requires relevant data on which decisions can be based. It is critical for practitioners to use best practices when identifying, gathering, and using appropriate data to improve adult-learner-focused programs and services.

The first step in gathering such data is to carefully articulate learning outcomes, program goals, or research questions. Learning outcomes refer to the specific knowledge or skills that students actually develop through their college experience (James Madison University, n.d.). The knowledge and skills may come from a specific course or experience or be developed over time from a collection of them. Adult learners have a variety of life and work-related experiences, so it is most likely that their skills and knowledge will be developed through practice (Knowles, 1980; Russell, n.d.). Learning outcomes, program goals, and research questions should all be specific and measureable. Strong outcomes should also be aggressive but attainable, results-oriented, and time-limited (Busby & Robinson, 2012). Furthermore, most student learning outcomes fall into two categories: cognitive and affective. Cognitive learning outcomes refer to the general skills, intelligence, and higher-order cognitive development whereas affective learning outcomes include those related to student attitudes, values, and self-concept (Bloom, 1956; Gagne, 1984; Krathwohl, Bloom, & Masia, 1964). Leaders of adult learner initiatives should consider establishing program outcomes across these categories.

If strong program outcomes exist, then gathering the necessary data to demonstrate progress toward those outcomes can follow. Many institutions have a wealth of readily available data that can be used to examine research questions, inform learning outcomes, and evaluate programs. Institutional data can include student demographic information (course completion, grade point average, amount of transfer credit, etc). Student demographic information can be obtained from the institutional student information system. Departments and institutions may also have survey data from proprietary or local surveys that can be used to support program outcomes and evaluation goals. In addition to

using institutional-level data, state agencies of higher education also maintain aggregated reports within and across institutions in their state. For instance, each year the West Virginia Higher Education Policy Commission and the West Virginia Community and Technical College System jointly produce an aggregated accountability report. The document examines national-, system-, and state-level data related to economic development, college access, cost and affordability, learning and accountability, and innovation (West Virginia Higher Education

QUICK TIP

Leaders of adult learner programs should establish strong working relationships with campus data stewards such as the registrar's office or offices of institutional research, effectiveness and/or assessment to ensure the integrity, accuracy, and appropriateness of the information being used for decision-making purposes.

Policy Commission, n.d.). Such data can be used to help inform campus leaders when developing their own goals and outcomes. Nationally comparative data are also readily available from the National Center for Education Statistics, which includes the commonly known Integrated Postsecondary Education Data System database. Unfortunately, some researchers have found the national databases lacking when it comes to data specifically related to adult learners and their experiences (Pusser et al., 2007). Extreme care should always be taken to ensure that all data requests are handled according to applicable institution, state, and federal guidelines.

When the desired data are not readily available, they must be gathered. Surveys and focus groups are among the most commonly used data-gathering techniques to measure the effectiveness of adult learner programs. Student surveys, particularly those created and administered at the local level, can yield important information. Faculty and staff working to establish a culture of evidence should use best practices in survey research. Dillman, Smyth, and Christian (2008) provided a broad overview of survey techniques designed to achieve a high response rate and reliable responses. More specifically, surveys should be administered with the needs of adult learners in mind. Surveys should be as brief as possible and items should be germane to the service or program being evaluated. Too often, program coordinators are tempted to add items that would be "interesting" to know but are not directly related to the evaluation of the stated goals. Lengthy surveys or those with poorly constructed items can be irritating to the adult learners completing the questionnaires. When developing a survey for the first time, additional time and effort should be spent in the pilot phase. This phase is often overlooked: neglecting it may save time during the development phase, but yields results that are not as strong as they could be had a pilot been conducted. Developing a robust survey is important, but it is also important to administer the survey carefully, keeping in mind that respondents who understand the purpose and importance of the survey may be more likely to respond (Knowles, 1980).

Surveys do not have to be developed locally. Several nationally administered surveys are designed specifically for adult learners, including the Adult Learning Focused Institution (ALFI) Assessment administered through the Council for Adult and Experiential Learning (CAEL) and the Adult

Student Priorities Survey administered by Noel-Levitz. Faculty and staff should take special care when considering whether a survey or assessment instrument is appropriate for use with adult learners or adult learner initiatives. When considering whether to administer a national survey, administrators should be sure it is applicable to adult learners because many surveys developed for college students are done so with traditional-aged students in mind. To go one step further, program coordinators may want to conduct a validity study to determine if a particular instrument is appropriate for adult learners.

Focus groups are often thought of as an alternative to surveys. However, the nature of the research question should dictate whether focus groups are used. When the research question is qualitative in nature, then focus groups or interviews might be a good way to gather data. Faculty and staff working to establish a culture of evidence should use best practices in planning and conducting focus groups. Morgan and Krueger (1998) provided a broad overview of focus groups designed to achieve high participation and reliable results.

Direct evidence of student learning cannot be obtained through a survey or focus group. Course-embedded assessment, portfolios, performance assessments, and standardized exams can be used to demonstrate student preparedness and student learning. Middlesex Community College (MCC) in Bedford, Massachusetts, has an emerging e-portfolio project with student learning and engagement at its center. MCC built its e-portfolio program on a strong foundation of institutional best practices and engaged faculty and other stakeholders to address any potential obstacles and highlight possible opportunities the e-portfolio project afforded students. The project allows students, especially adult learners, "to make connections between and among learning experiences" and demonstrate mastery of program and institutional learning outcomes (Martin, 2013, p. 15). Standardized tests can also be used for placement and the scores can be compared to a normed group. Standardized tests are available for adult literacy, job readiness, and basic skills, such as Educational Testing Service PDQ Profile, ACT WorkKeys, and Comprehensive Adult Student Assessment Systems instruments, respectively (Askov, Van Horn, & Carman, 1997).

Regardless of the measures used to evaluate program goals or assess student learning, it is the responsibility of the assessment professional, faculty member, or staff member overseeing the assessment process to ensure that all measures are appropriate for adult learners. One cannot assume that surveys or instruments that are appropriate for use with traditional-aged college students are appropriate for use with adult learners. In addition to appropriate measures, student motivation is also an important component of student learning outcomes assessment. Motivation is an individual concept, but generally adult learners are motivated differently than traditional-aged students (Lieb, 1991). It is important to keep student motivation in mind when developing and administering assessment activities.

PRIOR LEARNING ASSESSMENT

Adult learners possess numerous varied skills and experiences they have gained through work experiences, volunteer service, military service, and previous educational activities (Knowles, 1980; Russell, n.d.). Prior learning assessment (PLA) "is the evaluation and assessment of an individual's life learning for college credit, certification, or advanced standing toward further education or training" (CAEL, n.d., para. 2). The American Council on Education (ACE) is engaged in prior learning assessment through its Credits to Credentials strategy (ACE, n.d.). ACE collaborates with colleges and universities such as Ivy Tech Community College in Indiana and corporations such as McDonald's to design and implement pathways to educational and workplace advancement. A study conducted by CAEL indicates that PLA contributes positively to degree completion among adult learners. Specifically, students with PLA credit were more likely to earn their degree than those without it, regardless of institutional level, size, or control (Wertheim, 2010). These results support the aforementioned efforts to increase the number of adults with postsecondary degrees or credentials, and in many cases PLA includes the use of standardized exams or student portfolios. Best practices in PLA can be found in many institutions including LaGuardia Community College (http://www.laguardia.cuny.edu/home), Thomas Edison State College (http://www.tesc.edu), Western International University (http://west.edu), and Excelsior College (http://www.excelsior.edu).

STRUCTURING ASSESSMENT EFFORTS FOR ADULT LEARNERS

The purposes of assessing adult learners are much the same as they are for traditional-aged students. Assessment of adult learners is conducted to meet calls for accountability, as well as to provide faculty and staff with the necessary information to determine if student learning outcomes and program goals have been met. Although the purposes of assessment may be the same, assessment efforts should not necessarily be structured in the same manner for adult learners as for traditional-aged students. Grounding assessment efforts in an adult learning theory framework can provide for a more robust and appropriate approach to understanding and capturing student achievement (Kasworm & Marineau, 1997).

The complex and varied experiences of adult learners bring unique challenges to the practice of learning assessment among adult students (Kasworm & Marineau, 1997; Rose & Leahy, 1997). Many adult learners have attended more than one college or university, and formal education is interspersed with work and life experiences that contribute to practical application of theory, contribute to a deeper understanding of concepts, and can positively affect critical thinking skills. Traditionally, a great deal of emphasis is placed on constructing an appropriate structure for assessment efforts including the use of pre- and post-tests. However, lock-step assessment protocols may be inappropriate for adult learners and their programs because adult learners do not complete their college experience in a linear fashion (Borden, 2004; Kasworm & Marineau, 1997). Assessment practitioners and program coordinators should expect that adult student learning will come from a variety of sources, and students will bring a wealth of curricular, cocurricular, work, and life experiences that contribute to their achievement of program and general learning outcomes (Rose & Leahy, 1997). Performance-based assessment strategies are well-suited for adult learner programs as are assessment strategies that afford students the opportunity to demonstrate the connection and application of content knowledge to practical experiences and actual situations (Kasworm & Marineau, 1997). Leaders of adult-learner programs should also consider implementing rigorous processes to track student progress and including competency-based assessments as part of their overall efforts toward a culture of evidence (Borden, 2004).

QUICK TIP

Application cards allow students to assess their own understanding of a concept by writing down at least one possible real-world application for the idea(s) they just learned (Angelo & Cross, 1993).

It is important for student affairs educators to acknowledge the student learner when choosing assessment methods. Anderson (2001) explained that the selection or development of assessment instruments must account for diverse learning styles and cultural differences. Anderson noted that while learning can be modified, students have preferred styles based on how they receive, perceive, organize, process, and understand information. For that reason, student affairs educators may choose to administer a learning styles preference inventory. Data from such an assessment can assist student affairs educators in their selection or development of measures and simultaneously help adult learners reflect on their own learning styles.

Adult learners benefit greatly from feedback (Knowles, 1980; Lieb, 1991; Russell, n.d.). Using formative assessment with adult learners is particularly beneficial to the student and the assessment process. Formative assessment takes place throughout the course or initiative "with the purpose of providing feedback that can be used to modify, shape, and improve the program (or performance)" (Palomba & Banta, 1999, p. 7). Adult learners often seek such formative feedback and want to incorporate it into subsequent assignments and work products. Assessment practitioners and program coordinators should consider implementing more formative assessment in programs for adult learners to increase student motivation and benefits. Formative assessment results, sometimes thought of as "temperature checks," also provide student affairs professionals with valuable information that can be used to make immediate improvements to programs and services. All too often the focus is on summative assessment because of pressures of accountability and accreditation. Summative assessment takes place at the conclusion of the course or program and makes "judgments about its quality or worth compared to previously defined standards for performance" (Palomba & Banta, 1999, p. 8). Both formative and summative assessments should be included in adult-learner assessment models to meet the needs of the individual adult learner as well as internal and external stakeholders. In addition, including a self-assessment component in the assessment process provides adult learners the opportunity to reflect on, participate in, and own their acquisition of knowledge and skills (Kasworm & Marineau, 1997). Adult learners often self-assess in work, volunteer roles, and personal relationships. This technique can motivate them in the classroom and provide an opportunity to engage in their own learning process (Beaman, 1998).

USE OF TECHNOLOGY TO ADVANCE ADULT LEARNING

A culture of evidence in adult learning programs can be enhanced by the implementation and use of technology. However, the use of software or hardware to advance student learning and a culture of evidence is beneficial only if it is the right tool for the job and that tool is used correctly. There are several areas where technology can be used to build and maintain a culture of evidence, including artifact collection, progress tracking, information sharing, and assessment of student learning (Shay & Sweetland, 2010).

Portfolios, including electronic portfolios, have been suggested as a way to assemble and evaluate student work products to determine if learning outcomes have been met in particular courses, within a program of study, or as part of prior learning assessment. There is much to consider when selecting and implementing an e-portfolio system. Faculty and staff working with adult learning programs should collaborate with others on campus, including staff in technology services or institutional research, effectiveness, or assessment, so as not to duplicate efforts. E-portfolio systems can be purchased from a commercial vendor, built from open source software, or developed locally. Each option has advantages and disadvantages and each campus must carefully consider the available options and make a decision that fits within the institutional needs and constraints. Cambridge (2010) offered best practices in the use of e-portfolios and assessment.

Many campuses use software tools to manage the assessment or institutional effectiveness processes within academic and administrative units. Similar to e-portfolio systems, assessment management systems can be purchased from a commercial vendor, built from open source software, or developed locally. Often these systems are managed by offices of institutional research, effectiveness, or assessment. Adult learner programs should be active participants in campuswide assessment efforts and contribute assessment reports as necessary. Software that is readily available on most campuses such as Microsoft Access and Excel can also be used to track assessment efforts and provide progress reports for goals and outcomes. Offices that provide services to adult learners may find that using "standard" software in new ways will facilitate a culture of evidence. In addition, collaborative software products such as Microsoft SharePoint can be used to collect and disseminate assessment results. Using collaborative tools can strengthen a culture of evidence by facilitating the use of information for program improvement.

Leaders of adult learner programs and initiatives should proceed cautiously when selecting software systems designed to enhance assessment and evaluation processes. Technology cannot and does not replace the key components that contribute to a culture of evidence such as leadership, collaboration, and a focus on continual improvement.

Technology can also be used to deliver curriculum and assess students' skills and knowledge. Distance education has been a part of higher learning for decades and has been transformed by the widespread use of Internet-based instruction. Many adult learners have benefited from the ability to take all or some courses online as they pursue their degree. For example, Thomas Edison State College was founded by the state of New Jersey in 1972 specifically to provide adult learners with the opportunity to earn a postsecondary degree and offers online courses in addition to prior learning assessment and credit by examination. Western Governors University was founded in 1997 by the governors of 19 states as an online university offering competency-based academic programs. The use of online learning has enabled many adult learners to earn their degrees while managing work and family obligations.

More recently, massive open online courses (MOOCs) have been the focus of much attention in higher education. Anyone with Internet access can enroll in a MOOC, some of which enroll tens of thousands of students. Institutions such as San Jose State University in California and foundations such as the Lumina Foundation are piloting efforts to leverage MOOCs as a credit-bearing experience that will bring students closer to completing their degrees (Masterson, 2013). The impact of MOOCs on higher education, learning outcomes, and degree completion remains to be seen, but it is clear that technology provides faculty and staff in higher education with numerous opportunities to engage students in learning opportunities.

ILLUSTRATIONS OF IMPLEMENTATION

Tallahassee Community College (https://www.tcc.fl.edu) used disaggregated learning outcomes results to identify a group of students whose academic and social backgrounds did not adequately prepare them for college-level coursework. The institution emphasized readiness and academic achievement as key institutional priorities and implemented a program of individual learning plans to help students prepare for and succeed inside and beyond the classroom (McClenney, McClenney, & Peterson, 2007).

Excelsior College has a history of incorporating a variety of techniques in its assessment framework. Excelsior was founded in 1971 as Regents College, serves more than 50,000 adult learners each year, and offers an outcomes-based curriculum. Over the 40-year history of the institution, faculty

 IN THE SPOTLIGHT

Adult Learner Programs (ALP) at Kennesaw State University (KSU) exemplifies a culture of evidence because it provides model services and programs for adult learners. KSU is located in Kennesaw, Georgia, near Atlanta. In the 2012–2013 academic year, KSU enrolled approximately 24,600 students, 92% in an undergraduate program. Adult learners comprised 47% of the student body during that same year. ALP provides comprehensive academic support programs (mentoring, tutoring, career services, and child care resources) to help adult learners reach their education goals. ALP staff members have built a culture of evidence over many years and their approach to gathering and using data has evolved. Initial assessment and evaluation efforts consisted primarily of anecdotal evidence, student surveys, and focus groups. These efforts were successful and results of surveys were used to improve services and programs for ALP users; however, the staff wanted to learn more about the students who used their services. ALP began asking students to swipe their ID card as they entered the center for services and programs and subsequently analyzed the data that was extracted from the student information system. Specifically, ALP learned that freshmen used the center least often while seniors used it most often. This information allowed ALP to target its marketing efforts accordingly. ALP has also assessed the services of its tutoring center and conducted studies comparing student persistence among students who have used ALP services and those who have not (Todd Powell, personal communication, May 31, 2013).

have used nationally standardized exams such as the ACT COMP, locally developed standardized exams, licensure exams such as the NCLEX-RN, portfolios, oral exams, and performance assessments (Peinovich, Nesler, & Thomas, 1997). More recently, Excelsior uses instruments such as the National Survey of Student Engagement and the ETS Proficiency Profile. The institution communicates its student leaning outcomes and results of various assessment measures through the Institutional Effectiveness Plan and Institutional Assessment Plan for Student Learning, both of which are published online.

BUILDING A CULTURE OF EVIDENCE

Leaders of adult learner programs and initiatives may be asking themselves, "How do I know if a culture of evidence exists in my unit or at my institution?" The three exercises at the end of this module can be helpful in determining the current culture of evidence as well as identifying the desired culture of evidence. Faculty and staff responsible for adult learner programs can use these exercises as part of a professional development activity or strategic planning process to develop or strengthen the use of hard data to make program improvements.

Building a culture of evidence requires perseverance and commitment on the part of those leading adult-learner programs. The key components of leadership, commitment to the assessment process, and intentional use of the results must be developed over time within the context of the campus culture. As these components are refined and the culture of evidence grows, an increasing number of faculty and staff will use data to make informed decisions and improve programs, ultimately leading to increased success of adult learners.

APPLY THE CONCEPTS

Exercise 9.1—What Does It Mean to Have a Culture of Evidence?

Directions: Using a think-pair-share strategy, each person should complete the following worksheet independently. Then the group should share responses.

At Your Institution	
Describe the assessment activities within the division of student affairs and across the institution.	Describe the assessment activities of adult learner programs and initiatives.
Defining Your Culture of Evidence	
Describe your unit's current culture of evidence.	Provide your vision of a culture of evidence.
Closing the Gap	
What are the gaps between the current culture of evidence and the desired culture of evidence?	State possible solutions to close the gaps between the current and desired cultures of evidence.

Discussion: In what ways would adult learner programs be transformed by a culture of evidence? How would a culture of evidence affect the vision, mission, and goals of the division of student affairs? Of the institution?

Source: Busby & Robinson, 2012, p. 53. Adapted with permission.

APPLY THE CONCEPTS

Exercise 9.2—Navigating Barriers and Opportunities

Directions: Using a think-pair-share strategy, each person should answer the following questions independently. Then the group should share responses.

1. What are the barriers to developing a culture of evidence in your unit?
2. Which of these barriers can you directly influence?
3. What opportunities exist on your campus or in your division that could enhance a culture of evidence among adult learner programs?
4. How can your unit leverage available structures or opportunities to develop a culture of evidence?
5. Are there any opportunities to institutionalize current practices to foster a culture of evidence?

Discussion: How can you minimize the barriers that exist? How can you prevent new barriers from developing? How can you maximize the opportunities to enhance the culture of evidence? How can you promote additional opportunities in the future?

Source: Busby & Robinson, 2012, p. 54. Adapted with permission.

APPLY THE CONCEPTS

Exercise 9.3—Culture of Evidence Readiness Review

Directions: Check all the statements that apply to adult learner programs. Provide examples, where applicable, of how the statements are enacted in your unit. This checklist is not designed to be a test; rather, it should be used to facilitate discussion and reflection on the current culture of evidence.

_____ Unit/office has a vision and mission statement.

_____ Division of Student Affairs is committed to building a culture of evidence.

_____ Leader of adult learner programs is committed to building a culture of evidence.

_____ Staff members are committed to building a culture of evidence.

_____ Staff members are expected to use credible evidence to inform decisions.

_____ Unit/office has appropriate outcomes for programs and services.

_____ Unit outcomes are linked to broader division and institutional student learning outcomes/program goals.

_____ Programs and services are linked directly to outcomes.

_____ Unit/office has a practical and sustainable assessment plan.

_____ Assessment is conducted in a systematic manner.

_____ Data gathered and used are credible.

_____ Assessment results are communicated appropriately to stakeholders.

_____ Changes and improvements are connected to evidence-based decisions.

_____ Staff members use data in decision-making processes.

_____ Staff members have the necessary skills and knowledge to execute assessment.

_____ Assessment-related professional development opportunities are available for staff.

_____ Staff members are recognized for their assessment efforts.

_____ Unit/office celebrates and rewards activities that promote a culture of evidence.

_____ Partnerships exist with other campus units to gather and use data.

_____ Resources are available to conduct assessment activities.

_____ Best practices are used.

_____ New programs and initiatives include assessment and evaluation.

Source: Busby & Robinson, 2012, p. 55. Adapted with permission.

RESOURCES

Organizations

Association for Nontraditional Students in Higher Education (ANTSHE) (http://www.myantshe.org)

ANTSHE is an international partnership of students, academic professionals, institutions, and organizations whose mission is to encourage and coordinate support, education, and advocacy for the adult learner.

Council for Adult and Experiential Learning (CAEL) (http://www.cael.org/home)

CAEL is a nonprofit that works at all levels within the higher education, public, and private sectors to make it easier for people to get the education and training they need.

Instruments

Adult Learner Inventory (ALI) (https://www.noellevitz.com/student-retention-solutions/satisfaction-priorities-assessments/adult-learner-inventory)

The ALI is a Web-based satisfaction assessment administered by Noel-Levitz designed for adult students completing undergraduate programs.

Institutional Self-Assessment Survey (ISAS) (http://www.cael.org/alfi)

The ISAS evaluates a wide range of institutional activities, policies, and practices designed for adult learners.

Community College Survey of Student Engagement (CCSSE) (http://www.ccsse.org)

The CCSSE evaluates the curricular and cocurricular experiences of community college students.

Conferences

NASPA Annual Conference (http://www.naspa.org/events)

The NASPA Annual Conference is a 4-day gathering of student affairs professionals who come together to learn, grow, and be inspired. It includes panel discussions, poster sessions, concurrent sessions, and workshops that cover topics critical to the work of student affairs professionals.

NASPA Assessment and Persistence Conference (http://www.naspa.org/events)

This conference is designed to promote student learning and success by strengthening assessment, improving educational quality, and developing intentional persistence programming.

National Institute on the Assessment of Adult Learning (http://www.tesc.edu/national-institute)

The institute is an annual conference hosted by Thomas Edison State College with a focus on assessment of adult learning.

ANTSHE Conference (http://www.myantshe.org/ccpe.kennesaw.edu/antshe)

Annual meeting of the Association for Nontraditional Students in Higher Education (ANTSHE), with a focus on addressing challenges facing nontraditional students and programming designed to promote adult learner success.

REFERENCES

American Council on Education. (n.d.). *Credits to credentials.* Retrieved from http://www.acenet. edu/news-room/Pages/Credits-to-Credentials.aspx

Anderson, J. (2001, March). Tailoring assessment to student learning styles: A model for diverse populations. *AAHE Bulletin.* Retrieved from http://www.aahea.org/aahea/articles/styles2001.htm

Angelo, T. A. (1999). Doing assessment as if learning matters most. *AAHE Bulletin, 51*(9), 3–6.

Angelo, T. A., & Cross, K. P. (1993). *Classroom assessment techniques.* San Francisco, CA: Jossey-Bass.

Ashford, E. (2011, February 14). Initial ATD colleges build foundation for a "culture of evidence." *Community College Times.* Retrieved from http://www.communitycollegetimes.com/Pages/Academic-Programs/Initial-ATD-colleges.aspx

Askov, E. N., Van Horn, B. L., & Carman, P. S. (1997). Assessment in adult basic education programs. In A. D. Rose & M. A. Leahy (Eds.), *Assessing adult learning in diverse settings: Current issues and approaches* (New directions for adult and continuing education, No. 75, pp. 65–74). San Francisco, CA: Jossey-Bass.

Banta, T. W. (Ed.). (2004). *Hallmarks of effective outcomes assessment.* San Francisco, CA: Jossey-Bass.

Banta, T. W., Jones, E. A., & Black, K. E. (2009). *Designing effective assessment: Principles and profiles of good practice.* San Francisco, CA: Jossey-Bass.

Beaman, R. (1998). The urgent . . . even loud, andragogy! Alternative assessment for adult learners. *Innovative Higher Education, 23*(1), 47–59.

Bloom, B. (1956). *Taxonomy of educational objectives: The cognitive domain.* New York, NY: Donald McKay.

Borden, V. M. H. (2004). Accommodating student swirl: When traditional students are no longer the tradition. *Change, 36*(2), 10–17.

Busby, K., & Robinson, B. G. (2012). Developing the leadership team to establish and maintain a culture of evidence. In M. M. Culp & G. J. Dungy (Eds.), *Building a culture of evidence in student affairs: A guide for leaders and practitioners.* Washington, DC: National Association of Student Personnel Administrators.

Cambridge, D. (2010). *E-portfolios for lifelong learning and assessment.* San Francisco, CA: Jossey-Bass.

Carnevale, A. P., Smith, N., & Strohl, J. (2013). *Recovery: Job growth and education requirements through 2020.* Retrieved from http://cew.georgetown.edu/publications/reports

Council for Adult and Experiential Learning. (n.d.). *What is prior learning assessment?* Retrieved from http://www.cael.org/Whom-We-Serve/Colleges-and-Universities/Prior-Learning-Assessment-Services

Culp, M. M. (2012). Starting the culture of evidence journey. In M. M. Culp & G. J. Dungy (Eds.), *Building a culture of evidence in student affairs: A guide for leaders and practitioners.* Washington, DC: National Association of Student Personnel Administrators.

DeFao, D. J. (2012, June). *Finding the "I" in TEAM: Assessing student learning in academic support programs.* Paper presented at the 2012 National Institute on the Assessment of Adult Learning. Atlantic City, NJ. Retrieved from http://www.tesc.edu/national-institute/2012-Presentations.cfm

Dillman, D. A., Smyth, J. D., & Christian, L. M. (2008). *Internet, mail, and mixed-mode surveys: The tailored design method, third edition.* Hoboken, NJ: John Wiley & Sons.

Gagne, R. M. (1984). Learning outcomes and their effects: Useful categories of human performance. *American Psychologist, 39,* 377–385.

James Madison University. (n.d.). *Dictionary of student outcome assessment.* Retrieved from http://people.jmu.edu/yangsx/Search.asp?searchText=outcomes+assessment&Option=Term

Kasworm, C. E., & Marineau, C. A. (1997). Principles for assessment of adult learning. In A. D. Rose & M. A. Leahy (Eds.), *Assessing adult learning in diverse settings: Current issues and approaches* (New directions for adult and continuing education, No. 75, pp. 5–16). San Francisco, CA: Jossey-Bass.

Knowles, M. S. (1980). *The modern practice of adult education: From pedagogy to andragogy* (2nd ed.). Englewood Cliffs, NJ: Prentice Hall/Cambridge.

Krathwohl, D. R., Bloom, B. S., & Masia, B. B. (1964). *Taxonomy of educational objectives: The classification of educational goals.* White Plains, NY: Longman.

Lieb, S. (1991). *Principles of adult learning.* Retrieved from http://www.lindenwood.edu/education/andragogy/andragogy/2011/Lieb_1991.pdf

Lumina Foundation. (n.d.). *Goal 2025.* Retrieved from http://www.luminafoundation.org/goal_2025.html

Martin, E. (2013). Helping community college students "connect the dots" of their college experience with e-portfolios. *Peer Review, 15*(2), 14–15.

Masterson, K. (2013, March). Giving MOOCs some credit. *The Presidency.* Retrieved from http://www.acenet.edu/the-presidency/columns-and-features/Pages/Giving-MOOCs-Some-Credit.aspx

McClenney, K. M., McClenney, B. N., & Peterson, G. F. (2007). A culture of evidence: What is it? Do we have one? *Planning for Higher Education, 35*(3), 26–33.

MDC. (2006). *Increasing student success at community colleges: Institutional change in achieving the dream community colleges count.* Indianapolis, IN: Lumina Foundation for Education.

Morgan, D. L., & Krueger, R. A. (1998). *The focus group kit.* Thousand Oaks, CA: Sage.

National Conference of State Legislatures. (2013). Retrieved from http://www.ncsl.org/issues-research/educ/performance-funding.aspx

Palomba, C. A. & Banta, T. W. (1999). *Assessment essentials: Planning, implementing, and improving assessment in higher education.* San Francisco, CA: Jossey-Bass.

Peinovich, P. E., Nesler, M. S., & Thomas, T. S. (1997). A model of developing an outcomes assessment plan and the Regents College assessment framework. In A. D. Rose & M. A. Leahy (Eds.), *Assessing adult learning in diverse settings: Current issues and approaches* (New directions for adult and continuing education, No. 75, pp. 55–64). San Francisco, CA: Jossey-Bass.

Pusser, B., Breneman, D. W., Gansneder, B. M., Kohl, K. J., Levin, J. S., Milam, J. H., & Turner, S. E. (2007). *Returning to learning: Adults' success in college is key to America's future.* Retrieved from http://www.luminafoundation.org/publications/ReturntolearningApril2007.pdf

Rose, A. D., & Leahy, M. A. (1997). Assessment themes and issues. In A. D. Rose & M. A. Leahy (Eds.), *Assessing adult learning in diverse settings: Current issues and approaches* (New directions for adult and continuing education, No. 75, pp. 97–100). San Francisco, CA: Jossey-Bass.

Russell, S. S. (n.d.). *An overview of adult learning processes.* Retrieved from http://www.medscape.com/viewarticle/547417_2

Rutschow, E. Z., Richburg-Hayes, L., Brock, T., Orr, G., Cerna, O., Cullinan, D., Kerrigan, M. R., Jenkins, D., Gooden, S., & Martin, K. (2011). *Turning the tide: Five years of achieving the dream in community colleges.* Retrieved from http://www.achievingthedream.org/sites/default/files/resources/Turning_the_Tide.pdf

Seagraves, B., & Dean, L. A. (2010). Conditions supporting a culture of evidence in student affairs divisions at small colleges and universities. *Journal of Student Affairs Research and Practice, 47*(3), 307–324.

Shay, P. K., & Sweetland, Y. (2010). *Technology: A pillar for strengthening and sustaining assessment culture.* Paper presented at the 2010 National Institute on the Assessment of Adult Learning, Atlantic City, NJ. Retrieved from http://www.tesc.edu/national-institute/2010-Presentations.cfm

Southern Regional Education Board. (2010). *A smart move in tough times: How SREB states can strengthen adult learning and the work force.* Retrieved from http://publications.sreb.org/2010/10E06_Smart_Move.pdf

Suskie, L. (2009). *Assessing student learning: A common sense guide* (2nd ed.). San Francisco, CA: Jossey-Bass.

U.S. Census Bureau. (2012). *Current population survey, 2012.* Retrieved from http://www.census. gov/cps

U.S. Department of Education. (2011). *Meeting the nation's 2020 goal: State targets for increasing the number and percentage of college graduates with degrees.* Retrieved from http://www.whitehouse. gov/sites/default/files/completion_state_by_state.pdf

Wertheim, J. (2010). *Exploring prior learning assessment and individual learner outcomes – Findings from a new CAEL study.* Paper presented at the 2010 National Institute on the Assessment of Adult Learning, Atlantic City, NJ. Retrieved from http://www.tesc.edu/national-institute/2010-Presentations.cfm

West Virginia Higher Education Policy Commission. (n.d.). *West Virginia higher education report card.* Retrieved from http://wvhepcnew.wvnet.edu/index.php?option=com_content&task=view&id=23&Itemid=0

Zemke, R., & Zemke, S. (1995, June). Adult learning: What do we know for sure? *Training 32*(6), 31–34, 36, 38, 40.

MODULE 10

The West Virginia Story
A Case Study in Improving Access and Success for Adult Learners

Sarah Beasley, Susan Gardner, and Tammy Johnson

ABSTRACT

This module describes how the West Virginia Higher Education Policy Commission and the West Virginia Community and Technical College System partnered with NASPA–Student Affairs Administrators in Higher Education and the Lumina Foundation to launch *DegreeNow,* an innovative approach to increasing adult learner access and success in public colleges and universities across the state. The module also outlines the major strategies student affairs professionals in West Virginia used to bring about change, shares what college and university student affairs professionals learned from the experience, and examines the impact *DegreeNow* had on higher education in West Virginia. Finally, the module offers examples of changes occurring at individual institutions across the state as a result of *DegreeNow*: changes that strengthened the state's commitment to adult learners and improved adult learner enrollment and completion rates.

WEST VIRGINIA'S STORY

In 2010, the West Virginia Higher Education Policy Commission (HEPC), West Virginia Community and Technical College System (CTCS), and NASPA–Student Affairs Administrators in Higher Education received a grant from the Lumina Foundation to assist West Virginia in increasing the number of adult learners earning a postsecondary credential. The *DegreeNow* initiative targeted adults with some earned college credit but no degree and focused on enhancing student and academic services for adult learners. In year 2 of the grant, the HEPC and the CTCS also partnered with the Council for Adult and Experiential Learning (CAEL) to strengthen the delivery of instructional services. Over the past 5 years, overall adult (age 25+) enrollment in West Virginia public higher education institutions has increased by slightly more than 18%. Adult degree completion at the associate's level has increased by almost 33% over the course of the *DegreeNow* grant, while adult degree completion at the bachelor's level has increased by approximately 18% during that same time period.

Demographics

Higher education professionals in West Virginia face many of the access and success challenges their peers across the nation face. In addition, high poverty rates within the state correlate to lower college-going rates in many counties, and too many students who do enroll drop out before degree completion. Rural residents in West Virginia are often geographically isolated and less likely to attend college than their urban and suburban counterparts. West Virginia also has a higher percentage of veterans per capita than any other state (http://www.veteranshistory.wvu.edu), and effectively serving these students is a top priority.

Economics

For West Virginia, like many states, it is an economic imperative to increase the number of college-educated citizens. In 2010, Georgetown University's Center on Education and the Workforce concluded that West Virginia must add 20,000 citizens with postsecondary credentials by 2018 to sustain its economy. By 2018, 49% of West Virginia jobs will require some type of postsecondary education compared with 63% nationally (Carnevale, Smith, & Strohl, 2010). However, West Virginia cannot rely solely on traditional students to increase the number of college-educated citizens, because its high school population has been in decline since 2008 (Western Interstate Commission for Higher Education [WICHE], 2012). WICHE (2012) confirmed that declining high school populations is a national phenomenon and suggests that most states are entering a period characterized by a "modest decline in the number of [high school] graduates" (p. xi).

Higher Education System

To better understand *DegreeNow,* it is important to recognize the context in which the project evolved. West Virginia has a 4-year public college and university system and a 2-year public community and technical college system, each with its own coordinating board. The two coordinating boards

(West Virginia Higher Education Policy Commission and the West Virginia Community and Technical College System) and their staff frequently collaborate on projects and share information; they also share some staff members. Prior to 2004, however, the 2- and 4-year systems were combined. The separation of the two systems, particularly at the campus level, was at times a contentious process involving the division of resources, facilities, administrations, faculty, and staff. Therefore, reestablishing collaboration among higher education professionals remains a priority for the HEPC and the CTCS.

Both systems have flexible, statewide degree programs aimed at adult learners: the Regents Bachelor of Arts (RBA) and the Board of Governors Associate in Applied Science (BOG AAS). These programs offer baccalaureate and associate-level coursework in compressed formats and at convenient times to accommodate adult students. In conjunction with on-campus classes, many courses are offered online or in hybrid formats. Both systems allow students to receive credits for prior college-level learning. The 4-year institutions coordinate the RBA and the 2-year colleges manage the BOG AAS; campus coordinators for both programs regularly meet to discuss common issues and initiatives. Since *DegreeNow* began, enrollment in these programs has grown by more than 30%.

Student Affairs

In examining the status of student affairs in West Virginia, it is critical to note that the state's chapter of NASPA, called WVASPA, had been dormant for a number of years, depriving student affairs professionals of opportunities to network, share ideas and best practices, and engage in state-level initiatives. This changed dramatically as *DegreeNow* brought together student affairs professionals from across the state for a series of Train-the-Trainer workshops; Train-the-Trainer graduates were then paired to lead Leveraging *DegreeNow* workshops.

 IN THE SPOTLIGHT

"An increasing number of adult learners are retooling or changing careers because of the economic downturn. This creates a unique opportunity to educate a growing segment of the population that is motivated and committed to education. To meet the needs of adult learners, colleges and universities need to research best practices and conduct focus groups. On too many occasions, colleges and universities try to address the needs of adult students through the lens of the traditional college student. In most cases, this does not work. Adult learners have jobs, families, and responsibilities within the community. Colleges and universities must recognize these facts and design programs, processes, and support services that truly meet the needs of their adult students." —Brian O. Hemphill, president, West Virginia State University (personal communication, June 5, 2013)

THE TRAIN-THE-TRAINER APPROACH: BUILDING CAPACITY IN STUDENT AFFAIRS

Marguerite Culp, a national consultant with extensive experience as both a faculty member and a chief student affairs officer (CSAO), led NASPA's portion of the grant. To better understand higher education in West Virginia and the challenges associated with implementing *DegreeNow*, Culp met HEPC representatives and academic and student affairs leaders from West Virginia colleges and universities in March 2011 to set goals, develop guiding principles, agree on the best approach for NASPA's portion of the grant, and identify outcomes and assessment strategies. These conversations produced realistic guidelines for what eventually became a Train-the-Trainer approach to improving nonclassroom support services for adult learners and building a culture of evidence in West Virginia student affairs.

In 2011 and 2012, the West Virginia HEPC and the CTCS sponsored a series of 3-day Train-the-Trainer workshops that were attended by more than 60 state higher education leaders. Led by Culp, workshop participants completed a detailed SWOT (strengths, weaknesses, opportunities, and threats) analysis of higher education in West Virginia, assessed the student affairs climate on their own campuses and throughout the state, and evaluated their readiness to support *DegreeNow*. Participants also completed modules designed to increase their knowledge and skill sets in four essential areas: understanding the goals of *DegreeNow*; designing and implementing nonclassroom support services for adult learners; building and sustaining partnerships between academic and student affairs; and creating a culture of evidence in student affairs. Each module provided opportunities to apply theories and research results to real-life situations and offered numerous examples of best practices and processes.

Train-the-Trainer graduates became the nucleus for change on individual campuses and across the state. On their home campuses, graduates designed and implemented new support programs and services for adult learners, strengthened or redirected existing programs and services, and examined current processes to determine their impact on persistence and graduation rates for adult learners. Graduates collaborated with NASPA's consultant to design Leveraging *DegreeNow*, an 8-hour workshop to help student affairs staff members and nonclassroom support service personnel better meet the needs of adult learners. More than 180 people, including faculty members, completed the workshops led by teams of Train-the-Trainer graduates. Follow-up assessment activities documented how Leveraging *DegreeNow* participants used what they learned to implement change on their campuses. Both the Train-the-Trainer and Leveraging *DegreeNow* workshops provided participants with workbooks and leaders with a detailed instructor's guide. NASPA developed the workbooks and the guides with significant input from Train-the-Trainer graduates and has converted both to online formats. Student affairs professionals across West Virginia will be able to use the archived material to continue to build the state's capacity to serve adult learners.

BUILDING A CULTURE OF EVIDENCE IN WEST VIRGINIA STUDENT AFFAIRS

Train-the-Trainer graduates returned to their institutions and used strategies they learned during the workshop to assess the strengths and weaknesses of individual staff members, the student affairs area, and the institution. It soon became apparent that Train-the-Trainer graduates needed additional training and support in all areas related to building a culture of evidence. Culp and Gwendolyn Jordan Dungy, then executive director of NASPA, agreed to create a tutorial to help student affairs leaders and practitioners strengthen their assessment skill sets. The result was *Building a Culture of Evidence in Student Affairs: A Guide for Leaders and Practitioners* (Culp & Dungy, 2012), a tutorial that NASPA later made available to all of its members. To increase everyone's comfort level with using the tutorial, *DegreeNow* sponsored a 1-day workshop attended by more than 130 West Virginia higher education professionals, led by Culp. The interactive workshop incorporated strategies important to both academic and student affairs and began the process of intentionally encouraging collaboration between the two groups.

The renewed focus on the assessment of nonclassroom support services produced a variety of responses at colleges and universities across West Virginia. Leaders at West Liberty University developed a plan to help staff members increase their knowledge of and ability to create a culture of evidence. West Virginia University (WVU) dedicated significant staff time to increasing awareness of the need to design and implement cultures of evidence. WVU also implemented a 1-hour workshop to help student affairs professionals develop learning and program outcomes as well as assessment measures. Senior-level administrators across the state began encouraging—and arranging for—staff members to participate in culture of evidence webinars and assessment workshops.

In addition to the individual institutional initiatives, student affairs professionals revitalized the once defunct state association, WVASPA, and hosted meetings and conferences across the state that focused on the need to build a culture of evidence within student affairs. With the permission of the West Virginia HEPC and CTCS, NASPA shared *Building a Culture of Evidence in Student Affairs* with student affairs leaders and practitioners across the country.

DegreeNow and the CAEL Principles

DegreeNow focused everyone's attention on adult learners and created a climate for change across the state and within individual institutions. CAEL's Principles of Effectiveness for Serving Adult Learners offer a convenient framework for examining these changes. As outlined in Module 2, these principles include:

1. Outreach
2. Life and Career Planning
3. Financing
4. Assessment of Learning Outcomes
5. Teaching-Learning Process
6. Student Support Systems
7. Technology
8. Strategic Partnerships
9. Transitions (CAEL, 2014)

Because student affairs professionals used technology to address the other eight CAEL principles, this module does not feature a stand-alone section on technology. Instead, it incorporates technology into each section. One important observation is necessary at this point: Although this section is organized around individual CAEL principles, the most significant lesson West Virginia student affairs professionals learned while implementing these principles is that their impact is cumulative and interactive. Making changes associated with one principle frequently leads to changes that support other principles. Significant changes in an institution's culture occur when the institution addresses all nine principles, not just one or two.

Outreach

An important aspect of enrolling adult students in degree completion programs, outreach involves identifying and educating potential students about existing options and degree programs. Traditionally, the first step in enrolling a new student is recruitment or prospect generation. West Virginia discovered that recruiting adult students provided unique challenges to enrollment management professionals, including but not limited to:

- Obtaining accurate data to guide the development of recruitment plans specific to this demographic.
- Developing creative strategies for identifying potential students, because this population typically does not exist in one central location, such as a high school or college.
- Realizing that productive recruitment of adult students typically hinged on campaigns and communications directed toward specific populations targeted for certain academic programs or opportunities.
- Dealing with the reality that many adult students identify themselves only at the application stage, not by completing online or in-person interest cards or by attending open houses.

Two West Virginia institutions, Concord University (http://www.concord.edu/academics/rba-program) and Marshall University (http://www.marshall.edu/rba), reached out to adults who at one time had been enrolled in their institutions; as a result, both experienced significant gains in adult learner enrollments. Partnerships with employers granting full or partial reimbursement of tuition were particularly effective in generating interest in higher education. Even mass mailings, billboards, and other general advertisements (which are typically not highly effective recruitment strategies for traditional students) generated adults' interest in new or newly relevant programs. The state of West Virginia cross-referenced the names of adults who had attended a college or university in the state with current Department of Motor Vehicles records and sent letters or postcards to those individuals encouraging them to return to college. Many West Virginia institutions learned that one of the most influential factors in an adult's decision to enroll at a particular institution is word of mouth. If an institution launched a new program or recruitment effort without first verifying that the resources were in place to support that effort, dissatisfied prospective students would soon share their negative experiences with others, and the recruitment effort would falter. These experiences offer two significant lessons: (1) Partnerships between enrollment management professionals and everyone else on campus are essential, and (2) Attention must be paid to the support service infrastructure when launching outreach initiatives.

Websites dedicated to adult learner programs were very beneficial in conveying needed information to prospective nontraditional students. The *DegreeNow* initiative produced the expansion of the

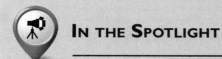

IN THE SPOTLIGHT

"Busy adults contemplating a return to college will quickly lose interest if they have to navigate the campus or website in search of answers. It is imperative that institutions provide a 'one-stop-shop' experience staffed by individuals who can provide answers or know where to direct students to get answers." —Mark Stotler, director of academic programming and statewide RBA/BOG AAS coordinator, West Virginia HEPC (personal communication, September, 26, 2013)

adult learner section on the College Foundation of West Virginia (http://www.cfwv.com) website, a statewide college access portal that includes financial aid resources for adults, information about the statewide RBA and BOG AAS adult degree programs, and a link to each institution's individual site for adult learners. Colleges and universities across the state used three principles to assess the effectiveness of existing or new websites created especially for prospective adult students: The sites must be easy to navigate, provide step-by-step instructions for students who wish to enroll, and include contact information for the person or office that serves as the dedicated contact for adult learners.

Life and Career Planning

Frequently, adult learners are more motivated than first-time freshmen to work not only toward degree completion but also toward gainful employment. Adult students typically return to college to earn a higher wage with their current employer or to train in a new field after being dislocated or becoming unemployed. This makes life and career planning an essential component of serving adult learners.

In most cases, traditional students come to college without ever writing a résumé, participating in a formal job interview or working in a business environment. Adult learners, on the other hand, typically come to campus with these experiences and are less likely to respond to traditional career planning approaches. Many institutions such as New River Community and Technical College used this information to partner with faculty to design and deliver career and life planning services targeted to adult learners. These partnerships produced an online career assessment component for life management courses and information on career paths for BOG AAS graduates. In addition, New River expanded its career services workshops to include information on using social networking sites for job searches, obtaining introductions to potential employers, and strengthening résumés. New River decided to limit workshops to 30 minutes because adult learners have so many competing commitments; to use instant messaging to reach adult learners wherever they are—at work or at home; and to allow students to log on to Blackboard, a Web-based learning management system, and chat one-on-one with the director of career services from anywhere (http://www.newriver.edu).

Location presents a significant life–career challenge for West Virginia residents, many of whom are "place-bound" and prefer to continue their education or find employment close to home. This perceived lack of mobility adds a unique challenge for those who assist adult learners in finding gainful employment after graduation. Because West Virginia is primarily a rural state, most students drive an average of 50 minutes to get to work or take a class. Another life–career challenge involves helping West Virginia adults establish realistic goals and translate these goals into realistic salary expectations. West Virginia University at Parkersburg educates students about these realities and helps them to establish reasonable goals and expectations via an online portal with links to information about jobs in their field as well as salary ranges within their geographic area (http://www.onetonline.org).

Transitions

Arguably, the most important contact a prospective student makes is the initial contact with an institution. This is essential in establishing a positive relationship and in generating positive public opinion. Many prospective adult students are already debating whether or not to enroll in college; inadequate initial information may motivate them to reassess their decision or to consider another institution. This was one of the most important lessons that West Virginia colleges and universities learned during *DegreeNow;* as Table 10.1 demonstrates, however, it was not the only lesson related to transitions.

Table 10.1

Assisting Adult Learners With Transitions

Issue	Lesson learned
Substance counts	Adult learners ask substantive questions from the outset. Well-trained staff must answer these questions promptly, professionally, and correctly. A significant number of colleges and universities in West Virginia provide adult students with dedicated telephone numbers, e-mail addresses, and websites. A few offer live chat opportunities.
There is a common core of questions	The top questions are: • What degree or certificate will help me to _____, and how long will it take me to earn it? • I know I need more education, but I do not know what I want to study. How can the college help me? • What credits will transfer, and how can I translate my work and life experiences into additional credits? • What will college cost, and how can I pay for it? • How can I make sure that I do not waste any time taking courses that do not count toward my degree? West Virginia increased the probability that knowledgeable staff would respond to these questions by identifying adult learner contacts at most institutions and providing these contacts with additional information and training.
24/7 information and support is important	The number of adults who e-mail, text, and shop online is growing. These adults expect the same services from colleges and universities that they receive from major online retailers. *DegreeNow* motivated many institutions to establish new or strengthen existing websites, online processes, and online assistance for adult learners.
Maps are essential	Adults appreciate "to do" lists that outline the entire enrollment process. They also respond positively to checklists and flowcharts that guide them through the process of becoming a student. Like many West Virginia institutions, Marshall University developed the *New Student Checklist*, a website with a detailed list of the steps in the enrollment process (http://www.marshall.edu/newstudentchecklist).

Issue	Lesson learned
Streamlined beats complicated every time	Adults do not want "dumbed down" systems, but they do want systems that accomplish their goals efficiently and transparently. Many West Virginia colleges and universities launched process improvement initiatives to examine current policies and procedures, streamline them, and remove barriers to adult students.
Advising is essential	Advisors who work with adult learners need a well-developed toolkit that includes, but is not limited to, knowledge of the following: • Individual degree requirements and the idiosyncrasies of the course scheduling process (e.g., courses that are offered only once a year, or only in the evenings). • Licensing and certification requirements. • Constraints with which many adult learners deal (e.g., child care, family and work responsibilities). • Nontraditional course and degree options (e.g., online and distance learning). • How to review all the data and assist students to realistically estimate the time it will take to earn the degree or certificate they want. • How to connect adult learners with the on- and off-campus support services that they need to succeed.
Mentors matter	Adult students tend to seek out one or two mentors who can assist them throughout their academic life. Through *DegreeNow*, West Virginia offered workshops and seminars to strengthen the ability of academic advisors to establish a connection with and mentor adult learners.
Orientation helps adults navigate an unfamiliar world	Adults are often confused by academic terms and systems, and need assistance acclimating to both. Adult learners benefit from connecting with other adults who have similar interests and are in similar life circumstances. Well-designed orientation sessions, whether online or in person, help adults both understand their college or university and connect with other adult learners. A number of West Virginia campuses implemented or are in the process of designing online orientation options for adult learners.

Financing

For most prospective adult students, the cost of college is one of the primary factors in the decision to attend; they need to know the costs of their education very early in the decision-making process. Colleges and universities must provide detailed financial aid packages before students make decisions regarding deposits, enrollment, and registration. When possible, adult learners need access to financial aid advisors who have specialized knowledge in three areas: (1) funding options for nontraditional students; (2) national, state, and regional scholarships and grants for adult students; and (3) dual enrollment and third-party payment options. West Virginia discovered that adult learners who know precisely how their previous credits will transfer, how long it will take to complete a degree, and

 QUICK TIP

"Many adults are employed and cannot visit a college or university during normal business hours. Institutions that require students to visit the campus cannot serve adult students effectively when essential offices are open only from 9 to 5 Monday through Friday. These institutions must extend operating hours to evenings and weekends and make every attempt to provide key services via the Internet and smartphones. Student affairs professionals also need to do a more effective job of leveraging technology not to replace the human experience but to enhance it." —Randall Friend, solutions consultant, Hobsons; former dean of admissions, Shepherd University (personal communication, August 23, 2013)

the approximate cost of the degree are far more likely to enroll than adult learners who receive general information about academic programs and financial opportunities. Information about specific programs may generate excitement and interest among prospective students, but it will not result in enrollment unless institutions offer customized information about time to degree completion and cost.

Aid programs that target adult students are particularly effective in generating interest among those who view the cost of college as an insurmountable obstacle. Such programs also may have a positive impact on retention rates for nontraditional learners, because these students often enroll part time and are not eligible for many traditional scholarships. To respond to this need, West Virginia created the Higher Education Adult Part-time Student Program to help financially needy students who must attend part time complete their education.

Assessing the Impact of Processes and Support Services on Adult Learners

There is no question that higher education has entered an era that demands proof from colleges and universities that they are doing the job society expects them to do. Recently, higher education's national focus has shifted from access to degree completion. Because adult learners care most about cost and time to degree completion, finding ways to help them complete their degrees quickly and efficiently is crucial to their enrollment and success.

 IN THE SPOTLIGHT

"Prior to creating an online version of new student orientation, either we watched adults tolerate a program that was not geared toward their needs, or we waived the requirement to attend. Either action sent the message that the needs of adult learners were not a high priority. Now, by providing adult learners with the information they need for a successful start and allowing them to access that information whenever they wish and in a streamlined fashion, adult learners get the message that Marshall cares about them and their success." —Beth Wolfe, director of recruitment, Marshall University (personal communication, August, 15, 2013)

IN THE SPOTLIGHT

"In 2013, Marshall University awarded the Higher Education Adult Part-time Student (HEAPS) Grant to the largest population of part-time students attending college in West Virginia. Out of the twenty 2- and 4-year colleges and universities in West Virginia, Marshall awarded 11% of all HEAPS Grants. Although Marshall University does not have the largest HEAPS funding level in the state, it makes HEAPS awards along with other financial assistance programs to as many part-time students as possible. Marshall's philosophy is to assist the greatest number of financially needy students while ensuring equity in the process." —Kathy Bialk, director of student financial services, Marshall University (personal communication, September 27, 2013)

There are many ways to determine if an institution is operating under "adult friendly" processes and procedures. Assessment tools, such as Noel-Levitz's Adult Learning Inventory or CAEL's Adult Learning Focused Institution (ALFI) Toolkit, are helpful in assessing the institutional climate in regard to friendliness and service to adult learners. Satisfaction, however, is only part of the picture: What students are learning and how that learning is contributing to degree completion are more important. Learning outcomes relative to courses and academic programs are already ingrained in the institutional culture. A stronger focus on assessment in student affairs, supplemental instruction, advising, and student support services is needed on many campuses to better determine the impact these services have on adult student learning and success.

At Kanawha Valley Community and Technical College (KVCTC), student affairs staff from all departments worked together to create learning outcomes for programs and services—from financial aid to career services. KVCTC linked the outcomes directly to the mission of the institution and the goals of the student services and enrollment division, an important first step toward demonstrating the contributions that student services makes to student access, learning, and success. New River Community and Technical College built assessment components into major programs and services

IN THE SPOTLIGHT

"Shepherd University tried an innovative approach to helping students finance their education by linking tuition for out-of-state community college transfers, many of whom are adult learners, to degree completion and grade point average at the community college." —Randall Friend, solutions consultant with Hobsons, previously dean of admissions at Shepherd University (personal communication, June 11, 2012)

offered by student affairs. New River also implemented Ready Assessment to verify that adult learners are ready to succeed in hybrid courses. Shepherd University developed procedures to conduct an in-depth analysis and needs assessment of adult learners during the recruitment and admissions processes. West Liberty University surveyed graduating students to establish a baseline for student satisfaction with nonclassroom support services and programs, and then disaggregated the data for adult learners. West Virginia University established student learning outcomes for orientation sessions and major campus life activities.

Supporting Teaching and Learning

As they increase efforts to enroll more adult students, institutions must pay attention to the unique learning needs of adults. Student affairs professionals and others charged with providing non-classroom-based support services also must address the unique support service needs of this rapidly growing population.

Adult learners who enroll exclusively in online courses face a distinctive set of issues that colleges and universities must address to ensure that necessary services and resources are available to online learners and that online learners know how to access these services. As more colleges deliver basic services over the Internet, they have an obligation to assist students who have not attended college for 10 or more years to acquire the skills they need to navigate these online systems. At the minimum, institutions need 24/7 help desks.

During the process of implementing the *DegreeNow* grant, student affairs professionals in West Virginia learned a great deal about preparing adult learners to benefit from instruction and to apply what they are learning, whether that learning takes place in the classroom or online. Table 10.2

IN THE SPOTLIGHT

"In 2011, the West Virginia Community and Technical College System and West Virginia University signed an agreement that articulated an online baccalaureate degree-completion pathway for place-bound adult learners, named the BA Pathway Multidisciplinary Studies Degree. Students who successfully complete their associate's degree at a local community college can pursue the degree at WVU. The agreement between WVU and the West Virginia CTCS increases access to college courses, provides more effective transfer systems and degree articulation, and effectively uses institutional resources. In addition, the partnership fosters ongoing communication between advisors at CTCS institutions and WVU, increasing the chances that students will receive consistent, correct, and timely information. Finally, the agreement allows adult learners to design their own program of study by choosing three minors instead of one major." —Lucinda Hart, director of online programs, West Virginia University (personal communication, August, 26, 2013) provides a snapshot of the strategies student affairs professionals developed or are in the process of developing to support learning.

Table 10.2

Supporting the Learning Process for Adult Students

Area	Support
College success courses	• Design a college success course specifically for adult learners or add elements to existing college success courses that address adult learner concerns and needs.
E-learning	• Provide adult learners with tools that they can use to assess their readiness to succeed in online or hybrid courses.
Math, test, or technology anxiety	• Design short-term seminars or workshops to assist adult learners to deal with math, test, or technology anxiety. • Provide adult learners with opportunities to acquire technology skills in a nonthreatening environment. • Collaborate with faculty colleagues to build participation in skill-building activities into the syllabus (e.g., requiring adult learners to participate in these activities, and rewarding them for it).
Targeted services for specific student populations	• Understand and educate the college community about the unique needs of student parents, student veterans, and adult learners with disabilities. • Design targeted support services to meet the unique needs of these student subpopulations and to connect them with other students who share their interests, challenges, or experiences (current and past). • Consider targeted advising, college success courses, organizations, orientation, and support groups.
Technology	• Leverage technology to provide adult learners with 24/7 services; to support a variety of instructional approaches (online courses, distance education, or blended courses); and to build community among adult learners. • Do not assume that every adult learner is uncomfortable with technology, but be prepared to offer targeted services to those who are. • Develop partnerships with regional libraries and education centers that allow adults to have access to computers. • Start viewing software as another way to reach out to students.
Tutoring	• Train tutors to understand who adult learners are and what they need to succeed. • Include current or former adult learners on the tutoring staff.

In West Virginia, one of the newest academic programs for adult learners is the West Virginia Remote Online Collaborative Knowledge System (WVROCKS), a statewide initiative first introduced by the West Virginia HEPC in 2011 that is designed to increase the number of available upper-division courses to students pursuing their RBA degree. Developed by several public higher education institutions in partnership with the HEPC, WVROCKS offers a selection of 8-week online classes.

SUPPORT SYSTEMS FOR ADULT LEARNERS

Student affairs professionals pride themselves on complementing the academic curriculum and providing supplemental and holistic experiences for students that contribute to student learning and development. On some campuses, however, these services are not always designed with adult learners in mind. In West Virginia for example, many community colleges operated initially under the same policies and procedures as the 4-year institutions to which they were previously linked, even though these institutions served a larger traditional-aged student population. John Gardner, founder and CEO of Excellence in Undergraduate Education, has argued very publicly that institutions participate knowingly and unknowingly in transfer-student discrimination (personal communication, August 5, 2013). According to Gardner, colleges and universities must reexamine campus programs, policies, and procedures to assess their effectiveness in supporting transfer students, many of whom are adult learners.

Adding services for adult learners does not require colleges and universities to abandon traditional students. West Virginia campuses already have started adding and enhancing services for adult learners without compromising support services for traditional students. In November 2012, West Virginia State University (WVSU), responding to a significant influx of student veterans, created a Military Student Center, one of four such centers at West Virginia public institutions. Staffed by VetCorps members, a federally supported service program, the Military Student Center connects veterans to tutoring, advising, counseling, disability services, and career planning resources. The center also hosts faculty seminars that focus on issues affecting veterans. Center staff members, in collaboration with colleagues in student affairs, also serve as advocates for veterans (http://www.wvstateu.edu/Current-Students/Military-Student-Services-Center.aspx). Two community and technical colleges, Kanawha Valley and Mount West, participate in the Future Soldier/Sailor Program that helps military enlistees earn college credits prior to beginning basic training and ensures that enlistees can continue their training during or after their military service.

In addition to working with veterans, WVSU created an Office of Adult and Commuter Student Services, where staff plan and implement adult learner programs. The center features a student lounge, computer labs, and a study area. Staff members assist adult learners with finding housing, child care, and transportation nearby. Student affairs professionals also work to connect students with campus resources such as tutoring, advising, and counseling and encourage adult learners to become involved in campus life and student organizations. At WVSU, more than 90% of students are commuters and more than half of those are adult learners.

Creating opportunities for staff to engage with adult students is critical to supporting their success and degree attainment. Institutions seeking to have a positive impact on adult student success must commit to that effort beyond fiscal resources. It means additional space, staff realignment, and institutional commitment.

Strategic Partnerships

Modules 7 and 8 demonstrate that building strategic partnerships within the institution and between the institution and the community increase access and success for adult learners. *DegreeNow* motivated West Virginia to increase its commitment to partnerships and to create a culture where internal and external partnerships are valued—and rewarded.

- Many community and technical colleges added faculty representatives to advisory boards and committees within student affairs.

- After West Virginia separated community and technical colleges (CTCs) from their host universities, the seamless movement of students from the CTC to the university was sometimes lost. *DegreeNow* rekindled the interest in creating articulation agreements that allowed students, most of whom are adult learners, to seamlessly transfer from community and technical colleges to upper-division institutions.

- Blue Ridge Community and Technical College designed an assessment instrument to gather data from faculty members on the effectiveness of student support services and used the results to both strengthen services and to build bridges.

- Concord University, Bluefield State College, and Marshall University strengthened a partnership that began prior to *DegreeNow*, a partnership that created the Erma Byrd Higher Education Center in Beckley, West Virginia. Targeting rural adult learners with little opportunity to start or complete a degree because of their location within the state, the center offers courses and degree programs in education, nursing, and business.

- Kanawha Valley Community and Technical College and Bridgemont Community and Technical College partnered with organizations like Dow Chemical and DuPont to train chemical operators for area plants. These partnerships allowed businesses to fill a need and contributed to the success of adult learners, who are now earning higher wages as a result of their participation in the programs.

- Kanawha Valley Community and Technical College and Mountwest Community and Technical College partnered with Goodwill Industries to allow Goodwill clients to take classes at their worksite.

- At Shepherd University, the dean of admissions, a Train-the-Trainer graduate, collaborated with the Teaching/Learning Center to offer Leveraging *DegreeNow* modules on adult learners to new faculty members.

- West Liberty University established the Early Bird Café to bring faculty and student affairs professionals together every Tuesday morning to identify and work on shared challenges.

- Many community and technical colleges partnered with Workforce West Virginia to recruit adult learners to either finish a degree or seek retraining through academic and workforce programs.

By emphasizing the value of internal and external partnerships, West Virginia sends important messages to the higher education system and to the community, that education is everyone's business—and that lifelong learning is the engine that will drive the state's economy and shape its future. By taking the lead in building partnerships across the campus and in the community, student affairs professionals demonstrate their value to students, faculty, the higher education system, and the community.

IN THE SPOTLIGHT

"For so many people who have some college credits but are no longer enrolled, the desire to walk across the stage to a degree is strong, but the prospect of returning to school is daunting. There are hosts of roadblocks, from finances to a lack of extra time and family commitments, so it is our job at the public higher education level to even out the road for returning students" (Hill, 2013).

DEGREENOW: THE BIG PICTURE

DegreeNow quickly taught West Virginia student affairs professionals the importance of involving and educating key players. Student affairs professionals and HEPC staff members met with administrators, staff, and faculty at colleges and universities throughout the state to analyze data on adult learner stop-outs (e.g., average age, median credit hours earned) and to discuss the importance of adult learners to West Virginia's economy, especially in light of the projected decline of the state's high school population. Probably the most effective tool for generating institutional buy-in for the *DegreeNow* initiative was the NASPA-led Train-the-Trainer workshops, whose graduates included both senior-level administrators and respected faculty and staff from across the state. These individuals served as *DegreeNow* champions on their campuses and as leaders of the 8-hour regional workshops. Additionally, HEPC staff presented *DegreeNow* updates to statewide groups such as the Student Affairs Advisory Council, the Academic Affairs Advisory Council, the RBA/BOG AAS Coordinators, and the Admissions and Registrars Advisory Council. HEPC staff members also presented *DegreeNow* updates at statewide higher education conferences. HEPC staff assigned to *DegreeNow* worked hard to strengthen relationships among student affairs professionals across the state as well as the relationship between the state higher education agencies and these professionals. Involving stakeholders in designing workshops and analyzing data created synergistic conversations that led to ownership of *DegreeNow* at the grassroots level.

Train-the-Trainer graduates believed that involving presidents in *DegreeNow* would generate support for needed changes and speed up the change process. In June 2012, *DegreeNow* was able to arrange a 3-hour workshop for CTC presidents led by Culp, NASPA's consultant on the *DegreeNow* grant. The interactive workshop focused on the role that student affairs must play in increasing access and success for adult learners as well as the importance of partnerships between academic and student affairs. Presidents had an opportunity to assess the effectiveness of programs and services offered by student affairs at their institutions and to evaluate recommendations to increase access and success for adult learners offered by 2- and 4-year college presidents across the country.

QUICK TIP

Identify and harness the enthusiasm of champions at each institution.

Chancellors of both the Community and Technical College System and the University System used a variety of public forums across the state to confirm the significance to West Virginia of reenrolling adult learners. The governor and first lady (a CTC president) echoed this message in speeches throughout the state. In addition, HEPC staff presented updates on *DegreeNow* to the Higher Education Policy Commissioners and to members of the Community and Technical College Council. With each update, HEPC staff reminded these policymakers about the importance of adult learners to West Virginia's economic future.

QUICK TIP

Involve and educate key players early: presidents, chief student affairs officers, respected staff, and administrators.

Building institutional and statewide buy-in was important, but it also was necessary to build capacity at the individual and campus levels. The Train-the-Trainers workshops built that capacity among leaders at colleges and universities across the state. However, student affairs leaders soon discovered that building staff capacity was the essential first step in any new endeavor. Asking staff to do something for which they lack knowledge or skills is a recipe for failure. Leveraging *DegreeNow* workshops led by Train-the-Trainer graduates and completed by hundreds of participants across the state helped staff members identify their strengths and weaknesses; develop a plan to build on the strengths and reduce the weaknesses; and connect student affairs to the mission, goals, and culture of the institution.

Higher education systems committed to changing their cultures and their systems must pay attention to the public policy aspects of the change process. West Virginia included adult learners in the new statewide master plan for higher education (HEPC). The reporting requirements associated with the master plan sent clear and consistent messages that adult learners were an essential component of West Virginia's higher education future. In addition, HEPC staff members are working with colleges and universities to create a statewide prior learning assessment policy that supports the master plan. Finally, West Virginia is considering a move to performance-based funding and adopting a formula that includes adult learners in the equation.

QUICK TIP

Change will not happen until people have a realistic picture of their strengths and weaknesses; the mission, goals, and culture of their institution; and the strengths and weaknesses of the area in which they work.

These policy changes allow West Virginia to sustain the initiatives associated with *DegreeNow* after the grant ends in 2014. The changes embed the importance of lifelong learning in the West Virginia higher education system and reinforce the importance of using the electronic, print, and "people" resources generated during the *DegreeNow* grant to maintain the state's commitment to adult learners.

LOOKING BACKWARD, MOVING FORWARD

In addition to the many Quick Tips and lessons learned scattered throughout this module, the experiences of educators and student affairs professionals associated with *DegreeNow* generated eight insights that may assist other colleges and universities that are struggling to increase adult learner enrollment, persistence, and completion rates.

1. The grant was structured to give student affairs a head start (Train-the-Trainers workshops). In retrospect, the West Virginia Higher Education Policy Commission realized that it should have built more joint activities between student and academic affairs into the grant after the first year.

2. It is more challenging and time consuming to move from an anecdotal culture to a culture of evidence than originally anticipated, but the investment of time and resources is worth it.

3. Lasting change must be grounded in and respectful of an institution's culture, even when a goal is to change aspects of that culture.

4. An approach that works at one institution may not work at another. Every student affairs educator and every institution within the state system must be moving toward the same point on the map, but they may follow different routes.

5. Change is an ongoing process that requires clear performance expectations, strong leadership, adequate resources, and the effective collection and use of data.

6. When people think about change, they think about changing other people or other areas. A major challenge is to help people understand that change needs to start with them.

7. To better serve adult learners, colleges and universities must examine their infrastructure, question assumptions, look objectively at data, and make data-driven changes.

8. It is relatively easy to implement a grant; it is more difficult to implement a grant in a way that matters.

West Virginia's efforts to serve its adult learner population and the lessons learned offer guidance to other states and higher education institutions looking to create data-driven, outcomes-oriented support services for adult learners. The Lumina-funded partnership between the West Virginia Higher Education Policy Commission, the West Virginia Community and Technical College System, and NASPA was a vital step in building and sustaining statewide support for increasing college completion rates for adult learners.

QUICK TIP

Think about sustainability from Day 1. Work must continue after the grant ends.

RESOURCES

Beasley, S. E., & Culp, M. (2012). Leading a statewide culture of evidence initiative. *Leadership Exchange, 10*(3), 14–17.

Gardner, S. M. (2013, Fall). The problem with transfer admissions. *Living Education eMagazine,* 38, 54.

Johnson, T., & Cantrell, S. (2012, August). *Adult learner considerations in admissions and enrollment.* Retrieved from http://www4.aacrao.org/semsource/sem/indexc93c.html?fa=view&id=5576

REFERENCES

Carnevale, A., Smith, N., & Strohl, J. (2010). *Help wanted: Projections of jobs and education requirement through 2018.* Retrieved from http://cew.georgetown.edu/jobs2018

Council for Adult and Experiential Learning. (2014). Discover CAEL's principles for serving adult learners effectively. Retrieved from http://www.cael.org/Whom-We-Serve/ Colleges-and-Universities/Adult-Student-Services/ALFI-Assessment-Tools

Culp, M. M., & Dungy, G. J. (Eds.). (2012). *Building a culture of evidence in student affairs: A guide for leaders and practitioners.* Washington, DC: National Association of Student Personnel Administrators.

Hill, P. L. (2013). Hitting "restart" for those who have stopped out. *The evoLLLution: Illuminating the Lifelong Learning Movement.* Retrieved from http://www.evolllution.com/opinions/ hitting-restart-stopped

Lumina Foundation. (2013). *A stronger nation through higher education.* Retrieved from http://www.luminafoundation.org/stronger_nation

Western Interstate Commission for Higher Education. (2012). *Knocking at the college door: Projections of high school graduates.* Retrieved from http://www.wiche.edu/knocking-8th

INDEX